The Wholly Book of Genesis

The Wholly Book of Genesis

By
Jay Dubya

eBOOKSTAND

http://www.eBookstand.com
http://www.CyberRead.com

Published by
eBookstand
Division of CyberRead, Inc
1928_4

ISBN 1-58909-256-2

Printed in the United States of America

Other Books by Jay Dubya
Adult Fiction

Black Leather and Blue Denim, A '50s Novel
The Great Teen Fruit War, A 1960' Novel
Frat' Brats, A '60s Novel
Ron Coyote, Man of La Mangia
So Ya' Wanna' Be A Teacher
Pieces of Eight
Pieces of Eight, Part II
Pieces of Eight, Part III
Pieces of Eight, Part IV
Mauled Maimed Mangled Mutilated Mythology
Fractured Frazzled Folk Fables & Fairy Farces
FFFF&FF, Part II
Nine New Novellas
Nine New Novellas, Part II
Nine New Novellas, Part III
Nine New Novellas, Part IV
Thirteen Sick Tasteless Classics
Thirteen Sick Tasteless Classics, Part II
Thirteen Sick Tasteless Classics, Part III
Thirteen Sick Tasteless Classics, Part IV
The Wholly Book of Exodus

Young Adult Fantasy Novels

Pot of Gold
Enchanta
Space Bugs, Earth Invasion
The Eighteen Story Gingerbread House

Contents

Contents (continued)

Background

On April 1, 2002 Mohammed Kareem Jihad, a fourteen-year-old April Fool Palestinian revolutionary, was ascending a rocky ledge along rugged cliffs that bordered the western banks of the *Dead Sea.* Exhausted from his climbing enterprise, young Jihad stopped to rest his weary body. The vernal radical lit a *Camel* cigarette and casually surveyed the landscape below. Everything seemed calm and serene.

When Mohammed Kareem Jihad lazily leaned backwards his gaunt frame slipped through a narrow crevice situated between two limestone crags. The disoriented youth rose to his knees, inspected his surroundings and soon realized that he had fallen into a cave (containing a remarkable ancient artifact). In the center of the small hollow was an urn, a well' preserved remnant from Hebrew antiquity that the intruder had interpreted as being a 'dumb piece of worthless junk.'

Instead of sticking his hand inside the urn to feel for any contents, impetuous Mohammed followed his terroristic instincts by pulling the pin of a hand grenade and tossing the explosive device into what was surely a great archeological discovery. When the bomb exploded prematurely Mohammed Kareem Jihad had not yet exited the cave. Besides pottery shrapnel, two leather objects bound with straps (strapnel) blasted out of the ancient urn and instantaneously collided with the back of the Palestinian lad's skull, knocking him unconscious.

When Mohammed Kareem Jihad finally regained his faculties *(his rich uncle owned two radical Arab universities),* he noticed and then grabbed the newfound leather pouches and fled the scene of destruction. After descending the perilous cliffs the young militant thought, 'I'll bet whatever is inside these two ridiculous leather packages is worth at least a carton of American cigarettes or a black market *World War II* mortar.' So the neurotic youth mounted his stolen desert "quad" and motored to the city of Jericho where his poor father owned a mediocre but popular café.

Inside the café Professor Phillip Collins of the Semitic Semantic Institute was seated at a table conversing with Dr. Allen Qaeda from the Arab Aramaic Academy. Mohammed Kareem Jihad rushed into the dismal dark café and approached the two distinguished scholars' cozy table.

"How much will you give me for these two lousy-looking leather pouches?" the obnoxious boy asked Professor Al Qaeda. "I won't be able to sleep again until I can buy a weapon and commit a blatant act of random violence!"

"Let's unravel the pouches and see exactly what ya' got!" the suddenly curious researcher replied. The good academic doctor gently unwound the dusty cords that bound the leather wrappings. Inside the bundles Dr. Al Qaeda found dozens of remarkably well' preserved papyrus sheets with ancient writings carelessly scribbled on the archaic scrolls.

"Holy Moses! Why it's the first two renditions of the Old Testament!" Professor Al Qaeda exclaimed in astonishment and awe. "*The Book of Genesis* and the *Book of Exodus*! These artifacts are totally amazing!"

Professor Phil Collins, who knew plenty about *Genesis*, rendered his impressions. "This translation has much more detail than the presently read first book of the Old Testament does!" Collins enthusiastically observed and articulated. "This type of papyrus dates back to at least 900 BC, which makes it a lot older than the Dead Sea Scrolls that had been re-written by the Essenes during an impromptu creative writing class."

"If this historical account is accurate," interrupted Professor Al Qaeda, "then this great discovery will present a *wholly* new perspective to religious history, which is presently very controversial to begin with. These ancient documents might prove to be a new paradigm and they possibly could spawn a contemporary theological revolution!"

Young Mohammed Kareem Jihad was growing very impatient with the scholarly adults' intellectual evaluation and excited speculation of his find. "How much are the papers worth?" the argumentative lad insisted on knowing.

"Two cartons of American cigarettes, definitely!" Professor Phil Collins promised.

"And we'll even throw in an authentic AK-47 and two slightly used hand grenades," Dr. Al Qaeda persuasively added. "We want to give you incentive to perhaps discover other ancient objects like let's say, the Book of Doo-Doo Rot-Emmy!"

"Sold!" an elated Mohammed Kareem Jihad ecstatically shouted. "Now I can blow up my' older sister's secret forbidden doll collection and her ugly Jewish friends too!"

And so Dr. Al Qaeda and the author's uncle Professor Phil Collins became the legitimate owners of the only bona fide "First Two Books of the Wholly Bible" even though both men were illegitimate children to begin with. But the remainder of the "unabridged" Old Testament texts had been thoroughly obliterated inside the urn when careless Mohammed Kareem Jihad's hand grenade had effectively exploded.

Fortunately Uncle Phil Collins had wisely made a computer file in English of his meticulous translation of the great archeological treasures. Uncle Phil thoughtfully had electronically sent "Wholly Genesis" and "Wholly Exodus" to me as e-mail attachments. The laborious deciphering represented my relative's fantastic interpretation of the ancient Hebrew writing, which I had electronically received on April 10, 2002. Regrettably on April 11th Uncle Phil and Dr. Al Qaeda were blown to smithereens by an errant Palestinian rocket while refining their academic study of the ancient scrolls inside Professor Collins' Jerusalem home. The papyrus sheets and the original computer file had also been destroyed in the malicious terrorist attack.

My e-mail translations are the only remaining evidence of *The Wholly Book of Genesis and The Wholly Book of Exodus.* Uncle Phil sincerely believed that the new versions presently in my possession are the original and most reliable documentation of the "Word of Moses," who was believed to be the organizer of the popular Genesis and Exodus interpretations that appear in the standard *Bible.* Uncle Phil Collins and Professor Al Qaeda strongly believed that Moses had fabricated the Biblical Genesis and Exodus stories around 1400 BC. But since formal writing (and sophisticated alphabets) did not appear until the time period after Homer and King David, around 1,000 BC, the Biblical stories had been awkwardly handed-down and distorted because of the practice of oral tradition with storytellers, minstrels and bards adding and subtracting various relevant and irrelevant details.

Uncle Phil Collins and Dr. Al Qaeda professed and maintained that young Mohammed Kareem Jihad's most important accidental discovery represented the true unabridged stories of Genesis and of Exodus. They insisted that the new versions are much more valid in scope and content since the accounts had been written hundreds of years earlier than the stories that now appear in the first two books of the *Bible.* Thus, young Mohammed's find is closer to Moses' original language and intent than later popularly read interpretations of Genesis and Exodus. "Careless Hebrew historians and ancient priests recklessly but deliberately modified the 'Wholly Genesis and 'Wholly Exodus' versions into more pious, moral and self-righteous texts," Uncle Phil stated in his final e-mail letter. "They intentionally did it to satisfy their own selfish purposes and agendas."

Uncle Phil also indicated in his' final missive to me that "Moses, who had lived approximately 1450 BC around the time of Pharaoh Thutmose III of Egypt, didn't know how to write, even though the wily prophet had very cunningly put the stories of *Genesis* and *Exodus* together just like the blind poet Homer had done with the *Iliad* and the *Odyssey*. In fact nobody knew how to write with any expression skills until half a millennium following Moses, circa 1000 BC. According to Uncle Phil's last letter, "Moses barely knew the numerals one to ten signifying the *Ten Commandments* etched on the twin stone tablets," my mother's older brother attested. "That is to say, if Moses had never had a thumb or finger severed off!"

Now that the background of *The Wholly Book of Genesis* and *The Wholly Book of Exodus* are fully known, only the astute readers of these volumes can be the best judges of the merits of Mohammed Kareem Jihad's extraordinary discovery and of Uncle Phil Collins' extravagant claims. I have painstakingly placed in *italics* the language that ancient scholars had shrewdly edited out of the *Wholly Book of Genesis* and I have clearly left the standard Old Testament script in Times New Roman type.

Jay Dubya

Chapter One
"First Story of Creation"

In the beginning when God created the heavens and the earth He asked Himself, *"Why do I need more than one Heaven? I don't want to appear to be too greedy!"* The earth was a formless wasteland and darkness covered the abyss, while a mighty wind swept over the waters. *God got wind of what was happening. "All land has form, even wasteland, and since it is dark, how in the universe do I know that water had swept over the abyss?" God told me, the anonymous author of Genesis, so that's how I know all about this illogical and seemingly fictitious stuff!*

Then God said, "Let there be light *so that some day in the distant future we can have huge electric utility companies and glittering Las Vegas casinos,"* and there was light. God saw how good the light was *so He' finally saw the light after a near eternity of living in darkness.* God then separated the light from darkness, *not realizing that He had to first make the earth spin and rotate on its axis in order to have night and day and day and night.* God then called the light "day," and the darkness He called "night." *Thus, if someone gets the daylights knocked out of them, then they will only see night in their subconscious minds.* And then evening came, and morning followed-the first day.

Then God said *to Himself,* "Let there be a dome in the middle of the waters, to separate one body of water from the other." *Then God thought, 'Why am I speaking when there's no one else around to hear Me giving My imperative commands? I must learn not to talk to Myself all the damned time!'* And so it happened: God made the dome, and the dome separated the water above the dome from the water below it, thereby making fresh water divided from salt water. God called the dome "the sky," *and then He' thought, 'Maybe some day there will be a Skydome.'* Evening came, and morning followed-the second day, *and God thought, 'Hey, this is fun! We're finally getting some kind of orderly pattern going here!'*

Then God said to *no one,* "Let the water under the sky be gathered into a single basin," *and although He couldn't at that moment think of the word 'continents,' the dry land appeared anyway.* And so it happened: the water under the sky was gathered into its basin, and the dry land appeared *thousands of years before the world would know dry cleaners or dry towns or even a mythical distant country like Canada being dry.* God called the dry land "the earth," and the basin of water he called "the sea" *since He hadn't realized His immense power had created Mars, Jupiter and Venus and oceans, too. Despite inadvertently using the wrong descriptive terminology,* God saw how good the dry land *(continents)* and sea *(oceans)* were.

Then God said to Himself, "Let the earth bring forth vegetation, *so this whole damned thing I'm doing here looks like evolution instead of creation.*" Every kind of plant that bears seed and every kind of fruit tree on earth that bears fruit with its seed in it appeared. *The earth suddenly made its first step toward becoming a seedy place.*

And so it happened: the earth brought forth every kind of plant that bears seed and every kind of fruit tree on earth that bears fruit with its seed in it, *and He admired the fruits of His labor, which really was the earth's labor.* God saw how good it was, *even though some day some men would eventually become fruits (gay) and others vegetables (severely mentally retarded).* Evening' came and morning followed-the third day.

Then God said, "Let there be lights in the dome of the sky, to separate day from light" *because He had not yet comprehended that day and night were happening because the earth had already been rotating for several days without His Almighty knowledge or permission.* "Let them mark the fixed times, the days and the years, and serve as luminaries in the dome of the sky, to shed light upon the earth *in case the sun ever burns out before batteries and flashlights are invented,*" the Lord stated. *And so, God became the first "spin-Doctor" using the earth as His model.*

And so it happened: God made the two great lights, the greater one *(the sun)* to govern the day, and the lesser one to govern the night *(the moon does not give off its own light but merely reflects light from the sun to the Earth). And He made the stars, not assessing that many of the stars out there were millions of times greater in magnitude than the sun was and that the sun was just a tiny star with the earth being simply a puny planet revolving around it. 'Who cares about such stupid things? I just care about the big picture, which is the earth!' God remarkably imagined.*

God set the stars in the dome of the sky, to shed light upon the earth *on non-cloudy nights,* and the sun was set 'to govern' the day and the stars 'to govern' the night. *And God said to His anonymous audience, "Damn it! I wish I knew more astronomy!" There were no humans around yet to elect or appoint their own governors to govern anyone or anything so the sun governed the day and the moon and stars governed the night.* God wanted to separate light from darkness *and also light from heavy.* God saw how good it all was. Evening' came and morning followed-the fourth day.

Then God said, "Let the water teem with abundance of living creatures. *I want to make this creation business seem like evolution so that confused future generations will argue about the same theories as being different, creation versus evolution.* And on *(above)* the earth, let birds fly beneath the dome of the sky." And so it *(those events)* happened.

God created the great sea monsters and all kinds of swimming creatures with which the water teems, and all kinds of winged birds. *'I really like sea monsters, sharks, barracudas, predators, eagles, buzzards and other dangerous animals,' God thought. 'They're all pretty neat!'* God saw how good it was, and God blessed them by saying, "Be fertile, multiply and fill the water of the seas, and let the birds multiply on the earth. *I really enjoy watching predators kill one another so I say to all you violent carnivores out there, reproduce before you are eaten and devoured. Survival of the fittest is a really fascinating idea that will challenge this entire Genesis thing!" God exclaimed to no one.* Evening' came and morning followed-the fifth day.

Then God said *because He enjoyed hearing Himself' speak to no one*, "Let the earth bring forth all kinds of living creatures: cattle, creeping things, and wild animals of all kinds *because the predators need prey to hunt and kill while providing Me' with excitement and entertainment from boredom.*" And so it happened: God made all kinds of wild animals *because He didn't want a tame nondescript planet.* He made all kinds of cattle, and all kinds of creeping things of the earth, *and He pensively thought, 'These' things give Me' the creeps.'* God saw how good it all was *in spite of Himself'*.

Then God said, "Let 'us' make man in *our* own image, after *our* likeness," *as He' spoke to other gods He' had invited over to observe His' grand experiments.* "Let them have dominion over the fish of the sea, the birds of the air, and over the cattle and over the wild animals and all the creatures that crawl on the ground. *Man, did I do a good job!" God marveled and exclaimed. "But I don't think I got all of the wild animals right. Some of them will eat man even though I gave man dominion over the dumb insubordinate wild animals. Oh well, back to the old drawing board!"*

God created man in His' image; in the divine image He created him; male and female He' created them, *and that was the beginning of gender profiling.*

God blessed them, saying: "Be fertile and multiply. *Someday we will have empty churches and synagogues to fill, so I'll need lots of people because most of the ungrateful arrogant fools will refuse to go to church and honor Me," God lectured to Himself*. "Fill the earth and subdue it, *and most importantly watch out for environmentalists that will want you to disobey My' divine commands about man's dominion of the earth.* Have dominion over the fish *and chickens* of the sea, the birds of the air and all the living things that move on the earth."

God also said, *"See, I'm really a Good Guy after all.* I give you humans every seed-bearing plant *including cactus, briars, poison ivy and stickers* all over the earth and every tree that has seed-bearing fruit on it to be your food. And to all of the animals of the land, all the birds of the air, and all of the living creatures that crawl on the ground, I give the green plants for food. *So damned it unborn future men, don't eat any vegetables for they are exclusively reserved for the animals," the Lord maintained. "Only eat the fruit off the tree, and when your mothers tell you to 'eat your vegetables', ignore them completely. You are to compete with the tame and wild animals that you have dominion over for food, but try to eat only fruits from trees and go easy on the veggies coming from plants. And if a lion or a tiger defiantly devours you against My' supreme will, report the incident to Me' immediately because sometimes I am unobservant while engaged in mentally relaxing reverie."* And so it happened.

God looked at everything He' had made, and He' found it *(them)* to be very good. Evening' came, and morning followed-the sixth day. *Everything was cool*!

4

Chapter Two
"Second Story of Creation"

Why we need two creation stories is beyond comprehension, but here it is anyway. Thus the heavens and the earth and all' their array were completed. Since on the seventh day God was finished with the work that He had been doing, He rested on the seventh day *(redundancy)* from all the work He' had undertaken (*more monotonous redundancy*). *He rested even though most of the work had been done by magic, imagination, by desire and by the remarkable earth as evidenced and inaccurately stated in chapter one. The fact that He rested shows that God has physical limitations, just like men do. So who the heck created whom?*

So God blessed the seventh day and made it holy, *therefore showing very evident prejudice against the other six days of the week.* He rested on the seventh day *(redundancy)* because of all the work He had done in creation *without the help of Zeus, Poseidon or Hades.* Such is the story of the heavens and the earth at their creation, *which is not confirmed or verified in any other text, atlas, history or encyclopedia anywhere. The creation story is widely believed by people that desperately need something irrational to believe.*

At the time when the Lord God made the earth and the heavens there was no field shrub on earth and no grass of the field had sprouted, *although the damned planet was amply loaded with an abundance of fruit trees and vegetable plants.* There was no grass and no shrub for the Lord God had sent no rain upon the earth, *so other gods like Zeus and Poseidon skeptically wondered how the heck fruit trees and vegetable plants could flourish all over the damned place without an adequate water supply!*

There was no man to till the soil, *so God decided He needed someone down there to keep those fruit trees and vegetable plants going and growing and to till the soil when rain would eventually make weeds and wild grass grow. The ground would have to be cultivated just like man would have to be.* A 'stream' was welling up out of the earth, *and since the organizer of this whole extraordinary tale was the first storyteller, this second story of creation is actually the real beginning of "mainstream" literature. Anyway,* when the stream watered all the surface of the ground, *logically the ground became wet. Mud could be found all over. No wonder that God was temporarily muddled from His magnificent enterprise.*

5

The Lord formed man out of the clay of the ground *(even though man had been already created in chapter one),* and He blew into his nostrils the breath of life, *thus creating artificial respiration before artificial respiration had ever been needed or any human had ever nearly drowned in any lake, pond, stream, river, creek, sea or ocean.* And so, man *miraculously* became a living being *after entering the world as an uninspired dead non-breathing being.*

Then the Lord God labored to plant a garden in Eden *because He had felt guilty using too much magic and creation by imagination.* He placed there the man whom He' had formed, *not knowing where the hell else to put him, except smack dab in the middle of the stupid but beautiful garden.*

Out of the ground the Lord God made various trees grow that were delightful to look at and good for producing food *because God had momentarily forgotten that He' had already created a wide variety of fruit trees on the sixth day of creation in chapter one. 'I must be getting amnesia or Alzheimer's disease,' He thought.* The tree of life was planted in the middle of the Garden of Eden and the tree of the knowledge and of the bad, *which suggests right away that knowledge' is bad, but not as bad as Alzheimer's. 'This exotic Garden of Eden now has a vast Central Park just like the distant island of Manhattan will have some day,' God thought.*

A *certain* river rises' in Eden *(actually East of Eden)* to water the garden; beyond there it divides and become four branches, *and later it becomes eight twigs.* The name of the first branch is Pishon, *and future humans will be absolutely forbidden to take whizzes there.* This branch winds through the whole land of Havilah, where there is gold *and plenty of other colors, too.*

The gold of that land is excellent; bdellium and lapis lazuli are also there, *and even dark clouds have silver linings in that land and the men all have brass testicles. This is enough idiotic deviation from the very boring main subject.*

The name of the second river is the Gihon; it is the river that winds all through the land of Cush *where future generations named Cushions will manufacture scads of soft comfortable pillows for fat-assed people to sit on.*

The name of the third river is the Tigris, *where female tigers hunt and bathe and the deer and the antelope do not play.* The Tigris flows east of Asshur, *and also 'East of Eden'. This I assure you about Asshur.*

The fourth river is the Euphrates. *All of those female tigers that are scared to swim and hunt in this river are known as "you fraidy-*

6

cats," and all the men that are frightened of female tigers are "you fraidy-cats," too! So don't mess with the Mesolithic Mesopotamians!

The Lord God then took the man and settled him in the Garden of Eden, which is nowhere near Busch Gardens, Boston Garden or Madison Square Garden. God wanted his own private gardener, so the man was assigned to cultivate and care for Eden.

The Lord God gave man this order, "Hoe, hoe, hoe until you learn to cultivate yourself! You are free to eat from any of the trees of this garden paradise except the tree of knowledge and of good and bad. From that tree you shall not eat; the moment you eat from it you will surely contract either ptomaine or severe bacteria poisoning and surely be doomed to die, which is probably better than being doomed to live forever on this very odd planet I have created. What a bummer immortality is, for I can speak from experience."

Also, if this story sounds a lot like Pandora's Box from ancient Greek mythology, Zeus has informed the Lord that Pandora's Box is an egregious plagiarism of the Biblical creation story and the chief Olympian has been paying God royalties for a full seven thousand years now. Zeus and the Lord both agree that man's knowledge and curiosity are evil. From knowledge and curiosity man has invented science and has developed technology, which have rivaled the accomplishments of both Zeus and the Lord God, and all their jealous peers.

The Lord God said, "It is not good for man to be alone, for he might masturbate all day long. I will make a suitable partner for him to keep him dumb thinking about sex all day long so that he is not influenced by knowledge and will not be able to develop science and technology to rival Me. I also want to prevent the abomination of homosexuality from happening!"

So the Lord God formed out of the ground various wild animals and various birds of the air (even though He had already done those same things in chapter one). He brought the animals to the man to see what He' would call them because God, besides having a poor erratic memory, also had a limited vocabulary and had run out of animal names to label His magnificent creations. Whatever the man called each of them would be its name, even though it was wrong and politically incorrect even way back in the Garden of Eden to call others (even animals) names.

The man gave names to all the cattle, and to all the birds of the air. However, man didn't know what on earth to call a penguin, an ostrich, an emu and a kiwi, in that those birds lived on land and couldn't fly in the air. The man then named all of the wild animals,

7

but none of them proved to be the suitable partner *for him. This was because the first man felt a natural disdain toward the ideas of beastiality and of having kinky sex with wild animals.*

So the Lord cast a deep sleep on the man, and while he was asleep, God took out one of the man's ribs and then closed up his flesh. The Lord God then built up into a woman the rib that He' had taken from the man. When God brought her to life, the man said: *"Are You' ribbin' me?* This one is at last bone' of my bones and flesh of my flesh. *Do I need medical insurance to pay for the damned operation? If I eat spare ribs will I grow back the one I have lost?"*

And God said to the *ignorant* man, *"Make no bones about it!* This one shall be called 'woman,' for out of her man this one has been taken, *you dumb egocentric bonehead!"*

That is why a man leaves his father and mother and clings to his wife, *even though the man in chapter two obviously has no father and mother. That is why the above statement is out of context and has no meaning whatsoever in regard to the rest of the text.* Then man and woman become of body, *especially during sex but hardly possible when not having sex.*

The man and his wife were both naked, yet they felt no shame *nor did they feel each other's genitals. There weren't any curious and horny peeping Toms around yet in the Garden of Eden to practice voyeurism on them, and even though the man and woman were not officially married, it was assumed that they had been wed. Indeed, God had not manufactured any priests, rabbis, ministers, bishops, cardinals or Pope to officially marry them, but the man and woman didn't give a crap about technicalities. They had companionship without any rambunctious homosexuals around to distract their interest, and that's all that really mattered.*

Chapter Three
"The Fall of Man"

The fall of man came right after man's first summer in what later was Sumeria. Now the serpent was the most cunning of all the animals that the Lord God had made, *so God put a viper's eyes on the first pair of dice. Why Someone' so perfect would want to create a shrewd sleazy snake has never been adequately explained.* The serpent *was very newsy and* asked the *gorgeous* woman, "Did God really tell you not to eat from any of the trees in the garden?"

The *alarmed* woman answered the *talking* serpent: "We may eat of the fruit of the trees in the garden; *but dear serpent, the trouble with eating is that you always have to defecate.* But serpent, it is only about the fruit of the tree in the middle of the garden that God said, 'You shall not eat it or even touch it, lest you die.' *What a wet blanket and teaser God is! The Guy needs to get a damned life I tell ya'!"*

But the serpent said to the woman: "You certainly will not die! *God has not created morticians yet to take care of dead bodies!* No my woman, God knows well that the moment you eat of the special fruit you will be like gods who know what is good and what is bad, *just like Prometheus when he gave the gift of fire to men over there in ancient Greece. Prometheus was punished but not killed for giving man the knowledge of fire!"*

The woman saw that the tree was good for food, pleasing to the eyes, and desirable for gaining wisdom, *since she was bored with being a dumb female all the damned time.* So she took of its fruit and ate it, *saying to herself, "An apple a day keeps monotony away."*

The *curious but generous* woman gave some of the apple to her husband, who was with her *all the time but was too busy getting an education watching two gay male lions having intercourse.* The husband ate the apple, *which at first lodged in his throat, making the man choke and consequently forming the original Adam's apple.*

Then the eyes of the husband and the wife were opened, *because up until now, they had been only dreaming, daydreaming, night-maring and sleepwalking.* The pair soon realized that they were naked *and not standing on a beach for nudists.* They sewed fig leaves together and *loined* to make loincloths for themselves, *even though the woman didn't have loins or any figs between her legs to cover with fig leaves. Hence, this was the beginning of female penis envy.*

When the husband and wife heard the sound of the Lord God moving about in the garden at the breezy time of the day, *they realized that the clumsy ponderous Deity might get wind of what they had done.* The man and his wife hid themselves from the Lord God among the trees of the garden, *not realizing that He was omniscient and knew the naked truth without having to see it with His own bare eyes.*

The Lord God then called to the man and asked him, *"Peek-a-boo,* where are you? *Are you ready for a good beating and spanking?"*

The man answered, "I heard You' approaching in the garden, *tripping over logs and stumbling through the bushes. Wouldn't it be easier flying than walking?"*

"Don't change the subject and the predicate too," the Lord God chastised. *"I got a few good Draconian ideas from another god over in Greece. Zeus told me about what he had done to Prometheus, to Epimetheus and to Pandora for not following his ridiculous martinet instructions. I'm gonna' employ some of Zeus's strategic methods right here in the Garden of Eden to penalize you!"*

"I was afraid because I was naked, so I hid myself," the man confessed.

"You wouldn't make a bad male centerfold," the Lord confided. *"You do have a decent bod'.* But who told you that you were naked? You have eaten then, from the tree of which I had forbidden you to eat! *That's a no-no, Bro'!"*

The man replied *by attempting to shift blame,* "The woman whom You' put here with me-she gave me fruit from the tree and so I ate it. *She made me do it! She made me do it! And besides, the apple was not sweet and has left a sour taste in my mouth for You, for the Garden of Eden and for the idiotic bullshit two stories of creation."*

The Lord God then asked the woman, "Why did you do such a thing? *Don't you enjoy obeying the tyranny of petty Lordly' male chauvinism? I am very vindictive, as you will soon find out!"*

The woman answered, *attempting to shift blame,* "The talking serpent tricked me into eating it so I ate it. *And You' tricked me by creating a talking serpent! I thought that vipers were only supposed to hiss and not speak! That's grossly unfair! Where can I file a grievance?"*

Then the Lord God said to the serpent: "Because you have done this, you shall be banned from the animals and from all the wild creatures *in zoos, circuses, menageries, the Discovery Channel, Animal Planet, well, you'll just be banned just about everywhere!"*

Then the Lord God continued, "On your belly shall you crawl, *for the first serpent I had made had three hundred and sixty-five legs, one for each day of the year, and the last one for leap year when the serpent was allowed to jump through My illogical hoops.* And serpent," God continued, "dirt shall you eat all the days of your life. *I hope you appreciate you're getting away dirt cheap for making the woman eat an apple from the forbidden Tree of Wisdom, for I am especially greedy and want all knowledge and wisdom to Myself!* And serpent," God proceeded, "I will put enmity between you and the woman *so that you will love your enmity as you love yourself.* And there will be enmity between your offspring and hers. *Good humans despise lowly snakes in the grass such as you are!* Man shall strike at your head while you strike at his heel, *and you better move to India in a hurry because that is just about the only place where you will ever be revered or respected."*

To the woman, the Lord God said: "I will intensify the pangs of your childbearing, *since I like seeing pain and sadism suffered by humans, especially women.* In pain shall you bring forth children, yet your urge should be for your husband, so whenever you get the hots for the man," *the Lord indicated, "that desire means more suffering through childbearing and more suffering through raising kids. Your husband shall be your master, and thank God for male chauvinism!"*

And to the man the Lord God said: "Because you have listened to your wife, you will be punished. *The rules of male chauvinism state that no man should ever listen to his wife, even though I don't remember ever officially ceremoniously marrying you two weirdos.* Your wife persuaded you to eat from the tree, which I had forbidden you to eat, *so your wife is like the serpent that had convinced her to eat from the forbidden tree,"* God chastised the man. *"Only I can eat from the tree of knowledge, get it moron! Women are evil because they have an excess of curiosity! That's why I am celibate and refuse to have or make a wife for Myself!"*

"But, but," the man replied.

"Cursed be the ground because of you! In toil you shall eat its yield all the days of your life. *I say these awful things because I am basically petty, greedy, shallow, vindictive and angry over one silly apple being consumed!"*

"But, but," the man penitently replied.

"Thorns and thistles shall it bring forth to you, *and I say this because I am a lousy poet and also because I enjoy watching and*

11

practicing *rudimentary sadism. You will feel My' wrath* every time you eat of the plants of the field. By the sweat of your face shall you get bread to eat *even though man can't live by bread alone."*

"But, but," the totally *frustrated man cried out.*

"No ifs, ands or buts about it Butthead," the Lord God *emphasized,* "until you' return to the ground from which you were taken. For you are dirt *and are actually getting away dirt cheap by merely being punished with misery for life for eating one of My' precious sacred apples. And to show you what a great Guy I am,"* God *continued,* "all of your *descendents will suffer for the remainder of history, all because you defied My' petty dictatorship and ate one of My' special apples."*

Next the man called his wife 'Eve', *because she had brought darkness into his life.* Eve became the mother of the entire human race, *which since then has been humanly racing toward self-destruction.*

For the man and his wife the Lord God made *non-union* leather garments, with which He clothed them *since no Goodwill Stores existed way back then in prehistoric antiquity.*

Then the Lord God said *to his friends Zeus, Poseidon and Hades:* "See! The man has become like one of us, *curious, knowledgeable and a threat that can challenge Divine Existence by developing science and technology.* The man now knows what is good and what is bad! Therefore, he must not be allowed to put out his hand to take from the tree of life also, and thus eat from it and live forever. *Zeus,"* the Lord *continued,* "you *were right hiding nectar and ambrosia from men so that they cannot achieve immortality over there in Greece. I must confess I get some of my best ideas from you inventive Olympians. I'll promptly destroy the Tree of Knowledge so that future men will know to fear My' supreme prowess and My' abundant wrath."*

The Lord God therefore banished the man from the Garden of Eden, to till the ground from which he had been taken, *which was not the same ground as in the Garden of Eden where the man had been originally formed.* When He 'expelled' the man *without first suspending him from the school of life,* God settled the man east of the Garden of Eden. And next He stationed the cherubim and the fiery revolving sword so that God could *have Hell's Angels* guard the return route to the tree of life, *which God had destroyed anyway but was very paranoid about having it all to Himself'.* God had already demolished the tree that He' sent the loyal cherubim to guard.

Chapter Four
"Cain and Abel"

The man wanted to have three sons: Ready, Willing and Abel, but God raised Cain about that and said, "You can only have two sons, Cain and Abel. And to accommodate Adam's (the man's) concern, God said, "Let there be erections!" And then there were erections. And God saw how good it was.

Adam had relations with his wife, *and at last there were five minutes of pleasure to complement the years and years of misery that God had cursed upon the man and his woman for simply eating an unauthorized apple. Adam and Eve had committed original sin, which was not that original or imaginative as far as the art of sinning goes.*

Eve conceived and bore Cain, saying, "I have produced a man with the help of the Lord," *and God said, "I just simply watched you and your husband going at it in the sack. Adam didn't need any help from Me', that's for sure!"*

Next, Eve bore Cain's brother Abel, *but because this book of Genesis is suspect and leaves a lot to be desired in terms of historical, factual and chronological accuracy, it is quite uncertain whether Cain and Abel were twins or were siblings born nine months apart.*

Abel became a keeper of flocks and Cain a tiller of the soil, *thus soiling all his clothes and loincloths all the time from tilling and from jerking off too often.* In the course of time Cain brought an offering to the Lord from the fruit of the soil, *not knowing that fruit grew on trees and that vegetables grew from plants in the soil.* Abel, *with a sheepish smile upon his countenance,* for his part brought the Lord 'one of the best firstlings' of his flock *instead of bringing 'his best firstling' for the Lord's pleasure.*

The Lord, *who loathed vegetarians and environmentalists,* looked with favor upon Abel and his "*one of the best firstling's* offering," but on Cain and his offering He did not, *preferring to exercise His contempt and discrimination against vegetarians in deference to human carnivores and omnivores.*

Cain greatly resented this rejection and was crestfallen. *The Lord God reviled Cain because being a fruit and vegetable harvester, Cain might eventually have figured out how to grow a dreadful Tree of Knowledge.*

So the Lord God said to Cain, "Why are you so resentful and crestfallen?"

And Cain asked the Lord, "Why do You' discriminate against fruit and vegetable farmers? Are You solely carnivorous, or what?"

"Cain," the Lord God said *while ignoring His' listener's objection*, "if you do well, you can hold up your head; but if not, sin is a demon lurking at the door; his urge is toward you, *and I call the shots in this silly life and death game we're playing.* You cannot be sin's master *until you come around and start 'pasturizing' your sheep like your brother Abel does daily."*

After the Lord left the premises to confer with Zeus and Poseidon, Cain said to his brother Abel, "Let us go out to the field *on a field trip."* When they were out in the field, *way out in left field,* Cain attacked his brother Abel *and was able to kill him.*

The Lord God returned from his conference with Zeus and Poseidon. "Where is your brother Abel?"

Cain answered, "I do not know. Am I my brother's keeper? *I have enough damned trouble being my own friggin' bookkeeper let alone my brother's damned keeper. I'm just glad there's no damned IRS around yet!"*

The Lord then said, "What have you done! Listen: Your brother's blood cries out to Me' from the soil. *He's screaming bloody murder!"*

And Cain replied, "I only killed my brother. I did not murder him. Murder is what a person does to another person. Killing is what a person does to an animal or what an animal does to an animal," Cain ineffectually argued. *"My brother was a bad-tempered beast, an animal that Your' blatant bias favored over me. That's why I killed the dirty bastard! You made me friggin' jealous of Abel!"*

"Cain," said the Lord God, "you shall be banned from the soil *and therefore can never be buried. The soil is sacred and* it opened its 'mouth' to receive your brother's blood from your hands!"

"I didn't know that the soil had a mouth!" Cain protested. "Must You' speak in bizarre personifications and metaphors?"

"Cain, if you try to till the soil," the Lord continued *while paying no attention to the profundity of Cain's exceptional words,* "the soil shall no longer give you its produce. *You will never be successful in fruit or in produce, I will see to that,"* God emphatically explained. "You shall become a restless wanderer on the earth, *and nothing more."*

14

Cain said to the Lord: "My punishment is too great to bear, *and I'm glad I also didn't eat any damned apple from that cursed tree besides killing Abel.* Since You' have now banished me from the soil, and I must avoid Your presence and become a wanderer on the earth, *can't You' at least give me a damned compass or weathervane to tell direction or which way the wind is blowing?" Cain pleaded.* "Anyone may kill me at sight." *All of this meant that there were thousands and thousands of other humans on the face of the earth besides (as erroneously presented in this fabled book) just Adam, Eve, Cain and Abel.*

"Not so!" the Lord God said to him. "If anyone kills you Cain, you Cain will be avenged sevenfold!"

"Then I'd really hate to be the guy who kills me," Cain frankly answered. "Humans can only die once, You' know! Why don't You' just bring my brother Abel back to life?"

"So the Lord put a mark on Cain, lest anyone should kill him on sight. *Cain liked his new tattoo, which had a big-breasted nude woman on his right bicep.*

Cain left the Lord's presence and settled east of Eden in the land of Nod, *where he would eventually go crazy because all of the people in Nod incessantly bobbed their heads up and down whenever they talked or whenever they listened. Even Nod's deaf, blind and mute residents followed the peculiar practice.*

Cain had relations with his wife, *which means that the Lord God had to marry him to someone somewhere in 'Nod', where everyone in the city was also winking and blinking while nodding. The wedding was a very easy ceremony to conduct with Cain and his new wife nodding their heads before, during and after they each had vowed: "I will!"*

Cain's wife (*notice that few women are named in the Bible because of the Lord God's chauvinistic philosophy and tendencies*) conceived and bore Enoch. *Cain also conceived.* He had an idea to 'found a city', *which he never again had to find because he had already found it.* He named the city after his son Enoch.

To Enoch (*and his nameless wife*) was born Irad, *who lived and was not 'iradicated' by God or by man.* Irad became the father of Mehujael. Mehujael became the father of Methusael, and Methusael became the father of Lamech. *All of this was rather remarkable because the four men became fathers without any women involved or ever giving birth.*

Lemech 'took' two wives; *the stolen women Lemech had pilfered had names, though.* The name of the first was Adah, and the name of the second Zillah, *so Lemech had everything going for him in the romance department from A to Z.*

Adah gave birth to Jabal, the ancestor of all who keep cattle and who dwell in tents, *or all who have tent sales on their lawns or who happen to wear tent dresses.* Jabal's brother's name was Jubal; Jubal was the ancestor of all who play the lyre and the pipe, *and all those who harp on others and also all plumbers who play around with pipes or others that smoke pot a certain way. All these people owe their ancestry to zany Jubal.*

Zillah, Lemech's second 'stolen' wife, on her part gave birth to Tubalcain, the ancestor of all who forge instruments of bronze and iron. *This clearly indicates that Adam's descendents were finally entering the bronze age hundreds of years after the Egyptians, the 'Cretans' and other ancient world cretins that had advanced to that less-than-mediocre low-tech' stage.*

The sister of Tubalcain was Naamah, *who was ugly, nasty, and miserable. Naamah had no children, but instead, she gave birth to the blues. Naamah later changed her name to En-Naamah.*

Lamech said to his wives: "Adah and Zillah, hear my voice, *since nobody else in this damned city of Nodheads fuckin' listens to me.* Wives of Lamech, listen to my utterances, *for I am pretending to be milking a cow and making the corresponding appropriate sounds and onomatopoeic animal noises.* I have killed a man for wounding me, a boy for bruising me," *Lamech confessed. "The bastard got what he deserved.* If Cain is avenged sevenfold, then Lamech seventy-seven fold, *for I know my damned mathematics as well as any of the hicks in this disgusting, drab city. Just give me the nod women and I'll continue my wild rampage!"*

Adam liked sex and he needed something to do with his huge erection. Adam again had relations with his wife, and she gave birth to a son whom she called Seth. *Adam preferred having kinky sex to naming the results of having sex, so that is why his wife named the boy.*

"God has given me more offspring in place of Abel," Eve said, *"because Cain slew him, and now we're gonna' have a whole slue of sons."*

To Seth, in turn, a son was born, *and this was the first time (we humbly believe) that a man had ever given birth to anything: animal, vegetable or mineral.* The child's name was Enosh.

16

At that un-momentous time *(we don't know exactly when because early religion is so vague and nebulous about such essential things as time)* men began to invoke the Lord by name, *cursing Him in vain for the lousy screwed-up world that He had either deliberately or haphazardly created.*

17

Chapter Five
"Generations: Adam to Noah"

This is the *very boring* record of the descendents of Adam. *Eve, like all other women in Genesis, is unimportant and not worth mentioning doing anything right.* When God created man *He got the idea from his good crony Zeus, who had created from dirt the first race of men, the Arcadians. The descendents of the Arcadians were the first mortals to play pinball and video game machines many millennia later.*

God created them (*pronoun antecedent problem*) male and female. When He' created them (*more pronoun antecedent problems*) He blessed them and named them "man" (*sexual antecedent problem*). *He was unconcerned with gender bias, let alone with gender. God just wanted to create man because He' had been inspired and influenced by His unpredictable buddy Zeus.*

Adam was one hundred and thirty years old when he begot a son in his likeness. *The first man desired a son after his image, because Adam wanted to imitate his Creator and also because Adam finally figured out what to do with his erection, which he carried around for over a century without a clue of its fabulous function.*

Adam named his son Seth (*in the last chapter Eve had named the boy*). Adam lived eight hundred years after the birth of Seth, and he had other sons and daughters *not mentioned here because they were rapists, pimps, priests, prostitutes, pedophiles, ball breakers and transsexuals. Also, primitive prehistoric people couldn't yet figure out the fundamental differences between male and female since God had called them both "man." It was indeed a very confusing time on earth.*

The whole lifetime of Adam was nine hundred and thirty years; then he died. *The early Hebrews didn't know too much about astronomy or mathematics, so they thought that months were years and that years were months. Hence, Adam's nine hundred and thirty years was really nine hundred and thirty months, so Adam died when he was seventy-seven and a half years old, or nine hundred and thirty months. This all was very confusing to early men considering that they were also bewildered about sexual definition and sexual orientation in addition to astronomy and mathematics. Men were still trying to figure out why women had big tits and wet pink pussies and they didn't.*

When Seth was one hundred and five years old (*really eight and three-quarters years of age*), he became the father of Enosh; *which indicates that Seth was very sexually precocious for his age and had plenty of adventurous sperm in his scrotum.* Seth lived eight hundred and seventy years after the birth of Enosh, and he had other sons and daughters too *because Seth liked to screw-around a lot, even if it meant having incest.* The whole lifetime of Seth was nine hundred and twelve years (*nine hundred and twelve months or seventy-six years*); then Seth died *not knowing the difference between months and years or the difference between the moon and the sun. He also knew little about astronomy, daily horoscopes and mathematics. Like Adam, all Seth knew how to do was screw-around and share his myriad erections by humping and pumping his brains out.*

When Enosh was ninety years old (*seven and a half-modern years*), he became the father of Kenan *to prove that he was more sexually precocious and hornier than his father, Seth.* Enosh lived eight hundred and fifteen years after the birth of Kenan, and he had other sons and daughters *because he had learned to screw around just like his old man Seth had done. Like father like son, so they say. And so, Enosh lived seventy-five and a half-modern-years without knowing or caring one iota about the significant difference between the moon and the sun (in terms of months and years) or the important distinction between astronomy and mathematics.*

When Kenan was seventy years old (*almost six*), he became the father of Mahalalel. *Kenan had a very overactive pituitary gland and super-powerful testicles in order to be super-fertile at age six.* Kenan lived eight hundred and forty years after the birth of Mahalalel, and he had other sons and daughters *not worthy of mention.* The whole lifetime of Kenan was nine hundred and ten years (*75 and three-quarters*); then he died *not achieving too much in his lifetime because all he did was screw-around like his un-inspired big-dicked ancestors Adam, Seth and Enosh had done. Consequently, real civilization hadn't started yet. Creativity was still just regarded as biological reproduction, and that undeniably proves that Adam and Eve did not eat the entire apple from the Tree of Knowledge.*

When Mahalalel was sixty-five years old (5.4 modern years), he became the father of Jared *just to show everybody that his erection could work at a younger age than his father Kenan's had.* Mahalalel lived eight hundred and thirty years after the birth of Jared, and he had other sons and daughters *because like his doltish male ancestors, he had trouble keeping his erect penis inside his loincloth.* The whole lifetime of Mahalalel was eight hundred and ninety-five years (74.5 modern years); *then he died from dehydration from loss of body fluids and from testicular dysfunction.*

Holy Moses! The organizer of Genesis likes to sound repulsively redundant. When Jared was one hundred and sixty-two years old he became the father of Enoch. *Enoch was already born in Chapter 4, but who gives a crap?* Jared lived eight hundred years after the birth of Enoch, and he had other sons and daughters *because his brain was in his penis and the man didn't accomplish too much in life other than pork ugly whores who were easier to entice and a lot cheaper to screw than pretty hookers.* The whole *lackluster* lifetime of Jared was nine hundred and sixty-two years *(eighty). On his deathbed Jared asked, "Is there a difference between the moon and the sun? And how can I tell the difference between months and years?"* Then the *puzzled and bewildered* man died.

When Enoch was sixty-five years old *(5.4)* he became the father of Methuselah, *and this was remarkable because Enoch never married or had sex with anybody, male or female.* Enoch lived three hundred years after the birth of Methuselah *and he had other sons and daughters just by masturbating without even ejaculating.* The whole lifetime of Enoch was three hundred and sixty-five years (30.4), *so Enoch was really never "as old as Methuselah." Enoch died when his ovaries and testicles coincidentally ceased functioning.* Then Enoch walked with God, and he was no longer here, for God took him. *"I'd better stay away from God if I want to stay around on earth and successfully screw every filthy slut I can find," Methuselah said to himself. "There seems to be a definite correlation between walking with God and then dying!"*

When Methuselah was one hundred and eighty-seven years old (15.5), *he got his first erection, used it wisely by planting it inside some unknown loose woman and became the father of Lamech, which was also mentioned in Chapter 4, indicating that the Book of Genesis definitely likes being redundant and chronologically inaccurate.* Methuselah had other sons and daughters *but it is unclear how many women or wives he had screwed to have them.* The whole lifetime of Methuselah was nine hundred and sixty-nine years of age (80.7); *then he became disgusted when he couldn't get any more erections and since he never did anything else constructive in life other than screw-around with whores, wives and prostitutes, he died being as old as Methuselah.*

When Lamech was one hundred and eighty-two years old (15*)*, *he got his first erection and said to himself'*, *"What the hell is this big gruesome-looking thing that's throbbing like crazy?"* Lamech *figured out what to do with his huge erection and begot a son via an anonymous woman*. Lamech called his offspring Noah, saying, "Out of the very ground that the Lord has put under a curse, this one shall bring us relief from our work and the toil of our hands. *Then I'll have more time to chase and grab big-breasted women, rape them, masturbate, get laid, and have a really good time,"* Lamech said to his erect penis. "Thank God for Noah to do some of my work! I'll now have more time to take a crap and to have non-stop sex. Relief at last!"

Lamech lived five hundred and ninety-five years after the birth of Noah, *whose coming was especially announced by an 'ark-angel.'* Lamech had other sons and daughters *who were deadbeats, pimps, felons, whores and annoying shit' heads, and those un-illustrious offspring are not deserving of inclusion in such a sacred text as the Wholly Book of Genesis*. The whole worthless lifetime of Lamech was seven hundred and seventy-seven years of age (64.7) *and he died having a strange vision of a slot machine window (777, which is a hell-of-a lot luckier than 666).*

When Noah was five hundred years old (41.6) he *married and porked Mrs. Noah* and became the father of Shem, Japheth, Ham', *Veal and Pork*. *"Who cares if we don't have priests around yet to marry us?"* Noah told his exhausted wife. *"We can now legitimately screw-around like our horny ancestors had done for centuries!"*

Chapter Six
"Origin of Nephilim"

When men began to multiple on the earth, *they also soon learned how to, add, subtract and divide.* Daughters were born to them, *even though many men had no wives, were gay, or were totally impotent.* The sons of heaven saw how beautiful the daughters of men were, *regardless whether the girls had mothers or not or whether they were kinky whores or horny hookers. So imitating Zeus and other chauvinistic Olympians over in ancient Greece,* many of the sons of heaven took for their wives the daughters of men.

Then the Lord *authoritatively* said, *"I am the Lord.* My spirit shall not remain in man forever, since he is but flesh, *including his pulsating erections.* His days shall comprise one hundred and twenty years *(you figure it out by dividing by twelve) as soon as we get this damned stupid month and moon and year and sun business completely figured out."*

At the time the Nephilim (prehistoric Giants of Palestine, *the idea taken from the Greek heroes such as Hercules, Phaethon, Theseus, and the Titans, the fifty-foot-tall ancestors of the Olympians),* came down from the heavens *without the use of ladders or stairs.* At the time *(we don't know exactly when)* after the sons of heaven had intercourse *(sex, but not oral)* with the daughters of man *(unknown females because women are unimportant but not un-impotent),* who bore them sons. They bore the Nephilim's sons *(because women were, as you know, unwanted or unneeded back in those despicable chauvinistic times).* They *(either the sons of Nephilim or the Nephilim themselves, we don't know which because of pronoun-antecedent problems and poor grammar and communications' skills exhibited throughout Genesis)* were the heroes of old *(notice, there were no heroines back then).* They were the men of renown *(since there was no place for heroines, because women's functions were to have sex, to have children and to be obedient subordinate housewives and cave wives).*

The Lord saw how great was man's wickedness on earth *(because man was made in His image and also because the first man had eaten a forbidden apple with his sinful curious wife).* The Lord observed how every desire man's heart conceived was evil, and He regretted that He had ever made man on the earth *in His image.* God's heart was grieved, *because all man ever thought about was getting laid and all women ever thought about was being laid, even though men and women were both 'man'. Thus is our heritage.*

23

So the Lord said, *"Screw this crap!* I will wipe out from the earth the men whom I have created, *even the ones that were born. What am I saying? I only created Adam and Eve and they're already dead!"*

Then the Lord continued saying to Himself', *"Since men do not listen to me, they have Me constantly talking to Myself! Anyway,* I will also destroy the beasts and the creeping things and the birds of the air, for I am sorry that I made them *and for I am essentially a destructive Deity Who' merrily relishes being a destructive Deity."*

But Noah found favor with the Lord. Noah was wimpy and obedient and did not challenge arbitrary, petty, tyrannical dictatorship and certain wild fits of Lordly' anger. Noah also never questioned why he got so many erections. The Lord favored Noah because of this, and Noah was blessed with many throbbing erections and healthy defecations.

"Noah, shape up or ship out!" the Lord commanded.

"I think I'll become an arkeologist!" Noah promised Heaven.

These are the descendents of Noah. Noah was a good man and blameless in that age, *even though his many perceptive peers called him a jerk' off.* Noah walked with God, *which according to past practice meant that he might soon die.* Noah begot three sons *(forget about Mrs. Noah who was the pregnant one in the family).* They were Shem, Japheth and Ham. *Veal and Pork were later illegitimate progenies that were not prodigies.*

In the eyes of God *were pupils, irises, corneas and optic nerves. God saw* "the earth" as being corrupt and full of lawlessness *despite the fact that the earth was not man and that man was made in His image.*

When God saw how corrupt "the earth" had become, *He believed He required the services of an optometrist.* Since "all mortals" led depraved lives on earth, He said to Noah *(even though Noah was himself' a mortal),* "I have decided to put an end to 'all mortals' on earth; the earth is full of lawlessness because of them. So I will destroy 'all mortals' and all life on earth *because this is My' game you're all playing down there, and if I can't have it My' way then I am going to pull rank around here, and show you mortal idiots exactly Who' the omnipotent Boss is around here!"*

Soon the Lord had a clever inspiration. "Noah, make yourself an ark of gopher wood. *You can also use groundhog wood, woodchuck wood, hedge 'hog' wood and termite wood if you'd like.* Put various compartments into the ark *but no glove compartments,*

24

please! Cover the ark inside and outside with pitch, *so that it will not only be pitch black inside the ark but also pitch black outside, too."*

The Lord proceeded with His marvelous dissertation. "This is how you shall build the ark: *very carefully!* The length of the ark shall be three hundred cubits, its width fifty cubits, and its height thirty cubits. *The metric system and the decimal system have not been invented yet, so you gotta' use stupid cubits, ya' hear?"*

Noah nodded his head up and down like his pathetic ancestors from Nod used to do in the city of Nod. Ham soon became the chief law enforcement officer of a Nod suburb where he was appointed the Sheriff of Noddingham.

"Noah, make an opening for daylight *even though it will be pitch black both inside and outside the stupid ark.* And Noah, be sure to finish the ark a cubit above it *because I said so and that's all that really matters in our relationship!" the Lord stipulated.*

"And Noah," the Lord continued, "put an entrance in the side of the ark, *and make it very entrancing to attract animals and creatures to the hatch.* Make the entrance on the bottom, second and third decks, *so you'll really need three entrances and not just one like I originally had told you, because next to destroying man and causing havoc, I often enjoy changing My mind and confusing mentally challenged humans like yourself."*

"This ark sounds like it's more trouble than it's worth!" Noah complained. "Can't I just commit suicide instead of enduring all this nonsensical grief and sacrifice?"

The Lord ignored Noah's reasonable entreaty. " I, on my part, am about to bring the flood waters on the earth, *so it's too bad your ark won't have floodlights to see what on earth is happening.* I want to destroy everywhere all creatures in which there is the breath of life, *so Noah, I guess you'll have to stop breathing for forty days and for forty nights because that's how long it's gonna' take for me to destroy the earth and its life forms.* Everything that breathes on earth shall perish. *My advice to you and to your family Noah is for you to stop breathing."*

Thinking about rain, then the Lord had a brainstorm. "But Noah, with you I will establish My' covenant, *which I am thinking about calling the Ark of the Covenant. So stop breathing when the rains begin and then the Ark of the Covenant will be your inspiration and also your expiration."*

"When will my ship come in?" Noah fearfully asked.

"You Noah, your sons, your wife and your sons' wives, *I forget their names because women aren't important in this book,* shall go into the ark *before it becomes pitch black outside.*"

"*Will there be a first class deck on the ark?*" *Noah inquired.*

God overlooked Noah's intelligent inquiry. "Noah, of all other living creatures you shall bring two into the ark, one male and one female, *and make sure that not even the tiniest insect is gay. Faggot animals have trouble reproducing even though I've allowed the males to get erections.* Keep these creatures alive with you, *for if you die, you will not know whether they are alive or not. And when it starts raining cats and dogs, do not let those cats and dogs inside the ark if you already have Dobermans and tabby' kittens stashed away inside the vessel.*"

"*Is there' anything else crazy or illogical You' have to say?*" *Noah asked.*

"*Yes,*" *the Lord replied.* "Of all kinds of birds, of all kinds of beasts, and of all kinds of creeping things, two of each shall come onto the ark with you, to stay alive."

"*The doomed boat's gonna' become a damned floating zoo,*" *Noah complained.*

"*Moreover,*" *the Lord interrupted,* "you are to provide yourself with all the food that is to be eaten, *so you had better invent refrigeration in a damned hurry if you want to live and endure.* Store the food away, that it may serve as provisions for you or for them."

"*Are there any other incomprehensible demands You're going to require?*" *Noah adamantly protested.*

"*Only one,*" *the Lord returned.* "*When your ark passes the ship of Gilgamesh of Babylonia on the high seas, you're allowed to wave at each other if you can see one another in the pitch blackness that exists both inside and outside the ark.*"

This Noah did. *Noah was a loyal fearful earthling and a silly fool who would believe and endorse anything, for Heaven's sake.* Noah carried out all of the commands that God gave him *(had given would be more perfect and more appropriate grammar).*

26

Chapter Seven
"The Great Flood"

Then the Lord said to Noah: "Go into the ark, you and all your household, for you alone in this age have I found to be truly just, *and all the rest of mankind and their families are stupid sinful morons. This is what I think and believe!"*

"Can't I just murder my family and then commit suicide instead of having to endure this great travail?" Noah pleaded. "I'd rather be dead than have to live through Your' stupid nonsensical game plan. You like supervising over ordeals, don't You!"

As usual, the Lord focused on what He wanted to say next and immortal deaf ears fell upon Noah's vain plea. "Noah, of every clean animal, take with you seven pairs, a male and its mate," the Lord commanded. "And of the unclean animals, one pair, a male and a female. *That way we can eliminate most of the terrible odor and stench in your already smelly ark. And of you and your family, take with you eight pair of underwear, each person in your company seven clean and one unclean!"*

"Is that all? I hope," Noah complained. "That's plenty of washing and scrubbing to do! What do You' think my wife is, a washing machine besides being a talking machine?"

"Likewise," the Lord said, *"of every clean bird of the air, seven pairs, a male and a female, because you don't want crummy dirty birds defecating on your exposed head for forty days and forty nights."*

"That crap sounds like it's for the birds," Noah agreed. "It sounds like foul fowl' play to me!"

"And of all the unclean birds, only have one pair, a male and a female, because those lousy birds smell like crap even before they defecate on your unworthy exposed head," the Lord insisted.

"That makes about as much sense as Your' grand retribution scheme," Noah asserted. *"Don't You' know anything besides pain, suffering, persecution, vengeance, torture, abuse and calamities!"*

"And Noah," God continued, "seven days from now I will bring rain for forty days and forty nights, *so make sure that your ark is in shipshape condition.* I will wipe out from the surface of the earth every moving creature that I have ever made, *because as you know, I am sometimes very cruel, vindictive, volatile and destructive. And if you and your family are lucky enough to survive this great ordeal, you might wind-up as refugees as far away as Arkansas, which hasn't yet been discovered by men."*

27

Noah did just as the Lord had commanded him. *Even Arkansas sounded better than death by drowning or by suffocating inside the ark in twenty-foot-high bird feces resulting from the putrid scummy rectums of clean and dirty birds.*

Noah was six hundred years old *(you figure it out by dividing by twelve)* when the great floodwaters came upon the earth, *hence the initiation of the first Watergate.* Together with his sons, his wife, and his sons' wives *(notice that the word 'wife' should have preceded the word sons),* Noah went into the ark because of the waters of the flood. *He couldn't swim or float and neither could anyone else in his family, so they nearly trampled over each other to quickly gain access to the ark's smelly interior.*

Of the clean animals and the unclean, of the birds, and of everything that creeps on the ground, two by two male and female entered the ark with Noah, just as the Lord had commanded him. *'It looks like I'm gonna' be shoveling a lot of manure and fecal matter before this crazy voyage to nowhere is over,' Noah woefully thought. 'I wouldn't wish this unsavory predicament on my worst enemy.'*

As soon as the seven days were over *(for the word 'week' hadn't been formulated yet),* the waters of the flood came upon the earth, *everywhere from Asia Minor to Arkansas. 'The best thing that could happen is for an iceberg to be out there so that the end will come soon and I won't have to endure any more illogical misery just to see the Lord's inane saga through to its silly end,' Noah candidly pondered.*

In the six hundredth year of Noah's life *(50 true years),* in the second month *(irrelevant picayune fact), on the seventeenth day of the month (absolute garbage trivia),* it was on that day that all fountains of the great abyss burst forth, and the floodgates of the sky were opened. *'I gotta' drown out all the sinful men and women on the earth before they use their clever intelligence to invent submarines or scuba gear,' the Lord reckoned. "And to think that man was created in My' flawless image! And I really like some of those stupid assholes too?" the Lord said out loud to no one in particular.*

For forty days and for forty nights heavy rains poured down on the earth *and every damp thing soon became wet. Every dedicated weatherman from Egypt to Mesopotamia was confounded by the meteorological phenomenon. Some became so angry that they even stormed out of their homes, huts, tents and caves.*

28

On the precise day named *(which escapes the memory of the author)*, Noah and his legitimate sons Shem, Japheth, and Ham, *and his illegitimate sons, Veal, Pork, Larry, Curly, and Moe,* and Noah's wife, and the three unimportant wives of Noah's legitimate sons had entered the ark's *animal enclosure. They reluctantly helped Noah with the horrendous animal fecal removal detail.*

Noah's family was together with every kind of wild beast, every kind of domestic animal, *and every kind of domestic dispute.* The family was also with the creeping things of the earth, *which still gave them all the creeps.*

Pairs of all creatures in which there was the breath of life *had* entered the ark with Noah, *who by now had entered the ark at least four times after having to survive being trampled on by his immediate family the first time his frail anatomy had entered the enormous vessel.*

Those that entered were male and female, *since no gay animals were allowed up the gangplank according to the Lord's edict.* All of the species they came, as God had commanded Noah. Then the Lord shut Noah in, *and consequently Noah became the first shut-in, sort of an invalid invalid.*

"Damn it!" Noah shouted to his nameless wife. "Why doesn't the Lord give me a wheelchair or something like that if he wants me to be a friggin' good-for-nothing shut-in!"

The flood continued upon the earth for forty days, *and since Noah was safe inside his ark, he really didn't give a dam or a reservoir what was going on outside.* As the waters increased, the waves lifted the ark, so that it rose above the earth, *and the boat had to be strong and the finished product of good 'arkitecture'.*

The swelling water increased greatly *and looked real swell,* but the ark floated on the surface *because it had no motors or propellers to whisk it through the water.* Higher and higher above the earth the waters rose, *and Noah said to Mrs. Noah, "We're gonna' get out of this damned mess come hell and high water."* Actually, that was the high water mark of the very boring and tedious forty-day voyage.

Soon all of the highest mountains everywhere were submerged, *even those that were at the peak of their existence.* The crest of water rose fifteen cubits higher than the submerged mountains, *which was more than enough to 'tide them over' until the next flood would eventually be visited upon the earth.*

All creatures that stirred on the earth perished, *and even the innocent dumb animals that never sinned or broke any of the Lord's arbitrary laws met their demise.* Birds, cattle, wild animals, and all that swarmed on the earth as well as all man' kind met their doom. *But naturally the fish in the sea didn't die. God was in His gory glory.*

Everything on dry land with the faintest breath of life in its nostrils died out. *Since there no longer was 'any dry land' anywhere on earth (not even Canada Dry), the last sentence was implausible and totally immaterial to the theme and text of this chapter.*

The Lord as usual during that epoch was in a violent, vindictive, destructive state of mind. Noah's ark didn't even have any lifeboats, lifesavers, or mints aboard. Considering the putrid animal and bird feces all over the place, the ark was a real 'mess', to say the least, and indeed the vessel should have landed in 'Mess-opotamia'.

The Lord wiped out every living thing on earth: man and cattle, the creeping things and the birds of the air, *enema bags and loincloths, and also gays and lesbians were systematically and demonstrably eradicated.* The birds of the air were gone, and all other life was wiped out from the earth *because the writers and organizers of Genesis like repeating themselves over and over. But the real losers were the humans and the animals that still occupied the ark. They were destined to have to suffer through hardship after hardship and would have definitely been much better off dead than alive.*

Only Noah and those stationed with him in the ark were left to live, *and as has been mentioned, that particular tragedy amounted to more of a curse than did death itself.*

30

Chapter Eight
"The Ark's Landing"

The waters maintained their crest over the earth for one hundred and fifty days *or for around six years if you buy into the theory that states years were really months back then in prehistoric times.* Then God, *Who was on a temporary mental holiday,* remembered Noah and all the animals, *but didn't recall the names of Noah's wife, sons, illegitimate sons and their unimportant wives.* God recalled that all the animals, wild and tame, were all with Noah in the ark, *which was still heading in the general direction of Arkansas.*

So God, *feeling a trifle guilty about His' lack of concentration and forgetting about Noah for a hundred and fifty days* made a wind sweep over the earth, *giving it a really good blow job,* and the waters began to recede *just like Noah's gray hairline. But the recession was not due to a bad economy as many Biblical scholars have hypothesized.* Soon the waters subsided.

The fountain of the abyss and the floodgates of the sky were closed *when the Lord shut off all of the heavenly valves manually.* The downpour from the sky was held back *and Heaven gave Noah a rain check ticket for a free admission to the next big deluge.*

Gradually the waters receded from the earth *(Are you readers thick, dense or what? How many times do we have to tell you this simple fact?)* At the end of one hundred and fifty days *(if you readers were smarter than the average cucumber, we wouldn't have to keep reiterating these obvious embellished details),* the waters diminished. So, it was the seventh month *(we finally got the idea of month straightened out, but we still have to work on the concept of year; it's hard to get Biblical scholars to agree on anything that is obvious or true).* On the seventeenth day of the month *when Mrs. Noah was to have her monthly period at age six hundred,* the ark was tired and came to rest on the mountains of Ararat, *somewhere in Turkey not far from the former villages of Chicken and Cacciatore.*

Noah said to his naughty nautical family, *"We must be at Sea World, on the other side of the earth somewhere near Arkansas."*

Japheth told his father Noah, *"Go tell it on the mountain."*

The waters continued to diminish until the tenth month, *when the Lord finally realized that the drain at the bottom of the earth's basin had been clogged, and so He used His plumbing skills and fixed the troubling problem.* On the first day of the tenth month the tops of the mountains appeared *(we mean to say here became visible because they had never disappeared at all but had been merely covered with excessive water).*

At the end of the forty days Noah opened the hatch he had made in the ark. *He then opened a goatskin of red wine, lifted it to his mouth and said to his thoroughly impressed family, "Down the hatch!"*

Noah sent out a raven to see if the waters had lessened on the earth; *however, the stubborn raven did not honor Noah's honorable intent but instead flew through the years and visited an American poet named Edgar Allan Poe. The black bird proceeded to tapping and rapping on the writer's door, pestering the poor fellow into becoming a chronic alcoholic just like Noah had been.*

The *itinerant* raven had been sent out to see if the waters had lessened on the earth, *since Noah was too lazy, scared and drunk to stand on a ladder, look out from the hatch and see for himself. Noah and his family then sang a rendition of their favorite song from antiquity, 'Bye, Bye Blackbird'. After traveling through time and space and visiting Edgar Allan Poe* the *totally disoriented* raven flew back and forth above the sea until the waters dried off from the earth, *which meant that the raven had to have powerful wings to be able to dry off the whole damned planet.*

Then Noah sent out a dove, *and told it to stay away from turtles.* But the dove could find no place to alight and perch, so it returned to Noah in the ark, for there were waters all over the earth, *so the raven hadn't done such a great job after all flapping its wings and evaporating the seas. And besides, the dove was just as lazy as Noah was, and it returned to the ark because it refused buying into the idea of flying all around on a wing and a prayer. Noah now believed that* there was water all over the earth. *No daaaa!*

'Putting out' his hand, Noah caught the dove, *and on the Lord's baseball scorecard, God gave Noah credit for a 'putout.'* Noah drew the dove inside the ark *without the use of any pen, pencil or writing paper, which is paper that is capable of doing its own writing without any dumb or intelligent humans involved.*

Noah waited seven days more *(remember, the snobby, backward incompetent Biblical scholars were still learning about the concept of week),* and once more sent the dove out from the ark *because the bird had again extensively crapped on the beleaguered captain's exposed bare head.*

In the evening the dove came back to Noah and there in its bill was a plucked-off olive leaf! So Noah knew that the waters had lessened on the earth *by the high water mark indicated on the olive* leaf. *'This damned olive leaf must be from a limb belonging to the Branch Dividians,' Noah facetiously theorized.*

Noah waited another seven days. *He had once been a waiter in a sleazy Mesopotamian restaurant so he was quite used to waiting.* Then Noah released the dove once more in the morning, *because he now knew that the dove was not a 'fly by night' operator.* This time the dove did not come back. *It was sick and tired of doing stupid chores and errands for the very lazy and drunken Noah.*

In the six hundred and first year of Noah's life *(I thought we had finally gotten this annoying and infantile year-month-day problem resolved),* on the first day of the month, *Noah got his monthly period.* The water began to dry up on the earth *(and to tell you the truth, we're tired of emphasizing that dumb monotonous fact).*

Noah then removed the covering of the ark and saw that the surface of the ground was drying up. *Noah said to everyone on the ark, "It's damned wet out there! But don't let it put a damper on your day!"* In the second month, on the twenty-seventh day of the month, *we're happy to report that no one on the ark was having hers or his period.* The earth was finally dry, *even in Canada and in Arkansas.*

Then God said to Noah: "Go out of the ark, *because I know you are too dumb to think of that all by yourself!* Go with your wife, and your sons and your sons' wives, *none of whom I know by name or even care to know by name."*

"What should I do next?" Noah impulsively inquired. "I can't swim, and I hate to wade or ford across shallow oceans and deep blue seas."

"Bring out with you every living thing that is with you-all bodily creatures, be they birds or animals or creeping things of the earth," *the Lord commanded.*

"Thank Heaven I don't have to be on the ark's shit-shoveling duty any more," Noah replied. "I've put up with taking a lot of crap from those animals and beasts."

"And Noah," the Lord continued, "let them abound on the earth, breeding and multiplying on it. *But make sure they don't subtract or divide, because I abhor subtraction and I loathe fission and fusion along with mitosis and meioses."*

Noah didn't know what the hell the Lord was talking about. So Noah came out together with his *nameless* wife and his sons and his sons' *insignificant* wives. And all the animals, wild and tame, all the birds, and all the creeping creatures of the earth left the ark, *which* now was stinking horribly to High Heaven and offending the Lord's super-sensitive olfactory senses.

Then Noah built an altar to the Lord, *which meant it was a very high altar because the Lord was situated way up in High Heaven. So, Noah had to alter his altar so that the pungent odor could ascend to that lofty height.* Noah chose from every clean animal and every clean bird, *which suggests that he had nothing to choose from since all of the animals were now filthy and unclean after forty days and forty nights standing in manure on that stench-laden ark.*

Noah offered his holocausts on the altar, *and the holocausts did not sit too pretty with the man's Hebrew wife, sons and their families, making them all feel quite uneasy. The smoke from the holocausts drifted all the way to Mesopotamia, and other Aryan skinhead nations of that distant time.*

The Lord smelled the sweet odor *(which was rather horrific stench from the animals standing in fecal matter inside the ark for a month and a half).* The Lord said to Himself: "Never again shall I use water to doom the earth because of man, since the desires of man's heart are evil from the start. *Next time I'll destroy all life on earth with fire and brimstone, with great hurricane-force winds or with tornadoes or volcanoes. But next time I shall only destroy man.* I never again will strike down all living beings as I have done this time."

And then the Lord continued, for lacking an audience, He often enjoyed speaking to Himself, "As long as the earth lasts, seed' time and harvest, cold and heat, summer and winter, and night and day shall not cease." *And then He said to Himself, "Now I have to get as far away from that ark as possible because it stinks worse than Hell ever will after I finally get around to inventing it!"*

Chapter Nine
"Covenant with Noah"

God blessed Noah and his sons and said to them, "Be fertile and multiply and fill the earth. *Get many erections and use them well and often. I need all of the worshipers I can get. Competition in the local god industry is getting hot and heavy. Don't get any vasectomies, and by all means, avoid castrations and double hernias. I need more devoted worshipers, you hear, so stay potent and keep hammering away!"*

Poor Noah, who was still seasick from his traumatic ark expedition, couldn't get a word in edgewise.

"And Noah, dread fear of you shall come upon the animals of the earth and all the birds of the sky, *and you will know the thrill of power like I do when everyone is afraid of you like they are of Me'.* The creatures that move about on the ground and all the fishes of the sea you shall have dominion over. Into your power and custody they were delivered. *And don't ask Me' any silly questions about prehistoric beasts, dinosaurs or the like because I don't remember or know a damned thing about them."*

Poor Noah still couldn't get a word in edgewise, nor did he even want to. He just wanted to be left alone after his wicked and traumatic ark ordeal.

"Every creature that is alive shall be yours to eat, *and even pigs are kosher right now, although that scenario might change in the future.* I give them all to you as I did the green plants," *the Lord specified.* "Only flesh' with its lifeblood still in it you shall not eat, *so whatever you do, don't devour any live animals. Make sure you kill them' first. If you like, you may, however, eat them raw should your fire expire."*

"But what if a lion, a tiger or a bear kills and eats me?" Noah anxiously asked. "I'm supposed to have dominion over them!"

"They should know better than that," the Lord responded. "Lions, tigers and bears should instinctively be aware that man is My' special creation and exempt from their harm," the Lord insisted. "But I must confess, accidents do occasionally happen when you get a rogue shark or a maverick leopard involved in the complicated equation. Some wild beasts just don't follow My' damned directions."

"That's a croc!" Noah screamed up toward Heaven.

"Are you defying My' supreme authority!" the Lord challenged.

"No, I meant to say there's a vicious crocodile over there," Noah meekly answered while pointing to his right, *"and it might be a rogue and have me for supper."*

"Anyway," the Lord proceeded, showing little heed to the basking crocodile, *"*I will demand an accounting: from every animal. And from man in regard to his fellow man I will demand an accounting for human life, *even though animals aren't supposed to have a free will like man does, they still have to live by the same rules and have an accounting when playing in My' ballpark. Therefore I plan to establish a new heavenly department, the IRS. The Internal Review Service will be loaded with angelic accountants and 'arkangels' doing reams of animal and human accounting."*

"That sounds like massive wasteful bureaucracy thousands of years before its time," Noah interrupted.

"Anyway Noah, if anyone sheds the blood of man, by man shall his blood be shed. For in the image of God man has been made," *the Lord maintained. "So Noah, kill all of the animals you want and stay away from dangerous rogue animals that might kill you, even if they aren't supposed to. Also, pay no attention to environmentalists that might try to talk you out of killing animals and having dominion over the earth."*

"Couldn't You' tell Shem, Japheth and Ham about this crazy stuff?" Noah objected. *"Why pick on me all the damned time? I am very deficient in coping mechanisms!"*

"Noah, be fertile, then and multiply *without the use of calculators or calcu-earliers.* Abound on earth and subdue it, *for this planet is your toy despite what those moronic environmentalists might scheme or say."*

At last Shem, Japheth and Ham reluctantly came over to join their father, who was on the verge of re-entering the ark and diving into a ten-foot-high mound of animal dung, which to him seemed a better alternative than all of the Almighty' bullshit he had been hearing.

God said to Noah and his sons, "See, I am now establishing My' covenant with you and your descendents after you. And My' covenant is also with every living creature that was on the ark with you, *even though the dumb animals can't speak or understand or think, they nevertheless are an integral part of our divine covenant."*

"Isn't that logic a little absurd, shallow and faulty?" Shem asked.

"Noah, so I say to you," the Lord said while ignoring Shem's contention, "all the birds, and the various tame and wild animals that

36

were with you and came out of the ark are part of our covenant," *the Lord repeated.*

"*Can't You take an advanced writing and logic course?*" *challenged Japheth. "You seem to be quite redundant, arrogant, monotonous, didactic, pedantic and overwhelmingly boring!*"

"*Son of Noah, for I forget your damned name and care little about it,*" the Lord abruptly continued, "I will establish my covenant with you, that never again shall bodily creatures be destroyed by the waters of a flood; there shall not be another flood to devastate the earth."

"*That's real great!*" *Ham butted in. "That really limits Your' cruel options to fire and brimstone, rainless hurricanes, tornadoes, earthquakes, cyclones, volcanoes and millions of crazy terrorists on the loose,*" *Ham observed and verbalized. "I'll now really be able to sleep much better at night because of Your' great generosity about eliminating floods.*"

God added: "This is the sign that I am giving for all ages to come, of the covenant between Me' and you (*who cares about proper grammar and etiquette*) and every living creature with you. I set My' bow in the clouds to serve as a covenant between Me' and the earth (*because I think of Myself' first*). When I bring clouds over the earth, and the bow appears in the clouds, I will recall the covenant I have made between Me' and you and all living things. *And if I get angry with you and your descendents,*" *the Lord indicated to Noah, "I will grab my bow and shoot from it fiery arrows and also fire-off male lightning bolts without nuts, just like my pal Zeus does.*"

"*But what if we don't want to be a part of this ridiculous covenant!*" *Shem vehemently objected. "Who needs such an insane plan to live by?*"

The Lord paid little attention to Shem's objective criticism. "*Son of Noah, the waters shall never again become a flood to destroy all mortal beings,*" *God reiterated.*

"*How many times do You' got to remind us of that?*" *protested Japheth. "Do You' think we're nincompoops or something?*"

The Lord laughed at Japheth's mortality and at his futility. "As the bow appears in the clouds, I will see it and recall the everlasting covenant that I have established between God and all living beings: all living creatures that are on the earth."

"*All right, already!*" *Ham retorted. "Do You' think You're talking to a bunch of retarded deaf and dumb idiots or what! You seem not to remember what You' had just said a moment before and You keep sounding like a parrot with an enormous brain tumor!"*

God then said to Noah, "This is the sign of the covenant I have established between Me' and all the mortal creatures that are on earth."

"I'm beginning to agree with my sons about all this stupid horse crap repeating," Noah replied.

The sons of Noah who came out of the ark *(this was way before gay humans had closets to come out of)* were Shem, Japheth and Ham. (Ham was the father of Canaan; *don't ask us how, because Canaan was a mini-country in those still prehistoric times)*. These three were the sons of Noah *(I honestly wish the organizers of Genesis had a more extensive vocabulary and better communications' skills),* and from them the whole earth was peopled *(of course, they needed women to help them do it I think)*.

Now Noah, a man of the soil, was the first to plant a vineyard. *He learned the idea from a woman named Martha.* When Noah drank some of his wine, he became drunk and lay naked inside his tent, *which was part of a local bizarre bazaar.*

Ham, the father of *the country* Canaan, saw his father's nakedness, and he quickly stepped outside the tent and told Seth and Japheth about it. *"He's trying to turn our bizarre bazaar into a bizarre strip mall!" Seth complained.*

Shem and Japheth, however, took a robe, and holding it on their backs, they walked backwards *and then disrobed.* With the robe they covered their father's nakedness. Since their faces were turned the other way they did not see their father's nakedness *(yes, we like repeating ourselves), nor did they want to because Noah had a rather ugly decrepit-looking ancient anatomy. So Seth and Japheth told Ham to place the robe over their father.*

When Noah woke up from his drunkenness, *he disrobed, because he preferred walking around stark naked in his bizarre bazaar tent.* He quickly learned what his youngest son had done to him, *because Noah knew that his two older sons Seth and Japheth didn't give a shit about anyone or anything. So naturally, according to Biblical tradition, the young innocent good guy who tried being helpful has to be mercilessly punished.*

Noah said, "Cursed be Canaan, the children of Ham! *May they never eat Pork!* The lowest of slaves shall be to his brothers." He also said, "Blessed be the Lord, the God of Shem! Let Canaan be His' slave."

Noah's mania continued, "May God also 'expand' Japheth *and make his body out of some new materials like rubber or plastic.* Japheth and his children shall dwell in the *bizarre bazaar* tents of Shem. Let Canaan be His' slave, also. *Ham and his sons and daughters must be punished for trying to help me when I was drunk and naked by finding his brothers to get a robe from the local bizarre bazaar."*

Noah lived three hundred and fifty years after the flood, *and who gives a damn about his nameless wife.* The whole lifetime of Noah was nine hundred and fifty years *(divide by twelve);* then he died *not knowing or caring one iota about the difference between years and months or between mathematics and astronomy. Such was the tradition of the Old Testament.*

Chapter Ten
"Table of Nations"

Here is the Table of Nations, which was really colossal in size to be able to accommodate everyone in the known world, and therefore was no picnic to build and assemble. These are the descendents of Noah's sons, *and notice that they are all males in that women were always and were only regarded as baby making machines way back then.* Noah's *legitimate* sons were Shem, Ham and Japheth, to whom sons were born after the flood, *and as you already know, women and girls didn't matter at all. But on the ark the sons and their unknown wives needed some diversion from shoveling animal manure so they also screwed-around a lot exchanging their anonymous wives when Noah wasn't supervising them.*

The 'descendents' of Japeth, *who all liked walking down steps all the time:* Gomer, *Pyle, Maggot,* Magog, *Eggnog,* Madai, *Mayday,* Javan, Tubal, *Cylindrical,* Meshech and Tiras.

The 'descendents' of Gomer, *who all liked falling and tumbling down steps all the time:* Ashkenaz, *Alcatraz,* Riphath, *Ripoff and* Togarsmah.

The 'descendents' of Javan, *who both walked and fell down steps backwards:* Elishah, *Doolittle,* Tarshish, *Tarshishkabob,* the Rodanim and the *whole* Kittam *and Caboodle.*

These are the 'descendents' of Japheth, *who all rolled down steps instead of walking or falling backwards down them.* From them sprang the maritime nations, *but don't ask me how unless you believe that their mothers' salt water bags broke.* Here they are in their respective lands, *which were not always respectful lands.* Each land had its own language-by their clans *and by their Nazi' Ku-Kluxers within their Aryan nations. And when there were hurricanes storm troopers were all over the damned land.*

The descendents of Ham: *Cured,* Cush, *Tush,* Put, *Push, Pull,* Caanan, and finally *Cannon.*

The descendents of Raamah: *Jungle, Cumbackaliddle,* Sheba, *Little Sheba* and Dedan.

Cush became the father of Nimrod, *who became the father of Diviningrod.* Nimrod became the first potentate on earth, *long before there were any Shriners or Grand Dragons around.* Nimrod became a mighty hunter by the grace of the Lord, *and he was a good friend of Orion, Artemis, Atalanta and Georgia.* The saying goes, "Like

Nimrod, a mighty hunter by the grace of the Lord," *so as you can plainly see Biblical history often repeats itself.*

The chief cities of Nimrod's kingdom were Babylon, Erech, and Accad, all of them in the land of Shinar, *where the 'shin are' in the bottom part of the legs located closer to the ankles than to the knees.* Shinar *actually* was ancient Sumer in southern Mesopotamia, *so why didn't we just discuss Sumer in the first place instead of having to define and explain all about the assholes living in Shinar.*

From that land Nimrod went forth to Asshur, *which is another name for ancient Assyria. The Ass-searians had developed a special surgical technique for cauterizing rectums and getting rid of all the big assholes in the world.* Nimrod built Ninevah, Rehoboth, *Rehoboth Beach*, and Calah, *but not all by himself.* Calah was the principal city, *so no vice-principals or school superintendents were allowed there.*

Mizraim, *who had overactive testicles and mucho hyperactive sperm to spare*, became the father of the Ludim, the Anamim, the Lehabim, the Naphtuhim, the Pathrusim, the Casluhim, *the Colosseum*, the Caphtorim *and the Cafetorium* from whom the Philistines sprang. *He did all that without any Biblical mention of a wife, hussy or concubine. Wives were unimportant way back then and hussies and concubines were even less important during the great chauvinistic age of early Genesis. And Biblical scholars were those hoary whoring-around rabbis and prophets that wore bibs.*

Canaan became the father of Sidon *and that was the first time a country ever became a daddy.* Sidon was Canaan's first born, and of Heth. *Heth was not a woman; it was the land of the Hittites, who were a barbarian tribe that only punched people that were wearing tight leotards. (We now have another serious grievous pronoun antecedent problem that follows right here).* Also of the *Jeb-bushites* were the Amorites, *the Last Rites*, the Girgashites, the Hivites, the Arkites, *the Arkettes*, the Sinites, the Arvadites, *the Troglodytes,* the Zemarites, *the Meteorites* and the Hamathites.

Afterward, the *fucked-up* clans of the Canaanites spread out, so that the Canaanite borders extended all the way from Sidon to Gerar, near Gaza, and all the way to Sodom and Gomorrah, Admah and Zeboim, near Lasha, *which were in truth the seven blunders of the ancient world.*

These are the descendents of Ham, according to their clans and languages, *which were mostly later forms of prehistoric Pig Latin slang and the like.*

42

To Shem, *who was no sham*, also, Japheth's oldest brother and the ancestor of all the children of Eber, sons were born *(of course, without any mothers or wives)*.

The descendents of Shem: Elam, Asshur, *Wiseasshur, Hambone,* Arpachshad, Lud, Aram and *Aram-a-danna-ding-dong.*

The descendents of Aram were the folowing men: Uz, *Us, Oz, Ozzie, Harriet,* Hul, Gether, *Gather',* Mash *and Mashed Potato.*

Arpachshad became the father of Shelah *without ever having sex with anyone, male, neuter, bisexual or female.* Shelah became the father of Eber *by following the abstinence pattern that had been established by his father, Arpachshad.*

To Eber two sons were born: *(He dared not have any girls and risk being stoned to death by his belligerent chauvinistic peers).* The name of the first was Peleg, *who later sailed on sea voyages with a captain named Ahab.* In Eber's time the world was divided, *(how and why we'll never know. Also, we'll never know how it was put together again without any Eskimos using e-glue).* The name of Peleg's brother was Joktan *(this is almost as much fun as reading the dictionary or studying an address book backwards and upside down). Joktan only had darker skin in his genitalia area.*

Joktan became the father of Almohad, *and this was remarkable because instead of being a potentate, Joktan was an impotent'tater like Mash was'.* And Joktan also became the father of Almodad, *Islamabad,* Sheleph, Hazarmaveth, Jerah, Hadoram, Uzal, *Uzarubber,* Diklah, *Dikhead,* Obal, *Offal,* Abimael, Sheba, Ophir, *Oprah,* Havilah, *Nageela,* Jobab and *Joebob.* All of these were descendents of Joktan, *and none of those imbeciles were ever listed in an address book or directory other than the infallible Wholly Book of Genesis.*

Their settlements extended all the way to Sephar, the eastern hill country, *and many locals maintained that the children of Joktan are "as old as the hills."*

These are the descendents of Shem, who preferred descending ladders than walking or falling down steps. *How they ever got to the tops of ladders remains a Biblical secret because the descendents of Shem preferred crawling to actual climbing.* The *skinhead* descendents of Shem are listed according to their clans and languages, by their lands and by their *Aryan* nations.

These are the groupings of Noah's three *horny* sons, *who, as you can tell, liked to screw-around a lot with anonymous, nameless trivial, unworthy of mention loose females.* They are listed according to their origins and by their nations *(so what else is new?).* From these groupings the other nations of the earth branched out after the flood, *and according to Biblical folklore even the unpredictable self-destructive Branch Dividians branched out.*

Chapter Eleven
"The Tower of Babel"

Moses was the 'principal' organizer of the Book of Genesis. Moses had assembled the book without the aid of any vice-principal, curriculum coordinator or school board members. The sage compiled the events and the facts many centuries after the episodes had occurred, thereby making much of what is recorded and reported in Genesis subject to hundreds of years of distorted logic, folk tales, gossip and extravagant myths. The authors' claim that the book's content contains absolute truths, even though they are written in poor grammar and reflect weak craftsmanship. When Moses finally got to Chapter Eleven, he strongly considered filing for moral bankruptcy.

The whole world spoke the same language, using the same words, *which meant that for once, everybody understood each other even though the world (and not people) was doing the speaking. Actually, the world didn't speak the same language; the thoroughly confused people on the earth did.* While men were migrating all over the known world *no one knows what the hell the anonymous horny kinky women were doing.*

The men came upon a valley in the land of Shinar, *ancient Sumer in southern Mesopotamia, so what's with this stupid repetitious Shinar business?* They said to one another, "Come, let us mold bricks and harden them with fire." *Others said in unison, "Come, let us mold fire and harden it with bricks," just to be funny and different.* They used stone, bitumen and *later bit-four men* for mortar.

The men then said, "Come, let us build ourselves a city and a tower with its top in the sky," *since everyone not only spoke the same language and used the same words but also said the exact same words at the exact same time after having the exact same thoughts. Harmony and uniformity persisted.* "And so, we shall make a name for ourselves *(because they all wanted to have the same name);* otherwise we shall be scattered all over the earth." *This asinine logic actually made a great deal of sense to everyone, who really never thought about what they were all saying together any way. They just liked the idea of chanting, which they somehow found enchanting.*

The Lord came down to see the city and the tower the men had built *because His telescope had temporarily ceased to function.* Then the Lord *sternly* said, "If now, when they are one people, all

45

speaking the same language, they have started to do this, nothing will stop them from doing whatever they presume to do. *I must stifle their harmony and their ambition." The Lord realized that men were becoming organized and He didn't like it one bit since it violated His' divine 'Divide and conquer' strategy, for the Lord didn't want to lose any of His* worshipers *to other area gods or to the birth of science or to the formation of labor unions.*

"Let us *(we don't know who the others were)* go down there and confuse their language, *just to bust their stones.* That way each one will not understand what another says," *the Lord spoke to His' anonymous listeners.*

Thus the Lord scattered them *(humans)* from there to all over the earth, *some of them even to remote settlements like Arkansas.* And they stopped building the city, *obviously because nobody was around Sumer anymore with everybody being scattered all over the damned wretched planet searching for opportunities to instigate trouble or to get laid.*

That is why the city and the tower are called Babel, because the Lord had confused the speech of all' the world *so that now none of the planet's blundering inhabitants could speak 'down to earth' language. The people were soon called Babblelonians, but that doesn't matter here in that the humans were no longer living in the city or were no longer trapped in the tower.*

This is the record of the descendents of Shem, *who had once journeyed to Giza, learned how to walk like an Egyptian, and formed a strange singing group there known as Shem the Sham and the Pharaohs.*

When Shem was one hundred years old *(divide by twelve)*, his *testicles were finally activated* and he became the father of Shelah. Arspachshad lived three hundred years after the birth of Shelah, *and spent most of his years wondering whether he should invent a sundial or a moon dial to accurately tell time.* Arspachshad had other sons and daughters *whose names were even more incomprehensible than his own ridiculous appellation.*

When Shelah was thirty years old he became the father of Eber, *so watch it when you become thirty or else you might automatically become someone's father without even knowing it.* Shelah lived four hundred and three years after the birth of Eber, and he had other sons and daughters. *Forgive the mentally limited author of Genesis for not ever taking a creative writing course.*

When Eber was thirty-four years old *he had lived four hundred and eight months*. He became the father of Peleg. Eber lived four hundred and thirty years after the birth of Peleg and he had other sons and daughters. *Forgive the author of Genesis but he's still trying to think of some kind of plot or theme to this very redundant and boring book.*

When Peleg was thirty-three years old, he *screwed-around and* became the father of Reu. Peleg lived two hundred and nine years after the birth of Reu. *Please forgive the author because he never learned to add too well to figure out the number two hundred and forty-two (thirty-three plus two hundred and nine).* Peleg had other sons and daughters, *who like their father, never accomplished much on the earth except living badly and having children without having known wives or husbands.*

When Reu was thirty-two years old, he became the father of Serug. Reu lived two hundred and seven years after the birth of Serug, *and no, the author/authors of Genesis never learned the importance or the skill of using sentence variety or transitional paragraphs.*

When Serug was thirty-three years old he became the father of Nehor *despite the fact that Serug had a low sperm count and a hairy ugly incoherent wife.* Serug lived two hundred years after the birth of Nahor *and was happy to die and get his butt off of the lackluster planet.* Serug had other sons and daughters, *but he was apathetic and left it up to Nahor to give them names and never learned what the heck their unimportant names were.*

When (*an awful lot of "Whens" introducing paragraphs in this tedious chapter*) Nahor was twenty-nine years old he became the father of Terah *(Do you see a definite pattern here, or what?)* Nahor lived one hundred and nineteen years after the birth of Terah, and he had other sons and daughters *but being lethargic left it up to Terah to name them. Terah kept the names secret to himself. So Nahor died not knowing the names of his other sons and daughters but he still remembered who' his brothers and sisters were.*

When Terah was seventy years old he became the father of Abram, Haran, and Nahor *(who incidentally was reincarnated as himself').*

This is the record of the descendents of Terah *as recorded in the deeds, birth certificates and official documents and statistics' registry office that was located somewhere in an alley in Ur, Mesopotamia.* Terah became the father of Abram, Nahor and Haran, *despite the fact that he had been born without a penis and testicles* and never had oral or natural sex with any unidentified, insignificant woman.

Haran became the father of Lot, *who later became the world's first real estate agent.* Haran died before his father Terah had, in his native land *where the natives were often restless and never slept during the night or during the day.* Haran had lived in Ur, the city of the Chaldeans, *and his motto was "to Ur is human, to forgive is to err."*

Abram and Nahor 'took' wives *that didn't belong to them;* the name of Abram's wife was Sarai, *who was six-foot-ten inches tall. Sarai also weighed four hundred pounds and told her husband Abram that her name better be placed in the book of Genesis or else she would kick his butt repeatedly until it would become tenderized meat and his testicles would become tender loins.*

Nahor's wife was Milcah, daughter of Haran, *and Milcah like Sarai was a big mama who told Nahor that his ass was grass unless her name would be mentioned in Genesis, also. But Nahor really got his ass kicked after he told Milcah to "go milka' the cows!"*

Sarai was barren, *so she could never be a barreness.* She had no child, *which confirms that she was barren. However, Sarai might not have been barren after all. Abram might have been barren, or might have had a bad epididymis or even a defective scrotum.*

Terah took his son Abram, his grandson Lot, son of Haran, and his daughter-in-law Sarai, the wife of his son Abram, and *the patriarch* brought them out of Ur of the Chaldeans *to get away from decent people who believed in the development of science and civilization.*

But when Terah and his family reached Haran they settled there, *even though Haran was a person and the father of Lot. (Yes, a noun is the name of a person, place or thing, and the name of a person can also be the name of a thing, even though Genesis never exactly clarifies that unsettling point with usage of the word 'Haran').*

The lifetime of Haran was two hundred and five years; then Terah died in Haran *(we presume the place in Assyria, where the science of proctology was just beginning to develop with the emergence of the Ass-seareans experimenting with cauterizing rectums, colons and semi-colons).*

48

Chapter Twelve
"Abram's Call and Migration"

The Lord said to Abram: "Go forth from the land of your *mentally deficient* kinsfolk and from your father's house to a land that I will show you, *for you have to get away from civilization, culture and science and only worship Me."*

Since Abram was dumbfounded by the Lord's dramatic statement, a long pause ensued and then God continued his dissertation. "Abram, I will make you a great nation, and I will bless you *if you obey My' arbitrary commands and not curse Me' because I occasionally take pleasure in breaking your all-too-vulnerable stones.* I will make your name great so that you will be a blessing."

"Can't I make my own name great without Your' assistance?" Abram asked the thunderous Voice from the sky. "I do have a degree of ability and intelligence, you know!"

"Abram, *it's all quite simple and elementary.* I will bless those that bless you and curse those that curse you. *I'll give it to you 'straight',"* the Lord stated. "All the communities of the earth shall find blessing in you, *except the ass' hole gay community. That means I am only kidding about cursing anyone who is really straight."*

Abram went as the Lord directed him. *Old Abram was gullible and had once bought Mt. Ararat for two healthy cows, three chickens and a donkey without ever even seeing Mt. Ararat.* Lot went with Abram *only because the real estate agent desired to look for beachfront property having location', location, location.* Abraham was seventy-five years old when he left Haran *and the patriarch only had three hundred more years to qualify for Biblical social security (only if he wore a bib for that long).*

Abram took his wife Sarai, his brother's son Lot *(which we've already mentioned) and* all the possessions, which they had accumulated. The leader also transported the persons *(slaves, harlots, concubines, prostitutes, whores)* they had acquired in Haran, and they set out for the land of Canaan, *which even the poorest and most impoverished caravan traders avoided at all costs.*

When they came to the land of Canaan, *Abram said, "This must be the land of Canaan."*

Abram passed through the land as far as the sacred place at Shechem, by the terebinth of Moreh *(a small European tree that somehow got transplanted between Assyria and Egypt).* The Canaanites were then in that land *and they didn't like trespassers,*

49

interlopers, poachers, preachers, intruders, used donkey salesmen or *moochers hanging around in their territory, which they reputedly were very territorial about.*

The Lord appeared to Abram and said, "To your descendents I will give you this land."

"And Abram skeptically replied, "What about the Canaanites? It's their land and they ain't gonna' like it too much if I claim it! Those guys are notorious territorial bastards!"

"They'll just have to live with it," the Lord cleverly answered. "They're gonna' have to play by My' rules or die by some great imaginative catastrophe I shall contrive!"

So Abram built an altar there to the Lord who had appeared to him *and then later disappeared, trying to impress Abram with His' most splendid magic. "Building this altar is a real sacrifice," Abram complained to Lot, who merely stood around shaking his head left and right while watching obedient Abram assiduously labor.*

From there Abram and his group moved on to the hill country east of Bethel to the west and near Ai to the east. There, Abram built an altar to the Lord *even before the Lord appeared to command it or later disappeared before thanking Abram for his efforts.* Abram invoked the Lord by name, *but the Lord never showed up, preferring to not recognize all of the poor man's hard work ambitiously and industriously constructing the second altar.*

Then Abram journeyed on by stages to the Negeb *although stagecoaches were not yet invented and even though Abram only had a cavalcade of cheap donkey carts and beasts of burden to transport his slaves, concubines and loose women across the hostile arid desert. The arid desert made the loose woman get hot in a hurry.*

There was great famine in the waste land *that the Lord wanted Abram to claim, and even the primitive people were hungry, too, just like the ancestors of the Hungarians.* So Abram went down to Egypt to sojourn there since the famine in the land was severe *(as of yet, we don't know if Lot, the slaves, the concubines or the loose women were still accompanying Abram).*

When Abram was about to enter Egypt, he said to his wife Sarai: "I know how beautiful a woman you are, *even though I am near blind and completely delusional.* When the Egyptians see you, they will say 'She is his wife'; then the Egyptians will kill me, but they will let you live. *Why did I ever listen to the Lord in the first damned place? I should have stayed safe and sound in Ur and enjoyed the development of civilization, culture and science!"*

"What should I do husband?" Sarai asked. *"What if the Egyptian men are better looking than you are and have better sexual equipment that actually work?"*

"Sarai," said Abram, "please say *to them* that you are my sister, so that it may go well with me on your account and my life may be spared for your sake. *I am not a warrior and am basically a cowardly, craven old man and will not fight over any woman, sterile, well-endowed or otherwise."*

When Abram came to Egypt the Egyptians saw how beautiful Sarai was; and when Pharaoh's courtiers saw her, they praised her to Pharaoh, *who was hot and horny and tired of putting the royal salami to scrawny and non-passionate frigid Egyptian women.* So, Sarai was taken into Pharaoh's Palace, *a local gambling casino not far from the Luxor, where everything was royally opulent and 'luxorious'.*

On Sarai's account it went very well with Abram', and he received flocks and herds, male and female slaves, male and female asses, *but the female slaves had nicer asses than the male slaves had.* Abram also received camels too, *all because he had been shrewd enough to give his wife to the Pharaoh in exchange for domesticated animals and primitive cancer-causing cigarettes.*

But the Lord struck Pharaoh and his household with severe plagues because of Abram's wife Sarai. *So, blame it all on the woman even though it was Abram's idea to prostitute his own wife that actually had been the grossly immoral decisive factor. Abram's selfish act had immensely angered the Lord, and then instead of punishing Abram, the Lord socked it to poor old Pharaoh, who only desired enjoying a good piece of ass.*

Then Pharaoh summoned Abram *to his throne* and said to him, "How could you do this to me? Why didn't you tell me Sarai was your wife?"

"Because first of all I didn't want to die by having your heartless soldiers kill me," shrewd Abram disclosed. *"Secondly, I wanted to see your jerk' off land suffer immensely and thirdly, I wanted the Lord to kick your ass good'! I know how vindictive and possessive He can be!"* Abram confided. *"He knows how to bust chops and even Cheops too!"*

"Why did you say 'She is my sister'? Then *naturally* I took Sarai for my wife!" Pharaoh ranted.

"I thought I would outsmart you in a neat manner," Abram replied. *"You might be a Pharaoh but you're also a stupid-ass conceited bastard to boot!"*

51

"Here, then, take your *voluptuous ready-to-pump* wife!" *Pharaoh yelled in a state of rage.* "Take her and be gone *from Egypt! I've never met such fucked-up people in all my goddamned life!"*

Then Pharaoh gave his men orders concerning Abram and they sent him on his way, with his wife and all that belonged to him. *The Egyptians wanted no more to do with the crazy unethical wanderer or with his vengeful jealous Lord.*

Chapter Thirteen
"Abram and Lot Part"

From Egypt Abram went up to the Negeb with his wife *(the Pharaoh's former wife) whom the patriarch had given to Pharaoh so that paranoid Abram would not be killed by bloodthirsty Egyptian guards. The neurotic old codger feared that the soldiers might have thought that Abram had been Sarai's husband or that Sarai might have been Abram's wife. But Abram did not discuss or complain about all of this insanity with Sarai. She was big enough to effectively pound him right into the desert sand', and the patriarch knew that perfect truth very well, women's liberation or no women's liberation.*

Abram also took all that belonged to him *that he had cunningly tricked and deceived the Pharaoh out of.* Now Abram was very rich in livestock, *pork bellies,* frankincense futures, silver and gold, *thanks to the generosity of Pharaoh who had been pressured into being generous because of a few simple plagues and famines that nearly destroyed his prosperous kingdom, thanks to the tenacious Lord.*

From the Neheb Abram traveled by stages toward Bethel *because his buckboard had broken a spring under its seat so stagecoaches were the only alternative mode of transportation. Also, Abram was allergic to camel dung.* Then he returned to the place between Bethel and Ai where his tent had formerly stood *at attention.* It was the same site where Abram had built the first altar to the Lord *while Lot had looked and laughed at him while shaking his head left and right a lot.* There, Abram invoked the Lord by name, *since sometimes when Abram silently prayed the full message didn't get through.*

Lot, who went with Abram, also had flocks and herds *and herds of flocks and flocks of herds.* Lot saw that the *infertile* land could not support all of his livestock, *of which most he had won while cheating Abram in an unscrupulous but addictive dice game.* Lot knew that Abram and he could not stay together *because they were not Siamese twins. Abram might get angry that Lot had cheated him out of the livestock in the dice game and then have his wife Sarai beat the crap out of him, thus affording Abram's nephew a poor Lot in life as a paraplegic.*

The wise-acre Lot knew it was time for him to separate his possessions from those of Abram *before the ruthless Amazon Sarai would in due time begin to swiftly pulverize and castrate him.* There

53

were quarrels between the herdsmen of Abram's livestock and those of Lot, *which meant lots of quarrels. (At this time the Canaanites and the Perizzites were occupying the land that the Lord's trespassers had invaded). This occupation of other clans verified that Abram and Lot and their people had been officially encroaching, but since there wasn't any Our Father' prayer in existence yet, it really didn't matter if they trespassed against others.*

So Abram said to Lot *(after he had communicated with the Lord, Who' was Abram's chief adviser, accountant and psychiatrist),* "Lot, let there be no strife between you and me, or between your herdsmen and mine, for we are kinsmen *akin to friendly enemies. Although you are young and can easily kick my butt, we both know that Sarai could kick yours into bacon and pork so that we will look like Ham."*

"What did you have in mind?" Lot asked. *"I think that a royal rumble between my people and your herdsmen would solve the problem in a hurry."*

"Forget a drastic solution. Is not the whole land at your disposal?" *Abram rhetorically countered.* "Lot, please separate from me *even though we are not Siamese twins. If I lose any more dice rolls to you, I will be a pauper and be reduced to one of your lowlife herdsmen.* If you prefer the left, I will go to the right; if you prefer the right, I will go to the left; *if you prefer the center, then I will go to the middle."*

"What the hell are ya' talkin' about, you old senile fool?" Lot *challenged.*

"Lot," said Abram, *"I can't afford to be around you any more. You're driving me to the poorhouse even though we aren't even in an oxcart. You're a good real estate man and you know the importance of subdivisions when they are needed. Besides that, you're a hell-of-a good dice roller."*

Lot looked around *in spite of his stiff neck, a stiff neck he had acquired from watching Abram meticulously build all those enormous altars.* Lot saw how "well watered" the whole Jordan Plain was as far away as Zoar, *even though there was no well water or water that was well' available from wells.* (This was before the Lord had destroyed Sodom and Gomorrah, *foreshadowing writing technique utilized at this crucial juncture' as the lackluster Genesis author becomes a trifle more imaginative).*

Lot, *being greedy,* chose for himself the whole Jordan Plain and set out eastward with his people and possessions. Thus Abram and

54

Lot separated from each other *despite the fact that only Lot and his herdsmen and his people left the area.*

Abram stayed in the land of Canaan *to annoy and pester the local inhabitants with his blatant trespassing, and if anyone challenged his presence, he had a false deed that had been shrewdly drawn up by Lot.*

Lot settled among the cities of the Plain, *which were just ordinary plain cities to begin with.* Lot 'pitched' his tent near Sodom, *but he couldn't throw it too far.* Now the inhabitants of Sodom were very wicked *so it was easy for Lot to fit right in there.* Their sins they committed against the Lord, *but Lot's sins were committed against Abram, who happened to be the Lord's chief human friend and principal resident worshiper.*

After Lot had left, the Lord said to Abram, "Lot has left."

Abram alertly replied, "Now we can connive and scheme in private without that curious busybody eavesdropping every time I build a new altar or re-condition an old one."

"Abram," the Lord's *booming Voice* said *from Heaven,* "look about you. Gaze to the north *to Gaza,* the south, the east and the west, *even though you appear to be both autistic and dyslexic. As you can determine, I really and truly know My' four directions well."*

"What's the catch?" Abram suspiciously inquired.

"All the land that you see I will give to you and to your descendents forever *even though it presently belongs to the apostate non-believer Canaanites," the Lord said.*

"But isn't that only going to cause conflict and disrupt area agrarian tranquility?" Abram protested. "I mean, just because those sinners don't worship You', why must I suffer from the contempt You feel in Your heart toward the people of Sodom. I know, You're trying to make the Wholly Book of Genesis into a decent novel with a plot and some action along with a moral theme by giving it a definite problem and intense friction between enemy factions that hate each other."

"Abram, *don't rub Me' the wrong way," the Lord threatened.* "I will make your descendents like the dust of the earth; if anyone could count the dust of the earth, your descendents too might be counted *since they will certainly be a smaller number than the number of dust and dirt particles in the earth."*

"What are You' really trying to say?" Abram demanded. "Stop being so damned vague and evasive with all of this warped symbolic, figurative language that You' have the bad habit of using all the

time! Take an undergraduate communications' course somewhere will Ya'!"

"Abram," said the Lord, "set forth and walk about in the land *so that the people of Sodom think that you're just aimlessly passing through their territory.* Walk its length and its breadth," the Lord emphasized, "for to you I will give it."

"But the land already belongs to the people of Sodom who will get really pissed if I declare ownership of it!" Abram objected. "And there are too many of them for my behemoth wife Sarai to beat up and knock the crap out of!"

The Lord's outline vanished into thin air *since there were no factories around at that prehistoric time to pollute the atmosphere with heavy smoke.*

Abram, feeling extremely frustrated, kicked the new altar he had recently diligently labored to construct. The patriarch moved his tents and went on to settle near the terebinth of Mamre at Hebron, *the tree somehow being miraculously transplanted from Europe by a bird that coincidentally had taken a crap there.* There, Abram built another altar to the Lord *and seriously thought about profitably mass-producing altar kits for other chosen worshipers to buy and use.* That is why Lot really left Abram. *Lot saw how futile it was to always have to build, to tear down and then rebuild altars all the time just to make new enemies by residing on and then battling over property that really belonged to the newfound enemies. (Just because the Lord always insisted on giving Abram property that really belonged to someone else, usually the happy-go-lucky peace-loving Canaanites).*

Chapter Fourteen
"The Four Kings"

In the days of *(we don't know and we don't care)* Amraphel, king of Shinar *(which as you already know is really Sumer in southern Mesopotamia)*, Arioch king of Ellasar, Chedorlaomer king of Elam and emperor of the city of *Cheddar Cheese, and* Tidal, king *of Waves* and ruler of Goiim became allies. They all made war on Bera, who was king *of both Yogi* and Sodom. Bera's allies were Birsha king of Gomorrah, Shinab king of Admah, Shemeber king of Zeboim *and also king of Spades* and the king of Bela (that is, king of Zoar *like an Eagle)*.

All the 'latter' kings *had many rungs they had to climb up to achieve power.* They joined forces in the Valley of Siddim (that is the Salt Sea, which is now called the Dead Sea *because it is even more salty than the Salt Sea was way back then, and no fishes or fishermen could live inside it then or now)*.

For twelve years *(maybe months)* the latter kings had been subject to Chedorlaomer, *the king of Cheddar and Elam and also the big cheese on the top rung of the local ladder.* However, in the thirteenth year the other kings rebelled *against the big cheese. They finally had become teenagers and the hormone and chemical imbalances in their bodies during their thirteenth year made them more rebellious and defiant than ever.*

In the fourteenth year Chedorlaomer and the kings allied with him came and defeated the Rephaim in Asteroth-karnaim, *an oasis with nifty two-seater outhouses,* the Zuzim in Ham *and in Bacon,* and the Emim in Shaveh-kiriathaim. Then Chedorlaomer, *the big cheese* and his allies *(the ancestors of the Curds)* defeated the Horites *(male and female bisexual prostitutes)* in the hill country of Seir, *yes Seir-ee,* as far as Elparan, close by the wilderness *and the outback outhouses.*

Chedorlaomer *and his cheesy friends* then turned back and came to Enmishpat (that is, *as everybody knows,* Kadesh) and they subdued the whole *fat people* country both of the Amalekites, *the Accolites,* and of the Amorites *(local love-makers) and the Meteorites* that dwelt in Hazazon-tamar. *Chedorlaomer was stabbed and wounded in battle by a brandished enemy sword, and everyone at the combat was vociferously yelling, "Who cut the cheese?"*

Thereupon the king of Sodom, the king of Gomorrah, the king of Admah, the king of Zeboim, *the king of Hoboken,* and the king of Bela (that is, *as everyone knows* Zoar) 'marched' out *in April.* The

57

kings marched into the Valley of Siddim, and they went into battle against them: against Chedorlaomer, *the big cheese* king of Elam, the Tidal *Wave* king of Goiim, Amraphel, king of Shinar, and Arioch, king of Ellasar-four kings against five, *in the first officially sanctioned no-holds-barred tag team checkers' match.*

Now the Valley of Siddim was full of bitumen pits, *which were all rather pitiful.* As the kings of Sodom and Gomorrah fled they fell into these deep bitumen pits. *The kings' ancient ancestors were dinosaurs that had fallen into tar pits, so they genetically and instinctively knew what to do when getting close to any tar pit or bitumen pit or coming to any particular pit stop in their prehistoric donkey carts.* The other kings and the rest of their peoples fled to the mountains *where they chose to be eradicated by volcanoes, landslides and earthquakes rather than perish inside nasty lethal bitumen pits.*

Famous historians like Herodotus, Thucydides and Josephus never recorded these obscure Biblical battles and events. The chroniclers were only concerned about major turning points in civilization and warfare, and so we only know about the big cheese king and his allies and enemies from the tedious hackneyed account erroneously provided in the Wholly Book of Genesis.

The victors' *(none from the futuristic University of Michigan as had been predicted in prophecy)* seized all of the possessions and food supplies of Sodom and Gomorrah and then went their way, *for in addition to being robbers and thieves, the conquerors enjoyed being out-of-control maniacal plunderers.* The victors took with them Abram's nephew Lot, *whom they found hiding in an empty desert sandlot. Lot was not in the kings' league, nor were his children in any local Little Leagues because they had only played sandlot league games like their father Lot had taught them in the hot arid desert.*

A fugitive *(also a refugee, here)* came with the headlines and brought the news to Abram the Hebrew, *the father of beer, since 'he brew' the best combination of hops and barley around those parts according to fallacious ancient stories and testimonies.*

Abram was camping *without a permit from desert rangers (the Old Testament's equivalent of forest rangers in the desert)* at the terebinth of Mamre the Amorite, a kinsman of Eschol and Aner. These men were in the league of Abram, *but the other kings in the area had more on the ball and were completely out of their league.*

When Abram heard that his nephew Lot had been captured he mustered three hundred and eighteen of his retainers, *which his dentist advised him to wear in his mouth all at the same time.* Abram *traded in his mouthpieces and from his retainers acquired the services of three hundred and eighteen lawyers, who advised the distraught patriarch to go in* pursuit of Lot all the way to Dan.

Abram and his party deployed against the victorious kings at night, defeated them, and pursued them as far as Hobah, north of Damascus. *Hence, they became the first 'men-in-nights' to gain victory by virtue of a surprise attack upon a drunken enemy.*

Abram recovered all the possessions that had been lost and he brought back his separated kinsman Lot, *since the patriarch missed being a sucker and losing all of those loaded dice games Lot had deceivingly won.* Abram also retrieved the women and the other captives *(slaves, whores, concubine sluts and male and female transvestite prostitutes and dysfunctional tri-sexuals).*

When Abram returned from his victory over Chedorlaomer and the kings that were allied with him, *the patriarch proclaimed, "I'm the new big cheese around here now!"*

The King of Sodom went out to greet Abram in the Valley of Shaveh (that is the King's Valley, *a cheap counterfeit reproduction model of the famous Valley of King's located along the Nile, where all the natives tended and pretended to have nihilistic tendencies). The King of Sodom wanted to introduce Abram to the joys of sodomy when a joystick was not associated with any novelty game device.*

Melchizedek, king of Salem *many millennia before the futuristic witch trials,* brought out bread and wine. Since Melchizedek was a priest of God Most High, *which suggests that there were many gods of lesser high around way back then,* he blessed Abram with these words: "Blessed be Abram by God Most High; the Creator of Heaven, earth, *and the Chief Instigator of aggravation and human grief.* And blessed be God Most High, Who' delivered your foes into your hands *when your hands were in the pockets of your robe, doing an obscene naughty no-no' thing."*

Then Abram *learned the decimal system quickly* and gave Melchizedek a tenth of everything, *even a tenth of the things Abram did not own such as the land of Canaan.*

The king of Sodom said to Abram, "Give me the people; the goods you may keep *because you just can't have good sex with goods. You need to have people to have good sex, as you might already know, you ignoramus!"*

But Abram had an apt reply to the king of Sodom. "I have sworn to the Lord, God Most High, the Creator of heaven, earth *and hell. I have vowed* that I would not take so much as a thread or a sandal-strap from anything that is yours', *including your despicable threadbare robe and your decrepit old sandal, you old fart.* Lest you shall say, 'I made Abram rich'."

"Abram, you're a trip and a half!" the king of Sodom exclaimed. *"How about teaching me how to play dice. Lot already has won from me all my personal concubines and all my treasured whores."*

And then Abram finished, *"No dice!* Nothing for me except all what my *parasitic* servants have used up and the share that is due to the men who joined me: *it is a good thing that I am a herdsman', otherwise I would have to make these newcomers sharecroppers.* Aner, Eschol and Mamre, let them take their shares, *and I'll then start a mighty corporation and appoint myself CEO!"*

Chapter Fifteen
"The Covenant with Abram"

Some time after these events *(we had forgotten what the incidents were and we really don't care to remember)*, the word of the Lord came to Abram in a vision, *although Abram was not really a good visionary*. The word came in a vision *because all of the angels and other heavenly messengers were on strike for higher compensation, better working conditions and shorter hours*.

"Fear not Abram!" the *frightening omnipotent and omniscient* Voice commanded.

"Why should I fear myself?" Abram answered. "I'm the only one I can trust around here!"

"Abram I am your shield," *the Voice indicated without any allusion to a helmet or sword.*

"Whose land do You' want me to trespass on now!" Abram insisted and rankled. "Can't I just be a squatter or a poacher instead? Give me some eggs! Or better yet, give me a decent toilet!"

"I will make your reward very great," *the Voice lustily indicated with strong persuasion.*

But Abram said to the Voice *(which he thought was a quirky quasi-hallucination)*, "O Lord God, what good will Your' gifts be if I remain childless and have Eliezer, my steward become the heir to my house?"

"Eat more tenderloin and your loins will become more tender and productive," the strange awesome bass Voice suggested. "Your tender loins will become more active and then will produce more seeds."

Abram then *rudely interrupted and* said, "See, You' have given me no offspring, and so one of my servants will be my heir *just so You' can play Your' big power game with a mere weak mortal. I am sick and tired of being Your' puny pawn on beckon call all the time!"*

Then the word of the Lord came to him *(even though it had been there all along since the beginning of this chapter)*, "No; that one shall not be your heir; *I don't like Eliezer any more than I like the garrulous talking Serpent.* Your own 'issue' shall be your heir *so maybe you ought to consider publishing a local newspaper or magazine. That edition may result in an addition to your family, and that's the gospel truth as far as I can see."*

He took him outside *(pronoun identification problem, here)* and said, "Look up at the sky and count the stars if you can, *but*

61

make sure it's nighttime when you do it. Just so," He *eloquently* added *(the supernatural Voice that visited Abram?),* shall your descendents be."

"My descendents are going to be stars instead of people?" *Abram incredulously asked.* Abram immediately put his faith in the Lord, *or in the Lord's Voice that gave him The Word (or in this case, the Words),* and the Lord credited it to Abram as an act of righteousness. *Abram was happy to get extra-credit despite his great wealth and great misery and lack of collateral.*

The Lord then said to him, "I am the Lord who brought you from Ur of the Chaldeans *because I didn't want to see you and your family become Ur-banized and exposed to a bad social environment or to negative human influences.* I wanted to give you this land as a possession."

"O Lord God," Abram asked, "how am I to know that I shall possess it *if Canaan presently belongs to the Canaanites? Isn't possession in this case theft or stealing?"*

The Lord answered Abram, *"Possession is nine-tenths of the law, moral or otherwise.* Bring me a three-year-old heifer, a three year old she goat *in that male goats are superior to female goats,* a three-year old ram *that is not too rambunctious,* a turtle-dove *with a soft shell,* and a young pigeon. *Do as I command in a hurry. I have another appointment with Zeus in half an hour. It seems that Hermes is on strike as part of the despicable International Winged Messengers Union Job Action!"*

Abram brought Him all these animals, split them all in two *while completely enjoying his butchering enterprise,* and placed each half opposite the other; but the birds he did not cut up *even though it was just stated that Abram split up all the animals in two. Everyone knows that birds aren't (land) animals. Divide and mutilate was almost as much fun to the ecstatic Abram as divide and conquer was to the Lord.*

Birds of prey *(pray?)* swooped down on the carcasses but Abram stayed with the dead meat *and refused to split.* As the sun was about to set, *it was sunset.* A deep trance fell upon Abram. Then a terrifying darkness 'enveloped' him, *but the trance did not place a stamp or a return address on the envelope, which somehow had originated from a distant place called Manila.*

Then the Lord said to Abram *(who was in a deep trance and couldn't think about or understand anything since he had been effectively hypnotized),* "Know for certain that your descendents shall be aliens. *Abram', that' is why I told you to look at the stars.* I didn't mean that your descendents were going to be space aliens. Your descendents shall be aliens in a land not your own, where they shall be enslaved and oppressed for four hundred years. *I really enjoy punishing and cursing My' most devout worshipers and their descendents. You, My' chosen people all must suffer greatly before I can take pleasure in eventually rewarding you."*

'*I must be having a serious bad-trip' nightmare!' Abram imagined in his deep trance. "Why must I and my people endure all this excruciating duress just because of a silly apple in the Garden of Eden? Isn't that overkill?"*

Then the Lord said to Abram *(who was still mesmerized and was incapable of being rational or conscious)*, "But I will bring judgment on the nation that your descendents must serve. *Sometimes I enjoy bringing cruelty toward your enemies, but first your people must agonize and anguish for four centuries.* In the end your people will depart their captivity with great wealth. *What do you think of My' masochistic game plan? I hold all the trump cards you know!"*

'*Why couldn't my descendents just thrive in great prosperity without the four centuries of ugly sacrifice and awful persecution?' Abram remarkably thought while being brainwashed in his deep obedience trance.*

"Abram, you shall join your forefathers in peace; you shall be buried at a contented old age," the Voice predicted. *"You will have peace and honor when you are dead."*

'*Fine consolation for leading a life of misery and oppression,' Abram's mind incredibly contemplated in its subconscious state. 'Can't I just die now and get it over with? Where is my last breath, please!'*

"Abram, in the fourth time-span *(don't ask what a time-span is; it is undefined and open to debate and interpretation)*, the others will come back here to Canaan; the wickedness of the *promiscuous* Amorites will not have reached its full measure until then. *Maybe I'll make a time span a century. Then I'll be able to communicate time better to you doltish mundane mortals."*

'*Look Lord,' Abram's subconscious mind considered and mentally communicated, 'if the Amorites are wicked and evil, then kick their butts instead of arbitrarily condemning my descendents to four centuries of unwarranted slavery. And next kick the butts of the conquering slave masters too, while You' are at it!'*

When the sun had set and it was dark, there appeared a smoking brazier, *the bra having two D-cups* along with a flaming torch, which passed between those pieces, *symbolizing some form of supernatural perverted sex act.*

It was on that occasion the Lord made a covenant with Abram saying, "To your descendents I give this land from the Wadi of Egypt to the Great River *(the Euphrates)*; I give you the land of the Kenites and the Kenizzities *and the Gesundheits. Just obey My' commands and you will be amply rewarded."*

'But those potentially hostile people already own the land that You're giving me,' Abram's integrity nobly argued in its subconscious state. 'Can't You' just give me peace of mind instead of the property of others.'

"And," the Lord continued, "I will give you the land of the Hittites, the Perizzites, the Rephaim, the Amorites, the Canaanites, the Girgashites, *the Gigabytes, the Plebiscites* and the *Jeb-bushites. Don't you get it? I really relish giving away other people's lands to you and your accursed descendents."*

'Why was I ever born?' Abram's bewildered subconscious mind evaluated. 'Why couldn't I just have come into this fucked-up world as a lucky Canaanite? Then I could lead a tranquil and passive pastoral existence. I'd be much happier simply having my own land stolen than having to go through the Lord's saga of pilfering the territory of others. Unfortunately, the Lord is writing the script to this entire bull shit drama and I am a mere actor on His Almighty stage!'

Chapter Sixteen
"The Birth of Ismael"

Abram's wife Sarai had borne him no children *but Abram himself might have been an impotent potentate. However, in those ancient times women always had to be the problem regardless of the circumstances, so it was stated that Sarai had borne Abram no children, and if she had borne him a girl, then that would have been worse than bearing him no child at all.*

Sarai had, however, an Egyptian maidservant named Hagar. Sarai said to Abram, "The Lord has kept me from bearing children. *He wants your descendents to live in the land of Canaan, yet He doesn't allow you to have any damned descendents that are supposed to be damned according to His decree.*"

"*The Lord works in mysterious ways,*" Abram cryptically replied. "*Sometimes I don't even think the Lord understands the Lord.*"

Sarai then said to her *befuddled* husband, "Have intercourse then with my maid, *who often shacks-up with Eliezer, your chief steward.* Maybe then I shall have sons *the round-about way* through Hagar."

Abram heeded Sarai's request. *He had wanted to have sex with Hagar for a long time but feared that Sarai would pound the piss out of him should she find out about her old husband's extra-curricular activities or his perverted sexual fantasies. And besides, Abram felt like he and his descendents were getting the royal shaft from Heaven by being given land that didn't belong to them and by being cursed into slavery for four hundred years after they would be given land that didn't belong to them.*

Thus, after Abram had lived ten years in the *desolate* land of Canaan, *(and after he had gotten up motivation to have sex by nightly attending striptease and erotic couch dance bars along the Gaza Strip),* his wife Sarai took her maid Hagar the Egyptian to Abram. Sarai gave Hagar *(her property)* to Abram to be his concubine *(his property).* "*At last my loins feel tender again,*" Abram proudly proclaimed. "*I'm finally ready to sow some wild oats at age eighty-five, and I don't mean eighty-five damned months either.*"

Abram had intercourse with Hagar, *which was the best sex he had ever had with anyone, including all by himself by putting it on automatic.* Hagar became pregnant, *and many of Abram's herdsmen*

65

(who were too poor to afford wives so they had to do it with their sheep) suspected that Eliezer was the true biological father.

When Hagar learned of her pregnancy she looked on her mistress with disdain, *because although the old patriarch Abram thought he had had terrific sex, Hagar preferred the embraces and caresses of Sarai, whom she enjoyed rolling in the hay more than with either Abram or with the studly Eliezer.*

So Sarai said to Abram, "You are responsible for this outrage against me, *you foolish old Gaza geezer.* I myself gave my maid to your embrace; but ever since Hagar became aware of her pregnancy, she has been looking on me with disdain. Abram, may the Lord decide between you and me. *My God! What the hell am I saying here?"*

Abram told Sarai: "Your maid is in your power. Do to her whatever you please *you filthy slut. I am through with the bitch now that she's officially knocked up and sporting a big belly and gross-looking flabby tits!"*

"Look Abram, you've made us the laughing stock of this camp," Sarai *vehemently* accused. *"Even the cattle and the sheep are laughing stock laughing at us! Laughing livestock, get it?"*

Sarai then abused Hagar, *performing acts of sadomasochism using giant desert cactuses that were too gruesome to describe. Sarai now hated and despised Hagar as much as she hated and despised "that little impotent squirt" Abram.* Hagar *was so distraught and confused that the poor innocent pregnant* girl sprinted away from Sarai. *Hagar didn't walk like an Egyptian any longer; she now ran like an Egyptian with a sore lacerated butt hole.*

The Lord's messenger *(an angel with wings on its back imitating Hermes, who had wings on his feet and helmet)* found Hagar on the road to Shur by a spring in the wilderness, *the spring being from one of Abram's dirty old mattresses.*

"What are you doing on the Road to Shur?" the messenger asked. "You oughta' be on the Road to Recovery you little fool!"

"I am running away from my mistress, *who no longer desires to be my mistress on my mattress,"* Hagar cried. *"I'm knocked up with one illegitimate heir in the oven."*

"How can you be running away when you are sitting next to the spring?" the puzzled messenger inquired.

"I'm knocked up, pregnant, and I don't like it one damned bit," Hagar responded. *"I never ever wanted to have kids, either as a wife or as a concubine."*

"Well this adventure all now makes a lot of sense to me," the courier from Heaven revealed. "You are an Egyptian slave. You are carrying Abram's child. Abram's descendents will be captured and enslaved by the Egyptians for four hundred years," the inspired angel marveled. "Who says the Lord doesn't know what the hell He's doing? What a great soap opera script, even though writing has yet to be invented!"

"What should I do?" Hagar pleaded during the height of her lamentation. "My life was great until I got involved in this crazy Biblical bull' crap! It's been all miserably down hill since then."

"Before all this Biblical stuff, nobody wore Bibs, and everyone always got crumbs all over their friggin' chests and tits!" the messenger amiably chuckled. "But seriously Hagar, go back to your mistress and submit to her abusive treatment. Women should be tortured and abused by those in power, be they men or simply other women. I mean," the angel qualified, "even your mistress has to relieve her frustrations any way that she could, and since you are the nearest female slave object, you just have to tolerate Sarai's arbitrary maltreatment. You have no choice in the matter. You're a female and also a female maidservant and dependent concubine. If anything's the pits besides the area under your arms, it's that!"

"You're even more cruel and crazy than Abram and the Lord put together!" accused Hagar. "You make about as much sense as the first fifteen chapters of this insane book of Genesis does!"

"I will make your descendents so numerous," added the Lord's messenger, who seemed to be taking on too much power by proxy, pretending to be the Lord. "Your descendents will be too many to count, even with the world's largest abacus."

"You're about as comforting as an ass' full of cactus stickers," Hagar grieved and complained. "And believe me, that's a royal pain in the ass that's hard to rectify!"

"You are now pregnant and shall 'bear' a son that will look like a bear," the messenger confided. "You shall name him Ishmael, but keep the child away from a messed-up sailor named Peleg and an insane captain named Ahab."

"Who the hell are they?" Hagar wondered aloud.

"Call the ugly infant Ishmael, and not something stupid like Air Mail or E-mail," the glorious messenger continued. "For the Lord has heard you with His keen and suspicious ears. God has wisely and judiciously answered you. Ishmael shall be a wild ass of a man attending wild-ass parties and orgies all over the place. His hand will be against everyone, feeling and savoring the genitals of both *males and females alike.* And everyone's hand shall be against him, *for Ishmael will be exceptionally well' equipped, if ya' know what the heck I mean."*

"What kind of demented twisted bull shit is this?" Hagar *boisterously challenged. "Why couldn't I have just been boiled to death in 'ancient grease' instead of being involved in this warped idiotic plot?"*

"In opposition to all his kin shall Ishmael encamp," *the messenger finished before dissolving and then evaporating into the atmosphere.*

"This fucked-up story is a really strong argument for abortion," Hagar *cried on her knees. "Ishmael should be aborted as well as the entire Wholly Book of Genesis. What a living nightmare let alone headache! There will never be peace in the valley of the Canaanites. Maybe if I took cold showers, or something crazy like that, I could save millions of innocent people from unnecessary physical pain, conflict and emotional distress in the future four hundred years."*

To the Lord Who' spoke to her *(through an anonymous messenger who had cleverly used the Lord's Voice),* Hagar gave a name, saying, "You are the God of vision *and of all optometrists; but sometimes Your childish antics make it look like You need 'super-vision' instead of mere eyesight vision."* Hagar really meant *(and this is a certified, bona fide fact),* "Have I really seen God and remained alive after my vision? *Or was my vision another callous desert mirage or a heartless illusion, or a diabolical deceitful hallucination?"*

That is why the well is called Beer-lahai-roi. It is between Kadesh and Bered, *and if there was ever an irrelevant fact presented in this chapter or in this preposterous book of Genesis, then that one was just it.*

The hag Hagar bore Abram a son, and Abram named the son whom Hagar bore him Ishmael. *That's precisely how Hagar became an Egyptian mummy. Abram knew that if he didn't do what Hagar had recommended, then he would have to spend every night back in the sack with Sarai, who might beat-up and maul (using ghastly and gruesome s and m methods) both Hagar and her feeble husband simultaneously.*

Abram was eighty-six years of age when Hagar bore him Ishmael, *but he wished he were really nine hundred years old so that he could finally die and be buried to be eaten by worms, insects and maggots. Even rotting away inside the earth without a working brain seemed better than living a cursed life on the earth, with a working brain to remind poor old Abram about how nasty the future of his blessed people was going to be. All of this happy horse crap was implemented according to the Lord's inexplicable divine plan.*

Chapter Seventeen
"The Covenant of Circumcision"

When Abram was ninety-nine years old *the hoary man had trouble getting and sustaining erections, let alone urinating.* The Lord appeared to Abram and said, *"My damned messenger is on vacation and I have to do this tedious visitation stuff all by Myself'. But still,* I am God the Almighty, *at least around these parts where there are just desert and scrub shrubs and your moronic nomadic tribesmen to rule over.* Walk in My' presence and be blameless, *for if you don't, I'll make you the blame for everything, I assure you.* Between you and Me', Abram," *the Lord elaborated,* "I will establish my everlasting covenant and I will multiply you exceedingly."

"Er Lord, shouldn't that be our covenant and not just Your covenant," Abram objected. "I mean, a covenant oughta' be a contract between two individuals."

"Look Abram, I run this show, and until you become a Lord, just do what I say," the Lord returned. "Life will be a lot easier for you if you just simply cooperate and enjoy being subordinate. We are not equal in rank. You are My' humble servant, and I have absolute dominion over you!"

"But Lord, You' keep stating the same things over and over again," Abram retorted. "I know I'll be given the Canaanites' land and I know my family will increase in numbers. And I'm fully aware that my descendents will be slaves for four hundred years! Do you think I'm some sort of slow learner or something? You sound like a broken oxcart wheel!"

When Abram prostrated himself, *something good happened to his prostate, suddenly making the patriarch's testicles function like young active horny testicles again.* God continued to speak to him, *but Abram was delighting in the fact that his penis was enlarging and also throbbing rather robustly.*

"Abram," the Lord said, "you are to become the father of a host of nations *that, thank goodness for you, you' will not have to host.* No longer shall you be called Abram, Your name shall now be Abraham."

"I get it!" the old man joyously exclaimed. "Since my penis is now longer my name should be longer too. I now have more ham in my penis. I am now called Abra-ham. I now have enough ham to fill a-bra or any damned vagina including Sarai's or Hagar's!"

"Abraham," the Lord continued, "I am making you the father of a host of nations, *for if something is true, it is certainly worth repeating over and over again.* I will render you exceedingly fertile, *just like the Fertile Crescent over there in Mesopotamia.*"

"*Yeah,*" said Abraham, "*but my boner is straight and the Fertile Crescent is freakin' crooked.*"

"Abraham, kings will stem from you, *even without the aid of a future process that will be known as cloning, so stop cloning around.* I will maintain My' covenant with you and your descendents after you throughout the ages as an everlasting pact."

"*Wow! You mean to say my erection will last for generations!*" Abraham proudly and happily uttered. "*What a fantastic orgasm I'll be able to have generations from now when I finally climax!*" Abraham ejaculated.

"Abraham, I will be your God and the God of all your descendents after you and the land in which you are now staying, the whole land of Canaan, you keep as a permanent possession; and I will be the Canaanites' God too," the Lord proclaimed *and predicted.*

"*Wowee!*" Abraham yelled. "*I haven't had a super hard-on for over forty years. This is great! And if the Canaanites are given erections like the one I presently have, they will gladly worship You' too! Then it will be easy for me to take over the Canaanites' land because they'll all be distracted by their enormous throbbing erections! Now Your' very excellent plan all makes plenty of sense!*"

God also said to Abraham: "On your part, you and your descendents after you must keep My' covenant throughout the ages. This' is My' covenant with you and your descendents after you that you must keep. Every male among you must be circumcised *by a certain cut off date.*"

"*Well Lord, that's no skin off of my back!*" Abraham sarcastically answered. "*Just give me a knife and I'll start digging and slicing right now!*"

"Abraham, throughout the ages, every male among you, when he is eight years old, shall be circumcised, including household slaves, *which are okay to have and those slaves acquired with money from foreigners, for they are okay to have, also. Slavery is a great institution and I wholeheartedly endorse it.*"

"*Lord, forget all about the Aryans. I can sew the cut off skin to my slaves' heads and we can then have skinheads as servants,*" Abraham proposed. "*The excess skin will make my slaves skinheads and some will also be dick heads too!*"

"Abraham, thus My' covenant shall be in your flesh as an everlasting pact," the Lord announced for the third time. "If a male is uncircumcised, that is, if the flesh of his foreskin has not been cut away, such a one shall be cut off from his people; even if he is a slave, he has broken My' covenant. *If one breaks My' contract, he will surely contract bad luck in its place, circumcised or not circumcised.*"

"*Lord, wouldn't it be a lot easier just to have my male descendents simply born circumcised so that they won't have to experience the pain of circumcision at age eight? My slaves can then experience pain and be circumcised while my privileged descendents could be born without pain and be born circumcised already. I mean, why should my descendents suffer if they are supposed to be blessed?*"

"Abraham, you too must be circumcised!" the Lord admonished. "It is My divine will and decree!"

"What!" the patriarch vehemently objected. "I am ninety-nine years old, and if I have to keep this amazing erection I am now having, the circumcision will really hurt for months and maybe even years. I thought that only eight-year-olds would have to be circumcised. I thought I would be exempt from the agonizing torture because of my age!"

As was His habit the Lord deftly changed the subject. God further said to Abraham: "As for your wife Sarai, her name shall be Sarah. *It doesn't really matter as anything important since birth certificates have not been invented yet.* I will bless Sarah, and I will give you a son by her. *But don't worry Abraham. Sarah will not have to be circumcised. Only males with the proper equipment are qualified for the honor and joy of circumcision. So don't try pulling any boners!*"

"*Lord, I am really enjoying this huge erection I am having ever since something phenomenal happened to my prostate while I was lying prostrate. Can't I just have sex with Hagar the Egyptian concubine instead of with my fat masculine butch wife!*" Abraham suggested. "*Sex with Sarah is cruel and unusual punishment of the greatest magnitude!*"

The Lord ignored Abraham's practical recommendation. "Abraham, your son also I will bless; he shall give rise to nations *and also give rise to the penises of the men in those same nations.* Rulers *and yardsticks* of people *will measure those gigantic erections,* and many more nations and peoples shall issue from him."

73

"But Lord, I already have a son Ishmael by Hagar," Abraham distraughtly replied. "You are shrewdly setting the stage for more conflict between Ishmael and a second more legitimate son. Can't we just have peace in the valley with the Canaanites having their erections and me stealing their land while they are marveling all day and all night long about their magnificent hard peters?"

"Abraham, you shall have a legitimate son to have future centuries and millennia of conflict with the offspring of Ishmael, your illegitimate son born by your concubine," the Lord argued. "I need amusement and diversion. Abraham, I must confess that being immortal is a big bore, so I like watching war and chaos down here on earth just for sport, for My' entertainment and for My' personal gratification. And don't forget about the four centuries of slavery either!"

Abraham prostrated himself and *indulgently* laughed, *and the tingling sensation in his prostate made his penis swell to an even greater length and breadth.* "Lord, can a child be born to a man who is a hundred years old? Or can Sarah give birth at age ninety?" *Abraham curiously asked his Superior.*

"Abraham, you are not thinking correctly at this moment because there isn't too much blood nourishing your brain right now. Most of your blood is trapped somewhere else, which, of course, is part of My' divine plan. You will not be able to think much as long as you have that marvelous erection, which I graciously provided to you so that you would not be influenced by the evils of knowledge and of science. You can now stay a mindless and obedient patriarch of shepherds and gratefully continue to exclusively worship and serve Me'."

Then Abraham said to the Lord, "Let but Ishmael live on by Your' favor! *He's really a good kid, even though he hasn't had his first solid orgasm yet!*"

God replied: "Nevertheless, your wife Sarah is to bear you a son, *and this one will not look like a bear like Ishmael does.* You shall call him Isaac. I will maintain my covenant with Isaac as an everlasting pact, to be his God and the God of his descendents after him."

"But what about Ishmael?" Abraham protested. "I think that he should be circumcised too! I don't want to see Ishmael winding-up becoming some stupid skinhead nomad wandering aimlessly around the deserted deserts!"

74

"As for Ishmael," God said, "I am heeding you. I hereby bless him. I will make him fertile and will make him multiply exceedingly. *His testicles will be enriched even when he doesn't prostrate before Me'.* Ishmael shall become the father of twelve chieftains and I will make of him a great nation *where the people will all be very clanish and clandestine. But for the umpteenth time,* My covenant I will maintain with Isaac, whom Sarah shall bear to you by this time next year. *So Abraham, you should get your motor running and start screwing around! It's time to rack in the sack!"*

When He had finished speaking with Abraham God departed from him, *and the Lord was off to create more havoc and to play favorites with doomed humans somewhere else on the doomed planet.*

Then Abraham stood, tucked his colossal erection inside his robe, stepped inside his tent and found his *illegitimate* son Ishmael and all of his slaves, *for it' was a very big tent.* It didn't matter whether the *tentative* slaves were born in his house *(here, a tent)* or acquired with his money-every male among the members of Abraham's household-and he circumcised the flesh of their foreskins on that same day, as God had told him to do. *Suddenly, Abraham was to have a thousand revolting belligerent skinheads in his camp.*

"I have to do this quickly," Abraham told his slaves, "because tomorrow is the 'cut-off date', and I have to honor the Lord's commands. So, all you big daddies give me some skin! And if you glue the removed foreskin to your corneas, you all then could be cockeyed!"

Abraham was ninety-nine years old when the flesh of *his* foreskin was circumcised. *The elder performed the surgery on himself as he was watching the reflection of his enormous erection while standing next to an oasis pond. "This hurts more than my stupid inflated hemorrhoids do!" the patriarch hollered in excruciating pain as he mentally criticized the Lord's wisdom while meticulously peeling and carving away at his manhood.*

Abraham's son Ishmael was thirteen years old when the flesh of his foreskin was circumcised. *Abraham fed the removed skin to his pet dog, which also persisted in licking the scalps of the patriarch's thousand bellicose skin-headed dick heads.*

Thus, on that same momentous day, Abraham and his son Ishmael were circumcised *according to the Lord's cut-off deadline.* And all the male members of Abraham's household', *(for the umpteenth-plus time)* were circumcised also, including the slaves born in his house *(tent)* and those that had been acquired by money.

Chapter Eighteen
"Abraham's Visitors"

The Lord appeared to Abraham *since Abraham was a mere man and therefore incapable of flying up to Heaven and appearing to the Lord. And also the aged mere mortal just didn't have the ability or the wherewithal to do the very complicated visible/invisible thing. And besides,* Abraham was uninterested in appearing to the Lord *because the Lord always wanted Abraham to construct Him an altar or to enact other eccentric unreasonable demands on the already encumbered elderly patriarch suffering from arthritis, Parkinson's disease and dementia. Since the Lord never ages, the complex mind games were all done as an activity promoting the Almighty's amusement, but to poor old Abraham, the series of bizarre episodes all meant blood, sweat, tears struggle, drudgery and relentless toil.*

The Lord's appearance to Abraham was by the terebinth of Mamre, *which as you know, somehow migrated or was transplanted from Europe to Canaan.* The patriarch sat in the entrance of his tent, while the day was growing hot. *His colossal erection was still growing longer and becoming heavier to carry around. Abraham was already disenchanted being encumbered by his weighty shaft so the old man was not too thrilled to see the Lord arrive on the scene. 'He might make me awkwardly till a field with my abnormal-sized tool,' Abraham fearfully speculated.*

Looking up, Abraham saw three men standing nearby, *at first thinking they were tax collectors, Canaanites or slaves wanting painful circumcision operations performed under very adverse conditions where death from serious infection was a high possibility.* When the patriarch saw his three surprise visitors he ran from the entrance of his tent to greet them, *because Abraham had always wanted to circumcise and to castrate tax collectors, Canaanites and cooperative slaves, if that was what the three guests happened to be.*

Bowing to the ground *(for ancient Abraham had a giraffe-like neck),* the old man said: "Sir, if I may ask you this favor, please do not go on past me, your servant. Let some water be brought so that you may bathe your feet and then rest yourself under the tree. *For you see,"* the patriarch continued, *"I dislike dirty feet and hate tired travelers."*

Then Abraham, receiving no answer from the appalled reticent trio, said: "Now that you have come this close to your servant, let me bring you a little food *since I don't want to see any of you overeating like gluttons and burping, belching and farting all over the damned place.* In this way you can refresh yourselves *with just a little food,* and then afterwards you may go on your way."

"Very well *old-timer*," the three replied in unison, "do as you have said."

Abraham suspected that one of the visitors was the Lord, the second a landlord and the third a warlord. But then the old man reasoned that it could have been the Lord with two angels tagging along as henchmen or hit men. That idea was junked when Abraham considered that ordinarily kings traveled with kings, princes traveled with princes, slaves associated with slaves and Lords traveled with other Lords. That's the way of the world and of Heaven.

Abraham nervously hastened into the tent and told Sarah, "Quick, three seahs *(about a half bushel)* of fine flour. Knead it into rolls. *Knead it because I need it!"*

Abraham thought that perhaps the Lord accompanied his Son and the Holy Ghost to the elder's tent, both of whom had time traveled into pre-history just to be in the Wholly Book of Genesis with the Lord. Next Abraham speculated that Zeus and Poseidon had been visiting the Lord, but those two Olympians were over fifty-foot-tall, and the three individuals that appeared at the tent were of only average height and size.

Abraham ran to his herd, picked out a tender, choice steer and gave it to his servant, who quickly prepared it *for the three carnivorous guests to devour.* Then Abraham got some curds *before then started curdling,* and he obtained some milk as well. He set these foods down before his three guests, *and although immortals, Gods and angels don't have to eat, the three divine visitors cooperated with the old man's folly.* They ate under the tree while Abraham waited on them *and then bused and cleaned their dirty messy table.*

"Where is your wife Sarah?" the three *strangers* asked, *apparently all thinking the same idea at the same time.*

"There in the tent," Abraham replied.

One of the visitors said, "I will surely return to you about this time next year, and Sarah will then have a son *even though her ovaries are shriveled-up like dried prunes and her nipples like baked raisins."*

Sarah was listening at the entrance of the tent just behind Him. Now Abraham and Sarah were advanced in years and Sarah had stopped having her womanly periods *and was glad that those horrible bloody messy days were behind her. Since then, Sarah and Abraham had no sex at all and that cessation of intercourse became known as the 'men-o-pause', because no men had had sex with her, either.*

So Sarah laughed to herself and said, "Now that I am so withered and my husband is so old, am I still to have sexual pleasure *with such a dry well between my legs? I think the Lord is out of His' warped mind! And who would dare put two old fogies like us through the travail of such a terrible ordeal as having children at our advanced age?"*

But the Lord said to Abraham, "Why did Sarah laugh and say, 'Shall I really bear a child, old as I am?' Is anything too marvelous for the Lord to do? At the appointed time *you will not be disappointed, I guarantee it.* I shall return to you and Sarah, and Sarah will have a son *and you will watch. But Abraham, if you give Me a hard time and disobey Me in the next nine months, then I will make you have the child and Sarah will do the watching."*

Because Sarah was afraid, she dissembled, saying, "I didn't laugh." *The Lord knew that she was 'lying', even though Sarah had been standing all along.* So the Lord said, "Yes, you did laugh *you naughty, naughty girl, you. Shame on you!"*

The men set out from there and looked down toward Sodom. *The three travelers were probably not Gods or angels at all but mere impostors and moochers in that the itinerants did not fly away or disappear like Gods normally would do after visiting Abraham. Walking constituted such a 'pedestrian' means of transportation.*

Abraham was walking with them, to see them on their way. The Lord reflected *like a mirror*, "Shall I hide from Abraham what I am about to do? Now, Abraham is about to become a great and populous nation *with all of those super sperms I had placed into his testicles.* All of the nations of the earth are to find blessings in Abraham *even though not one nation can actually fit inside him. It's really fun playing this power game using a mortal and his helpless, hapless descendents as puny pawns."*

The other two visitors pretended to be listening to the Lord's haughty prattle. "Indeed, I have singled Abraham out that he may direct his sons and his prosperity *to his posterity. His progenies shall be prodigies.* Abraham must keep the way of the Lord by doing what is right and just, so that the Lord may carry into effect for Abraham the promises He' had made about him."

"Lord," said Abraham, "I am here walking with you and these two gentlemen right now. Why are you speaking to the other two about me and not including me as part of Your' royal audience?"

The Lord did not heed Abraham's request. The Lord *had tunnel vision and* said, "The outcry against Sodom and Gomorrah is so great and their sin so grave, that I must go down and see whether or not their actions fully correspond to the cry against them that comes to me. *I mean to find out what's goin' on and then kick their fat, ugly sinful butts really good."*

Abraham thought that the two men walking with the Lord must have been deaf mutes. They never answered the Lord and pretended to not hear Him whenever He spoke about favoring Abraham and his fortunate descendents that hadn't descended yet.

While the two men walked on farther to *Sodom (What happened to the other two men?),* the Lord remained standing in front of Abraham, *which makes no sense at all.* Then Abraham *(let's start using some pronouns here!)* drew nearer to him and said, "Will You sweep away the innocent with the guilty? Suppose there were fifty innocent people in Sodom. Would You' wipe out the place, rather than spare it for the sake of the fifty innocent people within it?"

The Lord was thinking about something else and did not immediately respond to the patriarch's rhetoric that was really gaudy gibberish. Making Abraham pregnant seemed much more interesting to the Lord than merely destroying Sodom and Gomorrah with fire and brimstone.

Abraham did not realize that he was being tuned-out and snubbed, so he persisted to articulate like a rambling fool. "Far be it from You' to do such a thing, to make the innocent die with the guilty, so that the innocent and the guilty would be treated alike! *What kind of twisted justice is that?*"

The Lord finally heard and assessed Abraham's argument and contemplated destroying the old windbag with fire and brimstone instead of using fire and brimstone to obliterate Sodom and Gomorrah, the sin capitals (translation: fun cities) of the ancient world.

"Should not the Judge' of all the world act with justice?" *just as we are standing here?" Abraham prattled and inquired.*

The Lord replied, "If I find fifty innocent people in the city of Sodom, I will spare the whole place for their sake. *There is a technicality here in terms of definition. Innocent refers to crime and to accused criminals; whereas, immoral pertains to sinners."*

Abraham, *not knowing when the hell to shut up,* spoke again: "See how I am presuming to speak to my Lord, though I am but dust and ashes *aspiring to be intelligent.*"

80

"Pretty stupid dust and ashes, too, if I may add," the Lord commented.

But Abraham persisted in his arrogant interrogation. "What if there are five less than fifty innocent people? Will You' destroy the whole city because of those five? *You could be a real hazard to human civilization, do You' know that!"*

The Lord quickly realized that Abraham had again used the wrong terminology, saying the word "innocent" rather than the word "immoral." "I will not destroy the city," the Lord answered, "if I find forty-five there, *for you see, I can subtract much better than you can because you can only say fifty less five and I readily know how to say forty-five, you dumb ninny,"* the Lord haughtily remarked.

But Abraham *was a complete nincompoop and* persisted *in his inane questioning*, "What if only forty innocent people are found there?"

"I will forebear doing it for the sake of forty," the Lord responded, *for He knew that Abraham had neglected to use the magic word "immoral," instead of the wrong term "innocent." Immoral would most definitely mean instant vaporization of the city of Sodom, no doubt about it.*

Then Abraham, *like a complete and vintage retard* continued *the ludicrous dialogue*, "Let not my Lord grow impatient if I go on. What if only thirty innocent people are found in Sodom?"

Since Abraham again failed to state the key word "immoral," the Lord's reply was: "I will forbear doing it if the number is thirty 'innocent' people, *for I am a Judge of vile morality and not an evaluator of random criminality."*

Still, Abraham, *not having anything important to discuss*, proceeded, "Since I have thus dared to speak to my Lord *audaciously*, what if there are no more than twenty 'innocent' people in Sodom?"

"Abraham, are you dense or what?" the Lord vehemently *shouted.* "I will not destroy it for the sake of twenty innocent people, *but if those twenty were immoral and sinful people, then they'll have their sundials cleaned and their bones cremated by My' wicked vengeance and My' ruthless wrath. Get the message birdbrain!"*

But Abraham liked to hear the melody of his shrill voice: "Please let not my Lord grow angry if I speak up this last time *like the wiseass I am*. What if there are at least ten 'innocent' people left in Sodom?" *the old man asked.*

"Then Abraham, for the sake of those ten, I would not destroy Sodom. *I mean, grow a damned brain with a functional cerebrum, will ya',*" God angrily ranted. "*Can't you see a definite pattern to My answers here! Stop acting like a totally devout moron!*"

The Lord departed as soon as He finished speaking with Abraham, *finally fully realizing that the patriarch was a feeble old idiot who didn't know the essential difference between crime and immorality. Abraham returned home (to his small circus-like tent). We don't know what the hell ever happened to the Lord's two deaf and dumb companions. They were probably just as upset with Abraham's stupidity as they were with the Lord's thirst for vengeance, so apparently they nonchalantly and unobtrusively had exited the scene, completely disgusted with the attitudes and behaviors of both individuals.*

Chapter Nineteen
"Sodom and Gomorrah"

The two angels finally reached Sodom in the evening. *Why they had walked to Sodom is unknown, for it would have been much easier for them to fly there or to supernaturally teleport themselves there. Perhaps they were in one of the Lord's 'no-fly zones', or maybe the Lord had clipped their wings and the victimized angels were temporarily grounded, we don't really know.*

Lot was sitting at the gate of Sodom *since there was only one way in and out of the reprehensible sinful city. We say one way because no one ever left the city once they had entered.* When Lot saw the angels, *Abraham's nephew, who was attracted to beautiful male anatomies nearly had an orgasm as* he got up to greet them. The man was bowing down with his face to the ground *(which is stupid because Lot had just been sitting with his ass on the ground).* Lot said, "Please, gentlemen, come to my house." (He hadn't yet realized that the distinguished-looking men were God's messengers, *so why the heck did he bow his head down and almost have an orgasm standing up before bowing down?).* "You can spend the night there and bathe your *stinking* feet. *They appear very grimy, unkempt and smelly.* Then you can get up early to continue your journey *if you don't spend all night here washing the cruddy skin off your ugly dirty putrid-smelling feet."*

But they replied *(in that they both thought and spoke the same words in unison and were not individuals at all),* "No, we shall pass the night in the town square, *for we'd like to square dance with the local yokels."*

Lot urged his visitors so strongly however, they turned aside to his place and entered his house *to see if it was big enough to have square dancing.* Lot prepared a meal for them, baking cakes without leaven, *not knowing that the men were angels and also not knowing that immortal creatures didn't need to eat food like humans had to.* The three then dined, *even though it was almost breakfast time.*

Before they *(?)* went to bed, all the *town*speople of Sodom *(remember, the place was earlier described as a city),* both young and old-all the people to the last man *lacking anything more constructive to do (for women were not regarded as people)* - closed in on Lot's house.

The people called to Lot and said to him *(for just like the two angels, the people were not individuals either and they all coincidentally thought and spoke the same words),* "Where are the

83

men who came to your house tonight? Bring them out to us so that we may have intimacies with them *and intimately Sodomize' their butt holes."*

Lot went outside to meet the people at the entrance. *He was jealous and resentful that the people wanted to Sodomize the two visitors and not have deviant sex with him.*

Lot said to the *riotous* crowd, "I beg you, my brothers, not to do this wicked thing *without me.* I have two daughters who have never had intercourse with men *or with women, either." Lot said these words because he would rather see his two precious daughters raped by evil scoundrels than have the two strangers in his house commit unnatural sex acts with the nefarious residents of Sodom.*

Then Lot continued, "Let me bring them out to you, and you may do to my two daughters *with your erections* as you may please. *You can use sticks, clubs or watermelons as dildos if you like, but by all means, leave the two innocent strangers that are visiting my home alone.* Don't do anything to the two men, for you know that they have come under the shelter of my roof *and might only believe in straight sex after marriage."*

The *licentious* crowd *armed with a Sodomy License from Town Hall* replied *in unison,* "Stand back! This fellow," they all *objected* and sneered *at the same time,* "came here as an immigrant *whose ancestors just came off the ark,* and now Lot' dares to give 'orders' *outside of our restaurants.* We'll treat you worse than we'll treat your two visitors, *that's for damned fuckin' sure!"*

With that, the mob pressed hard against Lot, *who was hard-pressed for an appropriate response to their unbridled aggression.* They attempted to break down the door. *If the mob knew magic, they could have had a 'mental breakdown', but they didn't know any magic so they had to use force.* Lot's two guests put out their hands, pulled Lot inside with them, and then *vigorously* closed the door.

At the same time the angels had rescued Lot *when ironically he was ineffectively attempting to protect the angels from the ancient mobsters,* the two visitors struck the men at the entrance to the house. One and all, the *Sodomizers* were struck with such a blinding light that the sinners were utterly unable to reach the doorway. *This event happened in the 'daze' of what was known as the preternatural flash.*

Then the angels said to Lot, "Who else belongs to you here?" *Of course, the angels were supernatural creatures and knew the answer all along but they still had to pretend to be dumb, incompetent, superstitious human guests.* "Your sons, son-in-laws and your daughters and all who belong to you in the city-take them away from it! We are about to destroy the whole wicked place, *but unfortunately we don't have the power to mentally and divinely transfer you and your family out of Sodom. That skill is out of our ability range. Therefore Lot, you have to flee on your own."*

So Lot went out and spoke to his *prospective* sons-in-law, who had contracted marriage with his *nearly raped* daughters, *not knowing that the prospective sons-in-law sons-of-bitches had contracted venereal diseases by being Sodomized up the old wazoo by the other merry male residents of Sodom.* "Get up and leave this place," he told his sons-in-law to be. "The Lord is about to destroy the city *because its residents think that ass holes are entrances and not exits." Actually, the two angels were assigned by the Lord to destroy the city, but why should these trivial deviations from fact or truth really matter? The Lord might have changed His vacillating mind and decided to kill all the remaining residents all by Himself.*

Lot's sons-in-law to be thought that their' *prospective* father-in-law had been joking *since Lot had a bad reputation for being a facetious prankster and prevaricator. And besides, the future sons-in-law preferred Sodomizing' strangers and guests in the city than screwing either of Lot's two ugly virginal thick-bearded daughters*

As dawn was breaking (*everyone's balls and tits*), the angels urged Lot on, saying, "On your way! Take with you your wife and your two daughters who are here, or you will be swept away in the punishment of the city." *Now why the city should be punished is unknown, for it was the residents of the city who were Sodomizing' guests, each other and any pig, cat, dog or heifer they could find.*

When Lot' hesitated to act, the men *(angels),* by the Lord's mercy, seized his hand and the hands of his wife and his two daughters and led them to safety outside the city, *so the two angels definitely 'had a hand' in the routine rescue operation.*

As soon as they had been brought outside the city, Lot was told: "Flee for your life! Don't look back or stop anywhere on the Plain! Get off to the hills at once, or you will be swept away or turned to salt." *If this threatening command sounds a Lot like Orpheus being forbidden by Hades to turn around while climbing up from the depths of Hades, then you happen to be absolutely correct.*

"Oh no, my lord!" *replied Lot, for he realized that the angel he had been addressing was not the real Lord but just a regular ordinary lord without a capital letter.* "You have already thought enough of your servant to do me the great kindness of intervening to save my worthless life. But I cannot flee to the hills to keep the disaster from overtaking me, and so I shall die, *which ain't such a bad idea rather than to hang around and endure stupid shit like this impending catastrophe all the damned time. I'd rather die than loiter around this friggin' idiotic cesspool!"*

Then Lot continued, "Look, this town ahead is near enough to escape to. It's only a small place so let me flee there'; *so then, to hell with my family.* It's a small place, isn't it? That my life shall be saved *in that I am the only one I really care about in the final analysis."*

"Well then," the angel replied, "I will *play God and* also grant you the favor you now ask. I will not overturn the town you speak of, *and besides, it was not earmarked for demolition on my assignment work order.* Hurry up Lot and escape there! I cannot do anything until you arrive there." That is why the town is called Zoar *(extraneous fact presented out of context and irrelevant to the flow of the text).*

The sun was just rising over the earth as Lot' arrived in Zoar *to hunt for profitable real estate deals.* At the same time the Lord rained down sulfurous fire upon Sodom and Gomorrah, *which came down so heavily that the downpour was sul-furious.* God *was so in(sul)-furiated* that He overthrew those cities and the whole Plain, together with the inhabitants of the cities and the produce of the soil. But Lot's wife disobeyed the Heavenly command and looked back toward Sodom and Gomorrah and she was turned into a pillar of salt, *and was salted away for all eternity, and was thus eliminated from ever being able to become a pillar of any other corrupt community. And so, it could be aptly stated that Lot's wife was promptly 'a-salted'!*

As for himself, Lot's aspiration was to leave real estate and become a sailor, and his ultimate desire was to some day become a sailor and transform into an 'old salt' all by himself without any assistance from the Lord or His henchmen.

Early the next morning Abraham went to the place where he had stood in the Lord's presence. *His erection was now so long that it touched the ground and Abraham no longer required a staff or walking stick to support his body for his throbbing tool served that particular purpose. His enormous erection was sufficient to achieve being able to stand erect.*

As Abraham looked down toward Sodom and Gomorrah and the whole region of the Plain, *he wished with all his heart that he had been a resident of one of the doomed cities.* Abraham saw dense smoke rising like fumes from a furnace *and then the patriarch*

86

thought about how many more future altars he would have to build for the Lord, all because he had cruelly been spared from death during the major twin catastrophes.

Thus it came to pass: when God destroyed the Cities of the Plains, he was mindful of Abraham by sending Lot away from the upheaval, *despite the fact that both the patriarch and his numbskull nephew wished that they had died by fire and brimstone during those fierce holocausts.* God overthrew the cities where Lot had been living, *for Lot had the amazing ability to live in the two cities at the same time.*

Since Lot was afraid to stay in Zoar *because that city had plenty of Sodomizers that had not died in Sodom,* he and his two *nearly raped* daughters went up from Zoar to settle. *They took residence* in the hill country where he and his daughters lived in a cave *at night and could roll around in the tall grass during the day.*

The older daughter, *who did not like sodomy and only wanted to be a common ordinary prostitute,* said to the younger one: "Our father is getting old, and there is not a man on earth to unite with us as was the custom elsewhere."

"You mean you want to get laid by our father?" the younger daughter incredulously asked. "You must really be super horny if you choose incest with him of all people!"

The older nearly raped daughter replied, "Come let us ply our father with wine and then lie with him, that we may have offspring *having thirty toes on each foot, three heads without shoulders and two fingers on each of their deformed hands."*

So that night *the little whores* plied their father with wine. The older one went in and lay with their father, *who knew and appreciated exactly what his daughters were up to although he pretended* he was not aware of her lying down, *pumping the hell out of him* and then getting up.

The next day the older daughter said to the younger one, "Last night it was I who lay with my father *and screwed the hell out of him.* Let us again ply him with wine tonight, and then you go in and lie with him *while I practice being a horny voyeur and masturbate myself into ecstasy while watching you get father's rocks off while he is pretending to be sleeping.* In that way we may both have offspring by our *fucked-up* father."

So that night, too, the girls plied their father with cheap wine, and then the younger *horny* one went in*to the cave* and lay with her father *so that he could then enter her cave.* But again, Lot was *shrewd enough to pretend being* unaware of her lying down,

87

pumping her ass and tits off like there would be no tomorrow and then *finally* getting up.

Thus both of Lot's daughters became pregnant by their father *and by their extreme lust for regular normal straight sex.* The older daughter gave birth to a son named Moab, and she said, "From my father. *Oh what a night!*" He is the ancestor of the Moabites of today, *and who really gives a flying shit about that trivia!*

The younger daughter, too, gave birth to a *raunchy-looking* son, and she named him Ammon saying, "The son of my kin," *which is akin to saying, "Oh no, another crazy ass hole just like my father! I should have known better but I couldn't curb my compulsive sexual appetite."* Ammon is the ancestor of the Ammonites today, *and who really gives a double dump about Ammon or the Ammonites! Amen to the Ammonites!*

Chapter Twenty
"Abraham at Gerar"

Abraham journeyed on to the region of the Negeb, *using his huge erection as his trusty-thrusty staff to stabilize his poor posture. If only Lot's daughters could have been a bit more fortunate, they could have hopped into the sack with their great uncle Abraham instead of with their ornery ordinary lecherous old man.*

Abraham settled between Kadesh and Shur, *and that is for sure.* While he stayed in Gerar, he said of his wife Sarah, "She is my sister," *for that trick had worked in Egypt and had spared the patriarch's life while Pharaoh pumped the poop out of Abraham's wife, thinking all the while that Sarah was the patriarch's little horny sister.*

So Abimelech, king of Gerar, sent and took Sarah. *Abimelech hadn't popped a load in over two decades and he was ready to explode internally if he didn't soon explode externally, shooting and squirting semen all over the damned place.*

But God came to Abimelech in a dream one night *(not a white one either)* and said a nasty threat to him: "You are about to die because of the woman you have taken, for she already has a husband."

Abimelech became pissed off in his dream. The king figured it was six of one and a half dozen of the other. 'Either I will just die or I will surely die by exploding internally from excessive sperm accumulation, so who really gives a crap?' Abimelech thought in his frightening nightmarish dream.

Abimelech, who had not yet approached Sarah *(meaning porked her)* said: "O Lord, would you slay a man even though he is innocent? Abraham told me 'she is my sister', *the lousy conniving bastard. Where does that creep think he is, Egypt or some hillbilly place like that?"*

The Lord did not answer Abimelech in his wild and crazy dream but merely chuckled to Himself at the idiot's frustration'.

'And Sarah herself lied and stated *in his nightmare,'* Abimelech continued, 'He is my brother. I did it Lord in good faith and with clean hands,' *the king continued, 'for I am one of the few who knows that invisible things called germs can infect a king's genitals and make me want to scratch my damned balls off all day long!'*

God *finally* answered Abimelech in the dream: "Yes, I know you did it in good faith. In fact, it was I who kept you from sinning against Me'. That is why I did not let you touch Sarah."

"But You' should be punishing Sarah and Abraham for lying to me instead of threatening me with death for being accidentally innocent and gullible," the king angrily protested while tossing and turning in his bed. "I mean, if I awake and reveal this stupid dream to anyone that has a brain, they'll laugh their asses off and no one will believe a single word of my true and harrowing story."

"Abimelech," the Lord said, *"first of all you must change your name to one having only a single syllable.* I want you to know that I *can't stand your silly name. It really pisses Me' off!* Next, return the man's wife to him-as a prophet. Abraham will intercede, for you *see, I wish I knew how to express Myself' better and more concisely.* Then your life could be saved," *the Lord laboriously explained.* "If you do not return Sarah, you can be sure that you and all who' are yours will certainly die. *Abraham is my favorite person on earth and no matter how much he lies, the person he has lied to will suffer dire consequences should they not heed My threats. Abraham gets preferential treatment everywhere he goes and it doesn't matter whether he is right or if he is wrong. He's always right simply because I happen to say he is."* So, as you can clearly determine from the oddball conversation, the king's heavenly dream was really a grotesque hideous nightmare.

Early the next morning Abimelech called all his court officials and informed them of everything that had happened (*which really might have been nothing at all*). The men were horrified *to learn that they too would die over something as ridiculous as sleeping with a woman who had deceived the king in a dastardly scheme contrived by her paranoid conniving dementia-suffering husband.*

Then Abimelech summoned Abraham and said to him: "How could you do this to us? What wrong have I done to you that you should have brought such monstrous guilt on me and on my *peaceful* kingdom *for not doing a damned thing to either you or to your lying wife?"*

Abraham adjusted his huge erection under his robe but he did not answer the enraged king's accusations.

And then Abimelech proceeded, "You have treated me in an intolerable way. *You are supposed to be a guest in my kingdom and are expected to behave like one.* What were you afraid of?" the king yelled *like a maniac.* "Why would you do such a *lousy fuckin'* thing? *You give me no choice but to be hard-on you!"*

90

"King, I was afraid," answered Abraham *as he adjusted his hard-on underneath his robe*, "because I thought there would surely be no fear of God in this place, and so the people would kill me on account of my wife."

"Have you no self-esteem or confidence in yourself?" chastised the enraged king. "You would turn your wife into a whore just because you are paranoid about being killed in a strange land that was really a tranquil and peaceful place before you, your wife and your lunatic Lord arrived here!"

Abraham remained silent for a moment and then responded, "The woman is truly my sister, but only my father's daughter, not my mother's; and so she became my wife, *genetics or no genetics."*

"You are indeed the fool of fools!" Abimelech thundered from his throne. "Your pecker and your scrotum should detach from your body and fall to the floor and be consumed by rats right this instant!"

Abraham readjusted his enormous erection inside of his robe and scratched the itches off of his blessed fertile scrotum. "When God sent me wandering from my father's house," Abraham said, "I *had* asked Sarah, 'Could you' please do me this small favor? In whatever place we come to, say that I am your brother'."

"You are the biggest blundering disgrace on the face of the earth!" shouted Abimelech with much disdain in his heart. "If I ever have a son like you, I'd castrate the prick and make sure he became a daughter in a hurry! Turning you into a eunuch would be too good of a fate for you. Abraham, you raunchy stupid shit, you deserve far more pain than a mere castration!"

Then the incensed king took flocks and herds and male and female *(masculine by preference and also by bias)* slaves and gave them to Abraham *for trying to deceive the king and trick him into dying.* After *the horny and frustrated* king restored Sarah to Abraham, Abimelech said: "Here my land lies at your disposal; settle wherever you please. *Your Almighty Lord is very shrewd, indeed.* I have been bribed by my own life as a hostage. I have been threatened in a dream by your Lord, *all because you and your wife lied to me all because you are neurotic and grossly insane about being butchered by my friendly guards and by my amiable soldiers."*

And to Sarah, the livid king *candidly* said, "See, I have given your brother *or your husband, or whoever he happens to be* a thousand shekels of silver, *which is plenty of heavy metal.* Let the silver serve you as a vindication before all those that happen to be with you. *I don't want to be assassinated by your vengeful Lord or by His lunatic maverick angels just because you and your deceitful husband have slyly lied to me.* Your honor has been preserved *only because you have connived and lied and your' powerful Lord has threatened my existence in a very bad and frightening dream."*

Abraham then interceded with God, *who had done a terrific job threatening the crap out of Abimelech.* The Lord restored health to Abimelech, that is, to his wife and to his maidservants, *whom the king often screwed in the dark and therefore, had it' 'maid in the shade'.* The maidservants could now bear children *so thank heaven that Sarah never became either the king's concubine or the king's second wife. Such immorality would have been abominable in the eyes of the Lord and everybody in this chapter except Abraham would have probably perished.*

The king also did not know that God had tightly closed every womb in Abimelech's household on account of Abraham's wife Sarah being so enticing to the royal sex addict. *So it was a good thing that a settlement had been reached (here, not a village or town). Otherwise, the affected women in the king's household could not have been able to urinate, and all of them would then have exploded their liquid waste and accompanying flesh all over the king's ceilings, floors, walls and house. Then Abimelech would have really been pissed-off and pissed on, even more so then he already was. Everyone in Abimelech's household was finally relieved when the women could piss again, even the king, because when the spirit to have sex is strong, the flesh is weak (and might actually explode right out of someone's abdomen).*

Chapter Twenty-one
"Birth of Isaac"

The Lord took note of Sarah as He had said He would *and jotted down the needed information in His marble composition tablet, which was made of black and white marble that the Lord took for granite.* The Lord did for her as He had promised *even though Sarah couldn't remember what those things were, and didn't want to remember what they were, either.*

Sarah became pregnant and bore Abraham a son in his old age *despite the fact that the two senior citizens never could recall ever having sex.* All of this happened at the set time that God had stated *regardless of the fact that clocks hadn't been invented yet to set time.*

Abraham gave the name Isaac to the son of whom Sarah bore for him, *since in those primitive days women never wanted to be mothers and bear children for themselves; the ladies only bore them for their chauvinistic egocentric God-fearing husbands.* Abraham circumcised Isaac as God had commanded, *and the patriarch told Sarah that Isaac's penis looked skinnier after he had removed a little too much of the infant's foreskin.* Abraham was a hundred years old when his son Isaac was born to him. *So the old man had to be very happy that he still had sperm ducts in his scrotum even though he couldn't recall ever having any ejaculation inside of Sarah's womb, or for that matter, any ejaculation inside Hagar's womb, or any ejaculation, ever in his whole damned life.*

Sarah then said *(to whom?),* "God has given me cause to laugh, and all who hear of it will laugh with me."

Abraham overheard Sarah talking either to no one or to herself. "Sarah, what the hell are you talking about?" he requested to know. "They say people that speak to themselves are loony!"

"Who would have told Abraham," she added, "that Sarah would nurse children! Yet I have born him a son in his old age."

"Sarah," Abraham grumbled, "you're talking about me while you're talking to me while you're talking to yourself. Are you warped out of your mind or what? Why are you speaking in both the first and the third person?"

Isaac grew, and on the day of the child's weaning Abraham held a great feast *and invited all of the wieners and other area guests that acted like hot dogs to the wonderful event.*

Sarah noticed the son that Hagar the Egyptian had borne for Abraham playing with her son Isaac *(notice that Hagar's son Ishmael already has lost both his name and his identity).* Sarah

93

demanded of Abraham: "Drive out that slave girl and her son! No son of that slave is going to share inheritance with my son Isaac! *Do this right now or I will apply on you a wrestling submission hold and then body-slam you right through the son-of-a-bitchin' desert floor!" Being an intimidated wimp just like Adam was, Abraham listened to his wife and obeyed the abrasive woman's unreasonable command.*

Abraham was greatly distressed, especially on account of his son Ishmael *being disfavored. The patriarch should have suffocated Sarah with a gaseous camel's ass sitting on her face as she slept, but he didn't have the courage to assassinate or even smother the dominant unbearable woman with the bear-like son.*

But God said to Abraham (*Where? When? We need a setting here!*), "Do not be distressed about the boy or about your slave woman. Heed the demands of Sarah, no matter what she is asking you; for it is through Isaac that descendents shall bear your name *without looking like bears as that bruin-faced Ishmael's children will most certainly look."*

"But Lord," *the grieving* Abraham protested, "what You' are suggesting is cruel and unfair. You're the One that suggested that Hagar bear me my first born son!"

"Forget the small stuff!" the Lord insisted. "That's now ancient Biblical history. As for the son of the slave woman, *who has the double whammy of being both a slave and a woman,* I will make a great nation of him also, *even though we both know that a person cannot be a nation. Regardless, since* he too (*I forget his name*) is also your offspring, *the boy shall become a great nation just like Isaac will become a great nation. Anything is possible that involves your Lord. People can become nations and nations can become people."*

Early the next morning Abraham got some bread and a skin *(not a foreskin)* of water and *generously* gave them to Hagar, *who then would have to suffer crossing the desert while eating and drinking like a modern-day prisoner eats bread and drinks water.* Then, placing the child on her back, Abraham sent Hagar away. As she roamed the desert aimlessly in the wilderness near Beer-sheba, *she did not drink the local beer of the area residents but still only imbibed the water Abraham had given her.* Soon the water in the skin was used up.

So, Hagar put the *pathetic* child *(who had lost both his identity and his birthright)* down under a shrub, and then went and sat down opposite him. She sat about a bow's shot away *(some bows back* then could be shot over a hundred yards, so this means that Hagar sat next to Ishmael only three-hundred-feet away from him).

Hagar said to herself (in this respect she was very much like Sarah, who also liked speaking to herself), "Let me not watch to see the child die." As she sat opposite him three-hundred-feet away, he (no name) began to cry. "Stop whimpering, you un-grateful, starving wimp!" Hagar admonished her son, Ishmael.

God's messenger called to Hagar from Heaven. "Hello down there! Hagar, what is the matter? Don't be afraid. God has heard the boy's cry in this plight of his."

"Why do you ask me what is the matter if you already know what is the matter?" Hagar flippantly answered. "Would you happen to have a pacifier on You'?"

"Arise," said the voice (imitating the more formidable Voice), "and lift up the boy and hold him by the hand; for I will make of him a great nation, so forget about him being three-hundred-feet away from you and disregard that a person cannot be a nation. Just lift him up! Do you hear?"

"Doesn't my son have a name?" Hagar defiantly screamed to the cloudless sky. "And stop calling him 'boy'! Don't you know that slaves and their sons take offense to that derogatory and prejudiced title?"

Then God opened her eyes, for the slave woman's eyelids were temporarily not working and then Hagar saw a well of water. She went and filled the skin (she had brought along?) with water, and then let the now nameless boy drink, fully aware that both he and she would be better off dead than alive. Even poor Hagar had for the moment forgotten her abused son's name.

God was with the boy when 'he' grew up (God or the boy?), for it is far easier to grow up than it is to grow down, unless of course you are a potato, a peanut, a carrot or an onion. The boy lived in the wilderness and became an expert bow's man capable of hitting any object with his arrow within a three-hundred-foot-radius. His home was the wilderness of Paran. His mother got a wife for him from the land of Egypt and both the boy and his wife remained nameless and communicated to each other by simply saying "you" to each other all the time.

About that time Abimelech, accompanied by Phicol, the commander of his army, said to Abraham: "Damn it, God is with everything that you do. Therefore, swear to me by God at this place Beer-sheba that you will not deal falsely with me if we should be playing cards. Promise also that you will not deal falsely with my progeny *if they should be playing cards with you.* And finally, promise that you will act loyally toward me and this land in which you stay as I have acted toward you, *because if you don't I'll turn you over to the Ass-searians, and you know what the hell they'll do to your royal aristocratic nomadic butt hole!"*

"To this Abraham replied, "I so swear. *I assure you I'm too old to be cauterized up my butt hole by those crazy idiots!"*

Abraham, however, reproached Abimelech about a well that Abimelech's men had seized by force. *Abimelech's men knew that it is far easier to drill women than to drill wells.*

"I have no idea who did that," Abimelech *cunningly* replied. "In fact, you never told me about it, nor did I ever hear of it until now. *Usually, my epileptic soldiers have seizures and not wells of wellness."*

Then Abraham took *shaking* sheep and *quivering* cattle *that were having seizures from drinking from the aforementioned well* and the patriarch gave them to Abimelech. The two then made a pact *because epileptic sheep and trembling cattle fascinated the hell out of Abimelech.*

Abraham also set apart seven ewe lambs *that were hiding inside seven yew bushes.*

Abimelech asked Abraham, "What is the purpose of these seven ewe lambs that you have set apart from your flock? *Don't you know that I'm allergic to lamb chops and to wool?"*

Abraham answered, "The seven ewe lambs you shall accept from me that thus I may have your acknowledgment that the well was dug by me," *even though it had been magically produced by the Lord, who would certainly punish anyone except Abraham for claiming to have the Lord's magical powers. The Lord might eventually make Abraham build a thousand altars, but according to the theme represented and repeated in Genesis, such a command from the Lord would be an honor for Abraham and not a cruel and unusual punishment.*

This is why the place is called Beer-sheba. *The alcoholic residents wished that beer came out of the well and not just plain ordinary water coming out of it.*

Abimelech and Abraham then took an oath at Beer-sheba *to only drink beer and not water when anywhere near the well.* When they had thus made the pact in Beer-sheba *(who says the Bible is redundant?)*, Abimelech, along with Phicol, the commander of the army *(all right, already!)*, left and returned to the land of the

96

Philistines, *thinking that all was well in Beer-sheba except the well water, since many of the area residents used the well as a cesspool.*

Abraham planted a tamarisk at Beer-sheba, and there he invoked by name the Lord God the Eternal *and created the Eternal Revenue Service, which was established to collect a tax on all the beer that was drunk from the water well of Beer-sheba.* Abraham resided in the land of the Philistines for many years. *The drunks of Beer-sheba and the shepherds of Canaan wanted nothing at all to do with him, his wife, or his legitimate or illegitimate sons.*

Chapter Twenty-two
"The Testing of Abraham"

Some time after these events (*please review them*), God put Abraham to the test, *which means He' wanted to evaluate the patriarch's testicles and his epididymis.* The Lord called to him: "Abraham!"

"Ready!" Abraham *alertly* replied. *"I'll do anything either rational or irrational for You Lord. I am so ready that I'll even be ready-whipped!"*

Then God said: "Take your son Isaac, your' only one whom you love and go to the land of Moriah *Carrie.* There you shall offer him up as a holocaust on a height that I will point out to you."

"Then if I kill Isaac, that will be a great personal sacrifice for me!" Abraham yelled up to the seemingly apathetic sky. "Then Ishmael is to be my one and only heir. Why the hell did You' make me go through the ordeal of getting Sarah pregnant at age ninety and now I have to surrender my legitimate son to You' in a stupid nonsensical bloody sacrifice? You may be the Lord, but You' demand many barbaric inhuman insane things for little old me to perform!"

Early the next morning Abraham saddled his donkey, took with him his *legitimate* son Isaac, and two of his *donkey* servants also, and with the wood that he had cut for the holocaust, set out for the place of which God had told him. *He put two lanterns on the donkey's back, because if it became dark out, he could always use his 'saddle-lights' to guide him. 'I'll just get the servants to sacrifice me along with Isaac in the holocaust,' Abraham intelligently thought. 'I gotta' get the hell outa' this crazy screwed-up world one way or another!'*

On the third day Abraham got sight of the place from afar. Then he said to his servants: "Both of you stay here with the donkey *and the saddle-lights*, while the boy and I go over yonder. We will worship and then come back to you." *'If only I had the guts to kill myself then I would not have to agonize over having to kill poor Isaac. Oh well,' reckoned Abraham, 'it's either him or me, so it's gotta' be him.'*

Thereupon Abraham took the wood for the holocaust and laid it on his son Isaac's shoulders, *thus 'putting the wood' to Isaac before really putting the wood to Isaac later on.* Abraham himself carried a knife *that he had surreptitiously obtained in Moriah Carrie.*

As the two walked on together, Isaac spoke to his father Abraham: "Father!" he *imaginatively* said.

"Yes son," Abraham *imaginatively* answered.

Isaac continued *(even though Abraham was just speaking)*, "Here are the fire and the wood, but where are the sheep for the holocaust? *This sacrifice seems like it's gonna' be a real bummer!"*

"Son," Abraham answered, "God himself will provide the sheep for the holocaust, *for in addition to being a merciful and benevolent ball breaker, God is also kind and good. He won't let my sacrifice simply go up in smoke! This I assure you my beloved son!"*

Then the two continued walking forward *since that is the way walking is normally conducted by most people' all over the world.*

When they arrived at the place of which God had told Abraham, the patriarch built an altar there and arranged the wood on it *while Isaac twiddled his thumbs, scratched his rear end and then took a leak in an ant hole and then a healthy crap in a groundhog burrow.*

Next, Abraham tied up his son Isaac, and then put him up top of the wood on the altar. *"Father, I cannot help you sacrifice the missing sheep because I'm all tied up on the altar at present," the gullible unsuspecting boy complained.*

Then Abraham reached out and took the knife *to take a stab* at slaughtering his son. But the Lord's messenger called to him from Heaven, "Abraham! Abraham!"

"Yes Lord," he answered, *even though he knew he was speaking to the Lord's messenger.*

"Do not lay your' hand on the boy," commanded the messenger, *who really happened to be the Lord imitating His own Voice.* "Do not do the least thing to him. I know now how devoted you are to God since you did not behold from Me' your own beloved son. *Find an appropriate animal and make a killing in the livestock market, but I warn you Abraham, do not choose a bull or a bear. And pigs lose big all the time."*

As Abraham looked about, *he looked about as dismal as one could look.* He spied a ram caught by its horns in a thicket. So, he went and took the ram and offered it up as a holocaust in place of his son, *who was quite disappointed at not being sacrificed.*

"Father, please get me off the altar before you kill the ram and then light the fire!" Isaac reminded his father. "I don't want animal blood on my clean new white robe, and mom will really torment me if I get any stinky charcoal embers on my clean pink silk underwear. I don't mind being stabbed to death but I absolutely refuse to be

burned to death! That is my final position and decision on this silly matter!"

Abraham named the site Yahweh-yireh *because he had shouted Yowee-eerie!" when he ignited the bloody dead ram during the magnificent holocaust.* Hence, people now say, "On the mountain of the Lord will see (?)." *Why they included no direct object after the action verb we'll never know. One could only speculate that there was no object to any of those asinine people's conversations or to any of their idiotic utterances.*

Again the Lord's messenger called from Heaven to Abraham and said, "I swear by Myself', declares the Lord, that you acted as you did in not beholding from Me' your beloved son. S*ince I took great pleasure in making you endure great emotional and mental anguish,* I will bless you abundantly. I will make your descendents as countless as the stars of the sky and *as numerous as* the sands of the seashore. Your descendents shall take possession of the gates of their enemies."

"Lord, poor Isaac does not know how unfortunate it was that he was not killed by me," Abraham adamantly objected. "If You're gonna' bust his balls like You've perpetually busted mine, then my descendents are gonna' curse You, curse Isaac and curse me for all this unnecessary bull crap You are bestowing on innocent future generations."

The Lord *(or His' messenger disguised as the Lord)* paid no attention to Abraham's entreaty. "Your descendents in all the nations of the earth shall find blessing-all this because you obeyed My' Almighty command," *the irritating Voice reiterated and insisted.*

"Hearing crap can sometimes be more disgusting than actually seeing crap, smelling crap or tasting it!" Abraham protested. "And I most certainly know crap when I hear, smell or taste it!"

Abraham then returned to his servants *(and possibly left Isaac at the holocaust altar).* They set out together to Beer-sheba, where Abraham intelligently made his new home *near a beer garden that Abimelech had constructed not far from the magical water well that now miraculously spewed-forth countless barrels of tasty premium beer.*

Some time afterward the news came to Abraham: "Milcah too has borne sons, to your brother Nahor. Uz, his first-born, his brother Buz, Kemuel *(the father of Aram), Buz-Off,* Chesed, Hazo, Pildash, Jidlapth and Bethuel.

"Good," Abraham said, "when Uz and Buz are old enough to walk, send them out to the holocaust altar I had constructed to

retrieve my son Isaac, who was too stupid to follow me back to Beer-sheba. As for me, I'll just hang out in the beer garden and enjoy some delicious brew."

Betheul became the father of Rebekah, *even though he was a confirmed homosexual that never had a wife, a concubine or any other female partner.* These eight Milcah bore to Abraham's brother Nahor. His concubine, whose name was Reumah, also bore children: Tebah, Gaham, Tahash, Maacah *and Maacahis-stolin.* Reuhmah had been born without ovaries, *and who really gives a flying shit about her eight flunky kids and Nahor's superior gonads.*

Chapter Twenty-three
"Purchase of a Burial Place"

The span of Sarah's life was one hundred and twenty-seven fruitless and monotonous years. One *hot summer* day Abraham's wife *became so pissed off from having flabby deflated breasts and a dry hairless crotch that she shrieked out loud "Screw it all!" and then deliberately stopped breathing.* She died in Kiriatharba (that is *as everyone knows,* Hebron) in the land of Canaan. *Her husband Abraham said (to?), "Good riddance! Now I don't have to worry about my shrew of a wife administering painful wrestling submission holds on my feeble frame or savagely body-slamming me into the hot desert floor any more!"*

Abraham performed the customary mourning rites *the next morning. He was so upset mourning that he developed a bad case of morning sickness.* Then he left the side of his dead one and 'addressed' the Hittites *outside a primitive-looking post office, but the grieving fool failed to place any of the tribesmen in envelopes and then neglected to place stamps on the heavy-duty envelopes. The Hittites were all standing around in their leotards and tights smacking each other on the legs while vocalizing high-pitched male soprano voices.*

"Although I am a resident alien *without a bona fide green card,"* Abraham began *to his apathetic totally bored audience,* "sell me from your holdings a piece of property for a burial ground, *for we are all too stupid to think of the idea of having or building a much needed cemetery.* This way I may bury my dead wife *and all my unpleasant memories of her deep into the ground."*

The Hittites *(all ten thousand of them)* answered Abraham: "Please sir, listen to us! *Even though both democracy and representative government have not emerged yet into the mainstream of civilization,* you are an' elect of God among us. Bury your dead woman in the choicest of our burial grounds. *We don't want your vindictive Lord cursing us with savage plagues or having fire and brimstone sizzling up into our delicate ass holes! That's the worst kind of Sodomizing' imaginable! None of us would deny you his burial ground for the burial of your dead wife with your vengeful, volatile Almighty Lord and His lunatic angels hovering around our fine community. And if we behave ourselves, we Hittites might also escape the horror of circumcision being done without the comfort of any soothing cream, medication or anesthesia!"*

Abraham, however, began to bow before the local citizens, the Hittites. *He needed the services of an Egyptian chiropractor very badly. The Hittites, however, all had bad cases of phlebitis because of all the blood clots and bruises on their legs from continuously hitting each other's tights and consequently, they all required immediate major surgeries or drastic-measure leg amputations.*

Abraham appealed to the Hittites, *even though he was super elderly and was not capable of getting or sustaining erections in either his penis or in his back.* "If you will allow me room for burial of my dead," he said, "listen to me! Intercede for me with Ephron, son of Zohar, asking him to sell me the cave of Machpelah that he owns; it is in the edge of his field. Let him sell it to me in your presence, *for I do not trust the cheap dirty bastard as far as I can throw him with a bad back at my old age,*" Abraham said. "Let Ephron sell it at its full price, *despite the fact that it is presently not for sale and that it is his only family heirloom and possession. I want that damned cave, and that's that! I need a burial place for my beloved Sarah so that I can forget about her and go out into the desert beyond the beer garden and search for the curvaceous Egyptian concubine Hagar. Sarah came from a hole at birth and I insist she shall return to a hole at death.*"

Now Ephron was present with the Hittites, *but it is unsure here whether or not he was one of them. Perhaps he just took joy in having his legs thrashed. Ephron was slightly perturbed at hearing Abraham call him a "cheap dirty bastard." However, the desperate fellow needed cash in a hurry to pay off some atrocious gambling debts and he had been trying to unload his family heirloom cave for nearly a century but couldn't find any nomadic sucker interested in buying it.*

Ephron the Hittite *(now we finally know he was an authentic Hittite)* replied to Abraham in the 'hearing' of the Hittites, *and how he and Abraham got into the ears of all the Hittites is truly a real Biblical mystery.* The other *enigmatic* Hittites *(all ten thousand of them)* sat on his town council, *which met once a week in the basement of Ephron's modest tent. How the ten thousand Hittites got from the desert in the beginning of this chapter and into the town council meeting is not provided by the book of Genesis and remains another one of those cryptic Biblical mysteries.*

"Please Abraham," said Ephron, "listen to me *because you never really listen to anyone else including the Lord or His ferocious messengers.* I gladly give you both the field and the cave in it; in the presence of my kinsmen I make this *generous* gift. All we want *in return* is some guarantee *that your unpredictable Lord and His' intimidating angels will not kill us all in a violent fire and brimstone holocaust or in a wicked piss and shit storm."*

"*I cannot speak for the Lord,*" Abraham *nervously answered. "He is as unpredictable as the current silver, frankincense and gold markets."* Then the patriarch continued after bowing down *and having another bow movement* in front of his hosts, "Ah, if only you will please listen to me, *your tenuous relationship with the Lord cannot be predicted by someone as humble as me.* I will pay you the price of the field. Accept it from me, that I may bury my dead there *and get rid of my manly wife once and for all."*

Ephron replied to Abraham, "*Are you dense? I promised to give you the field for nothing and now you want to pay me for it. I gotta' keep on the good side of you otherwise your Lord and His' desperado angels will descend on the Hittites and sew up the wombs of all our women and then give us all perpetual hard-ons to suffer with!*" Ephron stated. "*It would then be very difficult for us Hittites to remain straight when our dicks are also straight, if you know what I mean. It is one of our most valued laws that states: 'All homosexuals shall be killed.' We had instituted that particular law after what your Lord had done to Sodom and Gomorrah, and if we all suddenly become gay for lack of female wombs around to pork and pump, then we would all have to murder each other according to our honored laws on homosexuality.*"

"Well, you'll just have to get over it!" Abraham attested.

Ephron replied to Abraham *in a distraught and urgent voice,* "Please sir *Ur-gent, please* listen to me'! A piece of land here *is worth as much as a good piece of ass. The price is* four hundred shekels of silver-what is that *small amount* between you and me, as long as you can bury your dead *and as long as my people can get a reprieve from dying by dreadful mass annihilation? I will gladly receive four hundred shekels of silver from your covetous hands to avert being eliminated in some bizarre natural disaster perpetuated by your vicious Lord and His' fanatical warped messenger commandos.*"

Abraham accepted Ephron's terms since *the old gent was not a good negotiator, did not recognize that he had held the trump cards, and because the fickle patriarch was basically a bumbling, bungling blundering moron.* Abraham weighed out to him the silver that Ephron had 'stipulated' *(What do you know, an actual four syllable word!)* in the hearing of the Hittites, *who all amazingly had heard the same understandings in their eardrums.*

"Four hundred shekels of silver *at the current market value back at the beer garden in Beer-sheba,*" Abraham declared *as he handed over the loot to the delighted Ephron.*

"*Thanks a lot, you stupid bastard!*" Ephron impolitely responded. "*You're paying for a worthless cave that I had wanted to give you for gratis. But now I can pay off my colossal gambling debts and start a new life with a clean slate as a con artist.*"

Thus Ephron's field in Machpehah, facing Mamre, together with its *worthless damp* cave and all its *barren and decrepit* trees anywhere within its limits, was conveyed to Abraham, *and that was remarkable because useful conveyor belts did not exist way back then in those despicable repugnant prehistoric times in the land of Canaan.*

The purchase was conducted in the presence of all the *astonished* Hittites, who sat on Ephron's town council *in the man's cold damp subterranean cellar that incidentally had no chairs. The other Hittites had to bite their tongues from excessively laughing at Abraham's ignorance and at his gross stupidity, since they feared the wrath of the patriarch's dangerous and mercurial Lord and His' bizarre and fierce angels. Then feeling once again secure the zany Hittites all returned to their tribal custom of wickedly thrashing each other's tights and leotards.*

Abraham buried his wife Sarah in the *shabby dank* cave of the field of Machpelah, facing Mamre (that is, Hebron *as already stated in the beginning of this most mediocre chapter). By that time, Sarah's flesh had decomposed, and her bulky anatomy had deteriorated into mere skeletal remains.* All of this took place in the land of Canaan. Thus the field had been transferred from the Hittites to Abraham as a burial place *(for the umpteenth time) and Abraham now only had to fear the Lord and His overzealous henchmen.*

Chapter Twenty-four
"Isaac and Rebekah"

Abraham had now reached a ripe old age *and if he were a tomato or a strawberry, he would have decomposed already from being excessively overripe and from being extremely shriveled up.* The Lord had blessed Abraham in every way, *including being excessively overripe and extremely shriveled up when the patriarch should have actually been long-time dead and pushing up daisies.*

Abraham said to the senior servant of his household, *"I think my ass is falling off. I feel as if I am also disintegrating internally. Where's my dick? I think I have to take a piss!"*

The senior servant, *who just the year before had been a junior servant and the year before that a sophomore servant,* had charge of all of Abraham's possessions *except the old man's buttocks, dick and internal organs.*

Abraham said to his senior servant, "Put your hand under my thigh *to keep my precious scrotum from falling off next.* Then I will swear by the Lord, the God of Heaven and the God of earth, that you will not procure a wife for my son from the daughters of the Canaanites among whom I *unhappily* live."

The senior servant was deeply surprised that Abraham was swearing by the Lord's name instead of cursing the Lord for making him' suffer having his chafed buttocks and his fragile scrotum almost disengage from the patriarch's much maligned body. Instead, Abraham was concerned about something absolutely ridiculous such as Isaac not marrying a silly Canaanite wench.

Then Abraham continued conveying his rather ludicrous request. "Faithful servant," he proceeded, "you will go to my own *former* land, *which I no longer own or never did,* and visit my kindred to get a wife for my son Isaac, *for I believe that incest is the best way to transmit my already inferior genes to future cursed generations."*

The senior servant raised a logical question. "What if the woman is unwilling to follow me back to this *new found* land?" he inquired. "Should I dare take Isaac back to the land from which you migrated? *Your son is rather wretched and grotesque-looking, and even a blind woman might not want to be courted by Isaac or desire to marry him, in spite of your great wealth and handsome bribery."*

"Never take my son back there for any reason," Abraham told his senior servant. *"Isaac's ugly face will scare the living shit out of all the cesspools in Mesopotamia!" ranted Abraham.* "The Lord, the

God of Heaven, Who' took me from my father's house *without my father's permission, really had spiritually kidnapped me.* He also took me from my kindred land, and He' confirmed by oath the promise He had made me, 'I will give this land to your descendents-*even though I don't own it.'* He *(meaning, Abraham or the Lord, I think)* will send his messenger before you, and you will obtain a wife for my son Isaac there. If the woman is unwilling to follow you to this newfound land (*which wasn't Newfoundland*), you will be released from this oath, *you big oaf.* But *my dear servant, I implore you to* never take my son there *to my former land. He might then be spiritually kidnapped by the Lord just as I had been."*

So the senior servant again put his hand under the thigh of his master *because he was a perverted gay senior servant who liked feeling up old disintegrating feeble men.* The servant swore to Abraham in this undertaking, *since the fellow would promise anyone anything while in heat to do naughty things.*

The servant then took ten of his master's camels and bearing all kinds of gifts from his master *as a dowry bribe,* the servant made his way to the city of Nahor, *who was Abraham's brother and not a city at all.* Nahor *(the city or the brother)* was in Aram Naharaim, *as if you really give a flying somersault flip.*

At evening, at the time when women go out to draw water, *which is very hard to draw anywhere on any surface without a piece of charcoal to use for graffiti,* the senior servant made the camels kneel by the well outside the city, *which had the name of Nahor. The slick servant was thinking that the well was a supernatural being and that the camels should kneel down to attentively worship it.*

Then the servant prayed: "Lord, God of my master Abraham, let this mission turn out favorably for me today and thus deal graciously with my 'master Abraham' *(who was also called that title when he was a young boy, Master Abraham).* While I stand here at the spring, the daughters of the townsmen *(for mysteriously there were no townswomen in the town)* are coming out *with their crayons* to draw water. If I say to a girl, 'Please lower your jugs so that I may drink,' and she answers, 'Take a drink *from both* my jugs and let me give water to your praying camels, too,' then Lord', let her be the one whom You have decided upon for your servant Isaac, *for I have heard that Isaac likes hussies that carry around big jugs.* In this way I shall know that You' have dealt graciously with my master."

The servant had scarcely finished these words when Rebekah *(who was born to Milcah, the wife of Abraham's brother Nahor)* came out *to the spring carrying large jugs.* The girl was very

108

beautiful, a virgin, untouched by man, *because in those gruesome days a girl lost her virginity if she was even tapped on the shoulder by a man.* She went down by the spring and filled her jugs with water, *which even in those days was very hard for a woman or girl to do.*

As Rebekah came up, the servant ran toward her and said, "Please give me a sip *from one of* your jugs."

Rebekah, *whose father owned a farm near a sunny brook,* replied, "Take a drink, sir. *Gulp down all the water you need from either of my wonderful jugs."* And lowering her hand *to her left breast,* Rebekah gave the servant a drink, *squirting a mouthful of watery milk into his throat.* When she had let him drink his full, she said, "I will draw water for your camels too, *but only if they like my original sketches.* They can also have their fill, *but I will not squirt watery milk into their mouths from my jugs as I had done for you."*

With that *conversation out of the way,* Rebekah quickly emptied her jugs into the drinking trough, *which also drank a lot, since it was a drinking trough.* She ran back to the well to draw more water into her jugs, *which by then had deflated because of lack of liquid content. Soon she had enough water in her jugs to fill the horizontal trough for the camels to drink out of.*

The *amazed* servant watched her the whole time, *observing her beautiful breasts inflate* as she drew more water *into her jugs.* Abraham's servant was waiting to learn whether or not the Lord had made his *absurd* errand successful.

When the camels had finished drinking *they pissed all over the damned place.* The servant took out a gold ring weighing half a shekel, which he fastened on Rebekah's nose *centuries before civilization instituted body piercing parlors, for in those ancient times women were easily led around by the nose.* And then the servant placed two gold bracelets weighing ten shekels, which he put on her wrists, *symbolizing that marriage in those days was slavery to one's husband and to the reverse-dowry that he gave to the girl's very fortunate father.*

Then Abraham's servant asked her: "Whose daughter are you? Tell me please, *who is the lucky man that will get a huge reverse-dowry so that you may be an unfortunate slave girl by marriage. And is there room in your father's house for us to spend the night, for you must first roll in the hay and the straw with me before Isaac can get his tiny stick wet."*

She answered: "I am the daughter of Bethuel, the son of Milcah, whom she bore to Nahor," *which in those horrible chauvinistic times was far more important than for the girl to tell the servant her actual name.* "There is plenty of straw and fodder at my fodder's place *for us to roll around in.*" And then Rebekah *aptly* added, "And *there is* room to spend the night," *as she batted her hairy eyelashes at the very interesting stranger having the ten very thirsty camels.*

The servant then bowed down in worship to the Lord saying: "Blessed be the Lord, the God of my master Abraham. The Lord has not let His constant kindness toward my master fail *despite all of the altars poor Abraham had to construct alone and all of the other demented bull crap he had to contend with from Heaven for many centuries.* As for myself, the Lord has led me straight to the house of my master's brother *because the Lord prefers incest in the perpetuation of Abraham's past and future generations. I was led straight to this place because I had a continuous erection that served as a divine divining rod all the way from Canaan to this desolate desert slum."*

Then the girl ran off and told her mother's household about her meeting. Now Rebekah had a brother named Laban. As soon as Laban saw the ring around her nose and the bracelets around her wrists, he heard her words about what the man had said to her. *And so, Laban was overjoyed getting rid of Rebekah, whom he had always perceived as a super-big pain in the ass.*

Laban rushed outside to the visitor at the spring, *which might have also been a well according to this Biblical description.* When Laban reached him, Abraham's servant was standing by the camels near the spring. So Laban said to the visitor, "Come, blessed of the Lord! Why are you *casually* standing outside when I have made the house ready for you? I also have a place for your camels, *who can sleep with you and Rebekah in the straw and hay room."*

The servant went inside: and while the camels were being unloaded and provided with straw and with *Rebekah's father's* fodder, water was brought to bathe the stranger's feet and the feet of the men who were with him. *In those days of yore men only bathed their feet and no other parts of their crummy bodies.*

But when the table was set for Abraham's visiting servant, he said, "I will not eat until I have told my tale."

"Do so," they replied *(all in unison), "for we always like to listen to stupid bull shit before we eat."*

110

"I am Abraham's servant," the visitor began. "The Lord has blessed my master so abundantly *that my master will shortly die.* Abraham has become a wealthy man *but he has paid the price in human tribulation and extensive aggravation.* The Lord has given my master flocks and herds, silver and gold, male and female *perverted homosexual* slaves, *bisexual* camels and asses, *and women with nice asses, also.*"

"*Your master sounds like a lucky jerk off indeed," Laban commented. "He has certainly been favored."*

"My master's wife Sarah bore a son to my master in her old age, *and everyone in the neighborhood suspects that the dull kid might be mentally retarded,"* the visiting servant revealed. "Abraham has given his *slow-learner* son everything that he owns *upon my master's imminent death.*"

"*This is definitely the stupidest most outlandish bull shit I've ever heard," Laban remarked. "Please continue. I'm rather fascinated!"*

"My master Abraham put me under oath, saying, 'You' shall not procure a wife for my son among the daughters of the Canaanites. *Their women are too smart and will know that Isaac is a dumb ass having a very small penis, when usually the opposite is true. Instead dear servant, Abraham told me,* you shall go to my father's house, to my own relatives, to get a wife for my *mentally challenged small-pricked* son. *Thus, incest will fuck up my family even more than it is already fucked-up right now'!*"

"*This crazy story is better than three orgies on top of each other!" Laban exclaimed. "Tell me more incredible lunacy! Ha, Ha, Ha!"*

"Then I asked my master this," *the servant proceeded to divulge.* "What if the woman *is intelligent like the Canaanite women are and* will not follow me?" My *clever* master replied, "The Lord, in Whose' presence I have always walked, will send His' messenger with you, *so that I will actually have two messengers, a spiritual messenger, and you, a screwed-up yahoo-type mortal messenger.* Your errand will be successful *dear servant," the visitor said to Laban while recollecting what Abraham had informed him, "because all of my ancestors, my family and my relatives practice incest, so most of the girls in my former land are just as dumb as I have been all my miserable accursed life."*

"*This zany story is enough to make me fart my ass hole right off my body from laughing too much," Laban cackled. "Please wrap it up before I start farting backwards and inadvertently blow my lungs right out of my throat!"*

"Abraham then told me," the servant said, "you will get a wife for my son Isaac from my own kindred from my father's house, *so that then my descendents can fuck-up a world that's already the fuckin' pits right now!"*

The servant waited for Laban and the others to stop their boisterous roaring and incessant farting. "Abraham then said," the servant continued, "you shall be released from my ban. If you visit my kindred and they refuse you, then, too, you shall be released from my ban, *for I cannot blame any woman for not wanting to marry Isaac for all my wealth and for every healthy camel in the desert."*

The visitor took a gulp of water and then presented the remainder of his intriguing narrative. "When I came to the nearby spring today, I prayed: 'Lord, God of my master Abraham, may it be Your' will to make successful the errand I am 'engaged' on!' *What the hell am I saying? It's Abraham that wants Isaac to become engaged! Anyway,* while I stand here at the spring, if I say to a young maiden who comes out to draw water, 'Please give me a little water from *one of your* jugs,' and if she answers, '*Okay,*' then *I'll be happier than a pig rolling around in shit.* And if she says, 'Not only may you have a drink from my jug*s*, but I will give water to your camels, too-*then I would be happier than a pig wallowing in tenfoot-deep shit!* Let her be the woman whom the Lord had decided upon for my master's son."

"This harebrained story is so bad that it's fantastically good!" screamed Laban in a roar. "Have you ever thought of doing standup or sit-down comedy?"

The slightly chagrined servant smiled at his amused hosts. "I had scarcely finished saying this prayer to myself when Rebekah came out *with her huge jugs* on her *chest.* After, she went down to the spring and drew water *when* I said to her, "Please, let me have a drink, *for I like to suck before I gulp.* She quickly lowered her jugs and said, 'Take a drink, and let me bring water for your camels, too.' So, I drank, and *true to her word* she watered the camels, too!"

"Well," said Laban, "at least my sister kept you abreast of the situation. I knew you sucked from the first time I saw you enter our house. Ha, ha, ha!"

"When I asked her whose daughter are you," the servant proceeded, "she answered, 'The daughter of Betheul, son of Nahor, born to Nahor by Milcah.' *Then I immediately knew that she had*

112

little self-esteem giving no name to establish her own identity but only showing her obedient subservience to arbitrary male chauvinism. Such a woman with a poor self-concept would naturally be the ideal mate for Isaac."

"Please excuse me," Laban said, "but I am laughing so hard that I think I'm gonna' start pissing from my mouth. Please finish your story before I internally explode and smear my flesh, blood and urine all over the walls, the ceiling and your hideous-looking face."

"So, I put the ring on her nose and the bracelets on her wrists to symbolize her slavery to my master and his mentally deficient son," the servant further divulged. "Then I bowed down in worship to the Lord, blessing the Lord, who really should have been blessing me and this stupid-ass mission I'm on. I thanked the God of my master Abraham, who had led me on the right road to obtain the daughter of my master's kinsman for his son. What a lot of red tape and bureaucratic nonsense this misadventure has entailed! Anyway, if therefore Laban you have in mind to show true loyalty to my master let me know; but if not, let me know that too. I could then proceed accordingly, which means I won't know what the hell to do next."

After merrily laughing for three consecutive hours, Laban and his household (Laban had a chanting chorus) said in reply: "This fucked-up thing definitely comes from the Lord; we can say nothing to you either for it or against it. Here is Rebekah, ready for you; take her with you, because we're all sick and tired of putting up with her whining and her adolescent asinine hypocritical bullshit. She deserves to become the wife of your master's mentally challenged son. But we're gonna' miss her nice jugs around here, yes siree we sure will!"

When Abraham's servant heard Laban's compromising answer he bowed to the ground before the Lord, even though he was facing Laban and his household. Then the servant brought out objects of silver and gold and articles of clothing and articles from old papyrus newspapers and presented them to Rebekah. He also gave costly presents to her brother and to her mother, who were both more than delighted to get rid of the egocentric bitch that had habitually tried hustling strangers at the community well. After Abraham's servant and the men with him had eaten and drunk (the women had to eat in another smaller room the size of a tiny closet), the fellows spent the night there and had a gay old time.

When the men were up the next morning they all perceptively noticed that the moon and stars had disappeared from the sky. The servant of Abraham said, "Give me leave so that I may return to my dying master. *And don't worry, none of you assholes have to attend his funeral even though you're his only remaining relatives!"*

Rebekah's brother and mother replied *(in unison, for that was a big thing back in those corny ancient times),* "Let the girl stay with us a short while, say 'ten days'."

"Okay, ten days. I said ten days," answered and reiterated the sly servant. "Now what?"

"After ten days, she may go," Laban and his mother' said, *for he was a dummy, and his mom often practiced ventriloquism and evil voodoo on Laban.*

But the servant of Abraham said, "Do not detain me. *I had enough detentions in elementary divination school to last me a lifetime.* Now that the Lord has made my errand successful, let me go back to my master *so that I can watch him die."*

They answered *(It's inappropriate and rude to begin new paragraphs with pronouns),* "Let us call the girl and see what she herself has to say about it." So they called Rebekah and asked her, "Do you wish to go with this man? *He might be kidnapping you into slavery and bribing us with a cheap dowry."*

"I do! *I want out of this lousy dump!"* she *emphatically* answered. *And that "I do" was the beginning of the first marriage vow, even though Rebekah was saying it to Abraham's servant and not to Isaac.*

At this they allowed their sister Rebekah and her nurse to take leave, *for although Rebekah was eighteen years of age, the young lady was still being nursed from the breasts of the family nurse.*

The family invoked a blessing on Rebekah by saying: *(all together, now):* "Sister, may you grow into thousands of myriads *(whatever the hell they are?),* and may your descendents gain possession of the gates of their enemies, *even if their enemies don't have walls around their cities, let alone gates."*

Then Rebekah and her *old* maids started out; they mounted their camels, *which were really horny camels that wanted to mount Rebekah and her old maids.* So the servant took Rebekah from her family and went on his way.

Meanwhile, *back at the oasis, all of Isaac's friends were eating their dates.* Isaac, however, had gone from Beer-lahai-roi and was living in the region of Negeb, *which couldn't be found on any ancient map anywhere in the known or in the unknown world.* One day toward evening *(which should have been one dusk toward night)* Isaac went out in the field, *either left or center field,* and as he

114

looked around, he noticed that camels were approaching, *but he at first failed to see any riders on them.*

Rebekah, too, was looking about, and when she saw Isaac, she alighted from the camel *(despite the fact that she was still five miles away from the virtually retarded boy)*. She asked her *blind* servant, "Who is the boy out there, walking through the field toward us? *He looks too young to even get a decent hard-on!*"

"That is my master," replied Abraham's servant, *who was also a very skilled eavesdropper, even out in the desert dunes where there were no eaves.* Then Rebekah covered herself with her *transparent* veil, *which was big enough to conceal her from her face way down to her toes.*

The servant recounted to Isaac all the things he had done *but Isaac was too mentally slow to remember anything that the servant had diligently disclosed.*

Then Isaac took Rebekah into his tent; he married her *without the aid of any rabbi or minister,* and thus she became his *unfortunate* wife. In his love for Rebekah Isaac found solace after the death of his mother Sarah, *who often repeatedly had beaten her son over the head with a stone model of Noah's ark to remind him of his messed-up heritage.*

Chapter Twenty-five
"Abraham's Sons by Keturah"

As has been mentioned, Rebekah went to the well once too often and was nailed by Abraham's servant to accompany him to Canaan to marry Isaac without any big ceremony. Most of that happened after Rebekah had said 'I do' to Abraham's servant. And so, Rebekah left the slavery of family and entered an incestual relationship into the slavery of marriage. And the whole world's genetics have been fucked-up ever since, so says the Wholly Book of Genesis.

Abraham *screwed-around and* married another wife, whose name was Keturah, *thus adding more incredible bullshit to his already crummy unenviable life.* Keturah bore him Zimran, Joksham, *Jockstrap,* Medan, Median, Ishbak and Shuah. Jokshan became the father of Sheba and Dedan *without ever getting married or having sex with anyone, male or female. Jockstrap became the father of hairy-arm-pitted female Hebrew broad jumpers everywhere, and all of his offspring were avid athletic supporters. Median was the first to build dual four-lane highways with grass islands in between the opposite dirt lanes.*

The descendents of Dedan were the Asshurim, the Letushim, and the Leummim and the *Aluminums, the birth of whom created the need for numerous mental hospitals, sanitoriums and sanitariums all over Canaan and vicinity.* The descendents of Median were Ephah, Hanoch, Abida, Eldaah and *Hoogivesashit.* All of these were descendents of Keturah, *who might have been having an early adolescent and a later adulterous affair with Abraham ever since the two were childhood sweethearts.*

Abraham deeded everything that he owned to his *legitimate* son Isaac, *despite the fact that Abraham had six other sons with Keturah and one illegitimate son with Hagar. Ishmael might have looked like a bear, but Isaac looked like a jackass, following in his father's footsteps.*

To his sons by concubinage *(this means that Abraham never really married Keturah because she had to be a concubine),* Abraham made grants while he was still living, *since it was extremely hard in those days to make a grant or a loan after a person was dead and buried. That was taken for granted by all patriarch loan sharks.* Abraham sent them away eastward, to the land of Kedem, away from his son Isaac *(it is unclear here whether "them" refers to the grants or his illegitimate sons through* concubinage that actually might have been legitimate sons by Keturah through legitimate marriage).

The whole span of Abraham's life was one hundred and seventy-five years. *Near the end the old man actually wished he had died in infancy.* On his deathbed Abraham said *to the ceiling, "Why couldn't my last breath have been my final one?"* Then he breathed his last, dying at a ripe old age after a full life *of struggle, incest, despair, concubinage and total bullshit.* Abraham was taken to his kinsmen *who said, "Take the dirty bastard somewhere else. He left everything to his jackass Isaac and nothing to the rest of us!"*

Abraham's sons Isaac and Ishmael buried him in the cave of Machpelah, in the field of Ephron, son of Zohar the Hittite. The cave faces the field of Mamre, the field that Abraham *had* bought from the *envious* Hittites, *despite the truth that the Hittites wanted to give it to him for free.* Abraham was buried next to his wife Sarah, *and one should make no bones about it. Sarah could care less which person had been buried next to her because she was dead and disintegrated and didn't or couldn't give a shit about anything or anyone.*

After the death of Abraham, God blessed 'his' son Isaac, *who was really Abraham's son and not God's biological offspring.* Isaac made his home near Beer-lahai, *which means that Isaac pitched his tent near the local beer garden where his dad used to hang out to get drunk and to escape the Lord's harsh reality.*

These are the descendents of Abraham's son Ishmael. *Even though Ishmael was illegitimate, his sons still are important in this story, much more so than any women in the Old Testament ever were.* Hagar was the Egyptian slave that had bore Ishmael to Abraham. *This means that when a patriarch screws around and cheats on his wife, bad things tend to happen to the patriarch, his wife, their legitimate children, his adulteress, his' concubine and to their' illegitimate progenies. Everybody caught in the domino effect is comprehensively and thoroughly punished.*

These are the names of Ishmael's sons, listed in the order of their birth, *which in later years became known as chronological order.* Nebaioth (Ishmael's first born), Kedar *(Ishmael's worst born),* Adbeel, Mibsam, *Sonofsam,* Mishma, Dumah, Massa, *Massacurs,* Hadad, Tema, Jetur, Mapish and Kedemah. *All of Ishmael's sons looked human except Massacurs, who looked like a pack of wild savage disfigured dogs.*

118

These are the *insignificant* sons of Ishmael, their names given by their villages and encampments, *which immediately changed their names after each individual son had been born;* twelve chieftains of as many tribal groups *that actually hated the other tribes' diatribe.*

The span of Ishmael's life was one hundred and thirty-seven years. *On his death bed Ishmael said to the ceiling, "What the fuck were all those wasted years all about?"* After Ishmael had breathed his last breath, *he had finally achieved peace and happiness.*

Ishmael was taken to his kinsmen, *most of whom' wanted to toss his remains onto the stenchy village rubbish heap.* The Ishmaelites ranged from Havilah-by-Shur, which is on the border of Egypt, all the way to Asshur, *and you can 'ass-your rabbi' if this is true or not.* Each of them pitched camp in opposition to his various kinsman, *which means that the book of Genesis defines life in those chauvinistic times as a combination of strife, conflict, adultery, incest, envy, jealousy, bloodshed, rivalry and tribal warfare.*

Now this is the family history of Isaac, son of Abraham *(notice that poor Sarah (like Hagar) had already been forgotten and erased from Biblical history).* Abraham had begotten Isaac *and had forgotten everybody else in his dysfunctional family.*

Isaac was forty years old when he married Rebekah *without any rabbi performing any elaborate ceremony and after Rebekah had said "I do" to Abraham's loyal servant.* Rebekah was the daughter of Betheul the Aramean of Paddan-aram, *where rams were heavily padded to protect them from bears like Ishmael and from jackasses like Isaac.* Rebekah was the sister of Laban the Aramean. *Laban had died laughing fifty years after Abraham's servant had told him the perverted history of Abraham and Isaac.*

Isaac entreated the Lord on behalf of his wife since she was sterile. *Isaac must have had doctor's credentials to determine this and since he was a devout male chauvinist just like his father was, no man could ever be impotent; therefore, only women were sterile, and that was the bottom line back then.*

The Lord heard Isaac's entreaty *(since Isaac was the only one praying to Him during that time)* and Rebekah became pregnant *even though she was certifiably sterile.*

But the children in her womb jostled each other so much *and that was simply because they were supposed to be fetuses and not actual children.* Rebekah exclaimed, "If this is to be so, what good will it do me! *What the hell damned kind of cursed pregnancy is this anyway! I should have stayed with my brother Laban and had incest there!"*

Rebekah went to consult with the Lord *without an appointment, and her womanly instincts told her exactly where He was hanging out.*

The Lord answered Rebekah *after she had amazingly located Him*: "Two nations are in your womb *and not two children; that's why your womb feels like it's going to burst.* Two peoples are quarreling while still within you, *even though they are merely embryos and cannot talk or communicate yet.* But one shall surpass the other, and the older shall serve the younger, *so whoever pops out second is going to ultimately be the victor. Or maybe it should be the other way around?*"

When the time of Rebekah's delivery came, there were twins in her womb, *and the fetuses were battling so terribly that there almost was a 'twin' killing'.* The first to emerge was reddish *like a radish* and his whole body was like a hairy mantel *over a skin-infested fireplace.* So Isaac named him Esau *because Isaac didn't like what 'he saw.'*

Esau's brother came out next, gripping Esau's heel, *suggesting that the younger brother already had thought that Esau was 'a heel'.* Isaac named the younger twin Jacob, *and since Jacob looked nothing like Esau, they probably were not identical twins but fraternal twins that shared little fraternity.*

As the boys grew up *(which is the only way they could grow),* Esau became a skilled hunter, a man who lived out in the open *and also a man who came out of the closet.* Jacob was a simple man who kept to his tents *because he maintained a wonderful harem of good-looking well' endowed prostitutes having clean vaginas inside all of them.*

Isaac preferred Esau, *whose tendencies leaned toward the homosexual side.* Rebekah preferred Jacob *since he was definitely straight and could ride all night in the saddle.*

Once, when Jacob was cooking a stew, Esau came in from the open, famished. He said to Jacob, "Let me gulp down some of that red stuff. I'm starving, *and maybe it is poison and I will be fortunate enough to expire right here and right now."* (That is why he was called Edom, *meaning from "the red radish land" where everyone was a hemophiliac and was slowly bleeding to death).*

But Jacob replied, *"Esau, you are always in some sort of stew.* First give me your birthright since you are the first-born; *otherwise, I will see to it that you starve to death right here and right now. I will*

120

give you *an ounce of* stew in exchange for your birthright *that I covet.*"

"Look *Bro'*," said Esau, "I am on the point of dying. What good would any *birth-mark* do me?"

"I said birthright, not birthmark you stupid ninny!" Jacob nastily hollered to his twin brother. Jacob then insisted, "Swear to me first!"

So Esau swore and said, "Fuck you, ass hole!" Then Esau sold Jacob his *coveted* birthright under oath for *an ounce of* stew. Jacob *was in a very generous mood so he* gave his older brother some bread with the lentil stew, and Esau ate, drank, got up and went his way *pissed off that the stew had not been poisoned.* Esau cared little for his birthright *or little for his pathetic condemned life, either.*

Chapter Twenty-six
"Isaac and Abimelech"

There was a famine in the land *(distinct from the earlier one that had occurred in the days of Abraham, so why don't we just simply say there was another devastating famine in the land?)* Isaac knew that the Lord was up to His old tricks making the victimized people down on earth suffer and struggle so Abraham's *favorite* son went down to Abimelech, king of the Philistines in Gerar, *a popular village/brothel.*

The Lord appeared to Isaac and said, "Do not go to Egypt. *I don't have too much power there and the many false gods the Egyptians have might gang up on us.* Continue to camp wherever I tell you in this *God-forsaken* land. *My famine is working really well here and it's making the residents really miserable, just like I had cunningly planned.*"

"You like to bust chops, don't you?" Isaac complained.

"Stay is this land *of famine* and I will be with you and bless you, *for I enjoy blessing people that I am making suffer multiple hardships.* For you and all your descendents I will give all these lands, *just like I had promised your dead old man Abraham, even if the Canaanites and the other tribes already own the land I will give you.*"

"Can't you just get the Canaanites to worship You'?" Isaac suggested. "That solution would solve a lot of crazy problems!" Isaac audaciously challenged. "I think it is grossly unfair to manipulate me the way You' do. I am but a man and You' are a supernatural entity. That's grossly unethical and against all fairness!"

The Lord did not heed Isaac's grievance. "Isaac, I will give all of these lands in fulfillment of the oath that I swore to your father Abraham."

"Look Lord," Isaac lividly retorted, "I know my father's name is Abraham and You' don't have to keep repeating it! And if You' swore the land to my father, why didn't You make sure he possessed all of it before he died feeling like a defeated fool because he had failed to own the land of Canaan? Do You' always make hallow hollow promises that You fail to keep?"

The Lord was so focused on what He was to say next that he had tuned Isaac's protests right out of His' divine preoccupied mind. "I will make your descendents as numerous as the stars in the sky and give them all of these lands *owned by others that are brutally plagued with famine."*

"Yeah, I've heard those crazy extravagant promises before!" argued Isaac.

"And Isaac, I predict all nations of the earth shall find blessing in your descendents, *even if they happen to be pathetic products of generations of incest and doomed to four centuries of slavery. This is because Abraham obeyed Me', keeping My' mandate (My' commandments, My' ordinances, My' bylaws, My' petty rules, and My' inane arcane insane instructions)."*

So Isaac *reluctantly* settled in Gerar, *much to the objection, frustration and aggravation of the local inhabitants.* When the men of the place asked questions about his *beautiful* wife Rebekah, Isaac answered, "She is my sister." *Isaac had intelligently borrowed a page out of shifty Abraham's book regarding how he had told the Pharaoh that Sarah was his sister. We don't know if Isaac instinctively knew how to tell the imaginative lie or if he had been merely imitating his zany father's crafty guile. Or perhaps telling the imaginative tale was a genetic matter that Isaac had inherited from Abraham. But nevertheless, Isaac was being either deliberately or unintentionally deceitful.*

Isaac was afraid. If he called Rebekah his wife, the men of the place would kill him on account of Rebekah, since she was very beautiful *and Isaac was extremely paranoid and a frail wimp, just like his father had always been insecure about losing Sarah to another more muscular man.*

When Isaac had been there a long time, Abimelech, king of the Philistines *and a 'confirmed' but not baptized or circumcised practicing voyeur*, happened to look out of a window and was surprised to see Isaac fondling his wife Rebekah. *If Abimelech had been looking into a window instead of out of a window, then obviously he would have been outside the house and Isaac and Rebekah inside the house where such fondling should have been taking place in the first place in absolute privacy.*

Abimelech called for Isaac and he said: "She must certainly be your wife! How could you have said 'She is my sister? *Don't you know the difference between a wife and a sister'? Are you the ultimate dunce or what?"*

Isaac replied, "I thought I might lose my life on her account. *My paranoia dictates to my brain that it is better for you and your men to screw my wife than for me to be slaughtered and die. I have a phobia for death, as you might know! And besides, Rebekah and I*

124

were only trying to make you horny, aroused and extremely jealous!"

"How could you do this to us!" exclaimed Abimelech. *"You're a bigger jerk off than your fucked-up father ever was, and that ain't no stretch!* It would have taken very little for one of the men to lie with your wife, and you would have thus brought guilt upon us," Abimelech bellowed. *"Worse than mere guilt, then your lunatic Lord would have gone crazy on us by giving my people and me a bevy of natural disasters to complement His' already devastating famine! When your Lord goes bananas, it means curtains for everyone including Peeping Abimelechs!"*

Abimelech therefore gave this warning to all his men *that just happened to be hanging out there at the time:* "Anyone who *sexually* molests this man or his wife shall forthwith be put to death *although I fully realize that Isaac and Rebekah ought to be the first ones executed."*

Isaac sowed a crop *(we don't know or care to know what kind of crop)* in that region and reaped a hundred-fold the same year. *The Lord had accomplished His' objective to make Isaac rich and to make the Philistines jealous of Isaac's prosperity in their land of horrible famine.* Isaac became richer and richer all the time, until he was very wealthy *and affluent* indeed. *So since the Lord blessed him, Isaac became a fat cat while he behaved and acted like a pusillanimous pussy.*

Isaac acquired such *myriad* flocks and herds and *he possessed* so many work animals that the Philistines became *extremely* envious of him *(which was the Lord's marvelous plan to begin with. It would be wrong for everyone to be happy and to live in peace and prosperity, so believeth the Lord).*

The Philistines had stopped up and filled with dirt all the wells that Isaac's father's servants had dug back in the days of his father Abraham. *(Is there something wrong with the previous sentence, or what? Whatever happened to word efficiency and to word economy let alone story originality?)*

So Abimelech said to Isaac, "Go away from us *you lying, cheating, conniving miserable lucky bastard!* You have become *fat and* too numerous for us *despite the reality that you are but one person!"*

Isaac left there and made the Wadi Gerar his regular campsite, *much to the horror and contempt of the natives of the area.* (Isaac reopened the wells which his father's servants had dug back in the days of his father Abraham and which the Philistines had stopped up after Abraham's death (*Isn't there any viable cure for this relentless redundancy?*). *The local yokels logically thought they had gotten rid of the daft patriarch and the grotesque curses that accompanied him once and for all; that's why they really clogged the damned wells*).

But when Isaac's servants dug in the wadi and reached spring water *in the summer* the shepherds of Gerar *(who were Canaanite shepherds and not German shepherds)* quarreled with Isaac's *obnoxious* servants. The shepherds said *(all together, now)*, "The water belongs to us!"

But Isaac intelligently and profoundly answered, "But the wells belong to me!"

So the well was called Esek, meaning challenge, *because it had become an object of challenge between the mentally challenged shepherds and the mentally challenged Isaac and his mentally challenged servants, who all lived in mentally challenged times prescribed by the Lord.*

Then Isaac's servants dug another deep well and they again quarreled with the *insolent* shepherds *(who didn't know how to dig wells) over that particular one too while the servants and the shepherds challenged each other to crossword puzzles having only horizontal and vertical 'cross words' in them.* That new well was called Sitnah, meaning "opposition." *So, all was not well that ended well between Isaac's well-intentioned servants and the thirsty shepherds that only knew how to shepherd and how to quarrel and start altercations, and nothing else.*

When Isaac had moved on from there, he dug still another well *(actually, it was Isaac's servants that dug the new well because they simply dug digging new holes in the ground).* But over this one they did not quarrel with the shepherds. *The shepherds had been left behind at the Sitnah "opposition well" and were not in the vicinity to bicker with Isaac and his belligerent servants at the new well.*

The well was called Rehoboth, because Isaac said, "The Lord has now given us ample room *as we systematically according to His directions made new enemies and confiscated their land,* and we shall flourish *or perish* in this land that *definitely* is not ours. *Thank you Lord for more problems and conflicts! Men, make sure you put the new well on the west bank!"*

From there, Isaac *got tired of drinking only water* and went up to Beer-sheba *where he could guzzle down some brew and tie one on.* The same night the Lord appeared to Isaac and said: "I am the God of your father Abraham. You have no need to fear, since I am with you. I will bless you and multiply your descendents *with*

126

multiple sclerosis, all of this for the sake of my *dead already rotted* servant Abraham."

"How many times do I have to hear this same old crap?" Isaac *muttered and complained. "Can't You' find some other flunky to play Your' insane power game with?"*

So Isaac *obediently (out of fear)* built an altar there and invoked the Lord by name. After he had pitched his tent there, Isaac's servants began to dig another *west bank* well nearby, *because by then, they were really into digging wells more than into anything else less exciting like group sex or wild orgies. They immediately knew that water could easily be found because the servants all got huge erections at the same time and their throbbing peckers acted like fleshy divining rods, pointing straight' down into the desert sands at Rehoboth, precisely where the next well should be dug.*

Abimelech had meanwhile come to Isaac from Gerar, accompanied by Phicol, *Fecal and Protocol, his indispensable military advisers.* Ahuzzath, Abimelech's *guidance* councilor was also present. Isaac asked them, "Why have you come to me, seeing that you hate me and have driven me away from you *without even using a chariot or an oxcart?"*

They answered *(in unison, which was an uncanny ability and custom everyone seemed to have in Canaan and vicinity):* "We are convinced that the Lord is with you, *in spite of the fact that none of us can see Him here in this foul place.* We propose that there should be a sworn agreement between our two sides, *even though we have a mighty army and you don't.* Between you and us, let us make a pact *or else your formidable Lord will get pissed and swiftly eliminate our entire civilization with all its terrific science and technology."*

"Look guys, all I want to do is dig a stupid well and then hang out at the local beer garden," Isaac nonchalantly replied. *"Who needs all of this dramatic bullshit?"*

"You shall not act unkindly toward us," the men said *in chorus,* "just as we have not molested you, and have always acted kindly toward you and let you leave in peace. Henceforth, the Lord's blessing is upon you. *Just don't have your servants beat the shit out of our wimpy shepherds near any wells and everything else will be okay."*

Isaac then made a feast for Abimelech and his advisers *and the Philistines ate two broiled shepherds without their knowledge.* They ate and drank, and early the next morning Isaac and Abimelech exchanged oaths *and oafs.* Then Isaac bade the king and his *military* advisers farewell and the visitors departed from him in peace, *licking their chops from their delicious cannibalistic meal.*

That same day Isaac's servants came and brought him news about the well they had been digging; they told him *in unison,* "We have *remarkably* reached *sea* water *and we are over fifty miles away from the sea!"*

Isaac called the *strange* place Shibah, meaning "seven." *He had aptly named the place after rolling two dice on the desert sand.* Hence the name of the place Beer-sheba, to this day, *and Isaac, feeling quite literary even wrote a short play about it titled "Come Back Little Beer-sheba."*

When Esau was forty years old he married Judith, daughter of Beeri-*beeri* the Hittite, and of Basemath, daughter of Elon the Hivite. *Basemath was often called the mother of arithmetic.* But Esau and Judith became the source of embitterment to Isaac and Rebekah, *who favored Jacob over Esau just like the Lord had played favorites with Abraham and Isaac over everybody else on earth. As they commonly say, "Monkey-see, monkey-do."*

Chapter Twenty-seven
"Jacob's Deception"

When Isaac was so old *a fart* that his eyesight had failed him *and the geezer no longer had eyes in back of his head* he said *to his chief servant, "Fetch me my damned blindfold so that I could see better."* Then Isaac called his older son Esau *(who was five whole seconds older than Jacob)* and *very imaginatively* said to him, "Son!"

"Yes father!" Esau *ingeniously* replied, *for the older son was almost as imaginative as his dying father was and a chip off the old block despite the notion that red-faced Esau was overlooked in favor of Jacob. No wonder why Esau was red-faced. His father was an Indian giver.*

Isaac then said, *"I sick! In fact, I am very sick,"* said Isaac. "As you can see, *I can't see.* I am so old that I may now die at any time, *which will be a blessing for me' and a really big blessing for your favored brother Jacob.* Take your gear *and invent a transmission or a watch or some contraption like that to put it in.* Take your quiver and your bow *but make sure that your hands do not quiver when you shoot your arrows.* Go out in the country and hunt some game for me, *maybe checkers or perhaps my favorite, strip poker."*

Isaac cleared his throat that had been clogged with heavy mucus and thick clumps of accumulated snot. "Esau, with your catch, prepare an appetizing dish for me, *so why the hell should you go hunting for game when I only want to eat the damned dish? At any rate my shunned son,* you know what I like to eat, *checkers or strip poker pussy. Incidentally, did I ever tell you that I had once spent a night at a restaurant/whorehouse that had a sign in front of it, 'All the pussy you can eat, only ninety-nine shekels?' Anyway my neglected and disfavored son,* after the appetizer *bring me a tasty entrée* so that I may give you my special blessing before I *hopefully eat the dish, kick the bucket and fuckin'* die."

Rebekah *was a nosy wife and she* had been eavesdropping while Isaac was speaking to his son Esau *(who was also in a way her son).* So when Esau went out into the country *(from the desert)* to hunt some *exotic* game like *checkers or strip poker* for his father Rebekah said to her son Jacob, "Listen! I overheard your father talking to your brother Esau."

"Mother, I know that Esau is my brother so you don't have to mention his name every single time you mention the common word brother," Jacob indicated and admonished, *"and you should really*

129

mind your own damned business and not eavesdrop all the time on Pop or anybody else. Unfortunately, common sense is not too damned common!"

"Your father Abraham told your brother Esau," Rebekah continued *pissing off her slightly younger son,* "bring me some game and with it prepare an appetizing dish for me to eat that I may give you my blessing with the Lord's approval before I die *and get my fat fanny off this totally repugnant planet.*"

"Father's blessings and the Lord's blessings are nothing more than wretched dual curses specifically designed to cause hatred and animosity between Esau and me," Jacob criticized and lamented, "and besides, father has eaten so many dishes in our house that we no longer have any plates or platters in the empty cupboards. Pop's eaten them all like a ravenous maniac and you no longer have any opportunity to throw flying saucers at him!"

Rebekah *ignored her son's bizarre statement and proceeded with her own ludicrous rhetoric, which was based on preposterous logic.* "Now son, listen carefully to what I tell you, *for as you might know, I am a very distrustful scheming woman just like Sarah was. Jacob, you must* go to the *nearest* flock and get me two small kids, *but make sure that the kids aren't little boys or little girls,"* the mother stipulated. "With those kids I will prepare an appetizing dish for your father, such as he likes *before he eats his entrée and then has dessert while skipping the main part of the meal.* Then bring the appetizing dish for your father to eat, *but don't be surprised if he eats the dish and leaves the delectable appetizer.* Then your father will bless you before he dies *from broken earthenware chucks caught in his windpipe and in his esophagus."*

"But my brother Esau is a hairy man," said Jacob *incomprehensibly* to his mother Rebekah, "and I am smooth-skinned!"

"You don't have to keep telling me Esau is your brother," Rebekah barked. *"Where did you ever acquire the stupid bad habit of always emphasizing and reiterating the obvious?"*

"But *Mommy Dearest,"* said Jacob *to the unheralded matriarch,* "*let's just* suppose that my' father feels me? *You know he's always been sort of a pedophile with his own sons, especially me. Pop's always been fond of fondling.* He will think I am making sport of him *and will not then be a very good sport about it.* I shall then bring upon myself a curse instead of a blessing, *but in this disgusting day and age it is increasingly hard to tell the difference between the two*

130

supposedly opposite-ended manifestations. Whatever happened to the phenomenon known as moral polarity?"

His mother, however, replied: "Let any curse against you son, fall on me! Just do as I say *and not as I do. Go and get me the kids, and make sure they aren't little human tykes that have not passed through puberty."*

So Jacob *like an obedient wimp* went and got the kids and brought them to his mother and with them she prepared an appetizing dish, *cooking them whole and alive without taking their skins and wool off.* This was just like Isaac had always liked the lambs prepared *when his enzymes and digestive juices were working well during his earlier days.*

Rebekah then took the best clothes of her older son Esau that she had kept in the house *(tent),* and she gave them to her younger son Jacob to wear, *hoping that someday Jacob would eventually become a cross-dresser.* And with the skins of the kids she covered up Jacob's hands and also the hairless parts of his neck. All of this *was done to pull the wool over poor dying Isaac's eyes, who' was already legally blind in the first place without any wool pulled over his wrinkled eyelids.* Then Rebekah handed Jacob the appetizing dish and the bread she had prepared.

Bringing them to his *almost comatose* father, Jacob said: "Father!" *This particular word "father" was ancient Hebrew slang for Daddio.*

"Yes?" replied Isaac, *who could never tell the difference between Esau's low and Jacob's high-pitched voices, even before he had become legally deaf, blind and certifiably insane.*

Jacob answered his father: "I am Esau, your' first *and worst* born. I did *exactly* as you *had* told me. Please sit up and eat some of my game so that you may *then* give me your special blessing *that everyone around here fully understands constitutes a not-so-special curse."*

But Isaac asked, "How did you succeed in the hunt so quickly, son? *Are you sure you didn't buy this succulent meat you are presenting at the local bizarre bazaar supermarket? I happen to know that all of the freakin' butchers there are on strike!"*

Isaac answered, "The Lord your God *has* let things turn out well with me. *He's a real gamer, yes He certainly is, Daddio!"*

Isaac then said to Jacob, "Come closer son, that I may feel you *just like I used to molest your cute little genitals in the good old days. I will soon learn by grabbing your hairy testicles if you are really my furry son Esau!"*

131

So Jacob moved up closer to his father *because he still craved being molested by the notorious old pedophile.* When Isaac felt him, he said, "Although the voice is Jacob's, the hands are Esau's. *(Isaac failed to identify Jacob because his hands were hairy, just like Esau's testicles).* So in the end, Isaac gave Jacob his blessing, *all the while thinking about how great it would be to feel, fondle and pet Esau's hairy balls.*

Again Isaac asked Jacob, "Are you really my son Esau?" *All the while the incontinent and incompetent Isaac didn't give a happy hoot who' the hell he was fondling and feeling, just as long as he was fondling and feeling someone.*

"Certainly!" Jacob *fraudulently* replied. *'Don't forget to feel my hairless testicles covered by kid's wool too,' he wished.*

Then Isaac said, "Serve me your game, son, *but make sure you don't serve me any tennis balls. I hate that fuckin' game!* Then I may eat the game and then give you my blessing."

Jacob served it to him and Isaac ate; Jacob brought his father wine and he drank. *'If general gluttony doesn't kill the demented old bastard,' Jacob thought, 'then I don't know what the hell will!'*

Finally, his father Isaac said to him, "Come closer son, and kiss me. *Then I will be inspired, excited and sufficiently aroused to continue my molestation and my fondling of you!"*

As Jacob went up and kissed Isaac the father smelled the fragrance of his clothes, *which smelled like crap from the terrible cooked lamb's wool and stenchy entrails.* With that, Isaac blessed Jacob, saying, "Ah, the fragrance of my son is like the fragrance of a field that the Lord has *sufficiently* blessed. *I think I need to see a nose and throat specialist right away.* May God give to you of the dew of the heavens, *but if you think about it, dew is something that only settles on earth and there should only be one friggin' dewless Heaven."*

Then Isaac paused to gather his twisted and distorted thoughts. "And *enjoy all* of the fertility of the earth *and the* abundance of grain and wine *so that the Philistines and the Canaanites will hate you even more than they do right now. Let people serve you my son, especially in bars and in beer gardens and in 'all the pussy you can eat' whorehouse/restaurants.* May nations pay you' homage *along with plenty of taxes and tributes, too.* Be master of your brothers, *for as you know, I wholeheartedly advocate slavery and slave trading for profit,"* Isaac elucidated. "And may your mother's sons bow down to you, *and if they don't, send your biggest servants to kick their disobedient butts and instantly crush their brass balls.* Cursed be those who curse you, and blessed be those who bless you, *even though it is hard to tell the distinction between curses and blessings in this brutal and barbaric Wholly Book of Genesis."*

Jacob had scarcely left his father, just after Isaac had finished blessing him, when his brother Esau came back from his hunt *and entered the tent stage left.* Then Esau too prepared an appetizing dish with his game, and bringing it to his father, he said: "Please father, eat some of your son's game, that you may give me your special blessing *that probably is disguised as an un-special curse." It was quite clear that both of Isaac's sons were trying to kill the old dying man by having him over-eat their putrid-tasting food while languishing on his deathbed.*

"Who are you?" his father Isaac asked him *after belching and burping and farting in a disgraceful undignified manner for a full hour and a half.*

"I am Esau," he replied, "your *condemned* first-born *ruddy-faced* son. *I don't give a shit if you recognize me or if you don't recognize me you old fool. I just want to see you outa' here as soon as possible! You've already fucked up my life once too often!"*

With that, Isaac was seized with a fit of uncontrollable trembling. "Who was it then," he asked, "that hunted game and brought it to me? I finished eating it just before you came and I *gullibly* blessed him. Now he, *the favored lucky recipient* must remain blessed *because of the nonsensical tradition I happen to honor."*

It was quite evident that Isaac couldn't tell the difference between cooked veal (baby lamb meat) and wild boar (adult pig meat). Perhaps the old geezer's taste buds were already dead. Isaac should have known that only a wimp goes out with a bow and arrow into a corral and then shoots two innocent little lambs to death. Esau on the other hand was an accomplished boar hunter.

On hearing his father's words Esau burst into loud bitter sobbing *when he should have drawn his knife and violently punctured Isaac's chest repeatedly for unfairly and undemocratically favoring Jacob instead of his very ugly first-born.* "Father, bless me too!" Esau *sincerely* begged.

When Isaac *accurately* explained, "Your brother came here by a ruse and carried off your blessing, *so just like my father Abraham had done with Ishmael and me, I have to honor tricks and deception because they probably originated with the Lord and are His' erratic* enigmatic wishes. *It is very important and appropriate that I should die as I had lived, as a complete asshole!"*

Esau exclaimed, "He has been well-named Jacob! He has now supplanted me twice, *once with stew for my birthright and here now with your blessing, which might in reality be a dreadful curse in disguise. And now you claim you must honor these injustices just because you believe that the Lord capriciously values dishonesty, corruption and favoritism! What a fuckin' old imbecile you really are!"*

"That's the whole game plan in a nutshell," Isaac *truthfully* admitted. *"You're smarter than the average boar or bear."*

Then Esau *desperately* pleaded, "Haven't you saved a blessing for me? Perhaps you should curse me, *for that might turn out to be an actual blessing in this fucked-up convoluted world I live in!"*

Isaac replied: "I have already 'appointed' Jacob your master, *so don't be so damned disappointed.* And I have assigned to Jacob all of his kinsmen and slaves, *including you, Esau.* Besides, I have enriched him with grain and with wine. What then can I do for you my *disfavored unprivileged* son, *when I have nothing left to give you? The damned bank is empty!"*

But *then* Esau urged his father, "Have you only that one blessing, father? Bless me too! *I too am your flesh and blood, your' true first born. Have you nothing more to offer me than a childish mind game with all the marbles at stake given to my younger brother by deceit. Frankly Pop, I think you have completely lost your marbles by giving them all to that greedy ambitious conniving bastard Jacob!"*

Isaac, however, made no reply and Esau *sobbed and* wept aloud, *even though he was not allowed to cry by austere family tradition and custom.*

Finally Isaac spoke again and said to him: "Ah, far from the fertile earth shall be your dwelling. *Esau, you are shunned by me and deserve no better according to the Lord's discretion;* far from the dew of the heavens above, *despite the fact that it rains from only one Heaven and also that dew appears only on earth.* By your sword you shall live," *Isaac specified and equivocated,* "and your brother you shall serve *with a huge tennis racket;* but when you become restive, you shall throw off your yoke from your neck *when you finally realize that the yoke's been on you. Ha, ha, ha!"*

"It's bad enough that I have to see and smell bull shit out in your stinking pastures, but now I have to hear stupid corny

134

unmitigated bull shit inside your sacred tent!" Esau yelled as he stormed out of the place with great enmity in his heart.

Esau bore *(for good reason)* Jacob a grudge because of the blessing his father had *capriciously* given the younger brother. *Isaac knew that he had made a mistake in judgment but he failed to correct or alter his unjust conscious decision.* Esau said to himself *(for the injustices of Isaac had the abused fellow talking to himself)*, "When the time of mourning for my father comes, I will *without compunction* kill my brother Jacob."

When Rebekah got the news of what her older son Esau had in mind *she couldn't figure out how she had received the confidential information since Esau had only uttered it to himself.* Rebekah called her younger son Jacob *(we know the names already about who is who in this peculiar story)* and said to him: "Listen! Your brother Esau *(I mean, how many brothers does Jacob have?)* intends to settle accounts with you by killing you. *He might have a good and simple solution there.*"

"Mommy, what should I do?" Jacob implored with great apprehension.

"Therefore son, do what I tell you: flee at once to my bother Laban in Haran. *To my knowledge he has not yet died from laughing about what Abraham's servant had told him.* Stay with Laban a while until your brother's fury subsides *about being cheated by you and your father over his birthright, his blessing and his genuine inheritance, which you have skillfully stolen from him. Eventually* Esau will forget what you did to him, *but if it were me that had been so deceitfully cheated, I would cut your damned balls off right now and hang them in the bizarre bazaar marketplace for all to see and admire and gossip about. When the coast and the mainland are clear,"* Rebekah advised, "I will send for you and bring you back. *On second thought, if I send for you how can I possibly bring you back? Anyway Jacob, must I lose both of you in one day, for indeed, that is impossible because you are only one person to lose.*"

Rebekah *later* (time transition problem here) said to *her failing husband* Isaac: "I am disgusted with life because of the Hittite women. *I'm messed up in the head because they're messed up in the head, so I guess I really regret and resent being a Hittite woman that is messed up in the head.* If Jacob should also marry a Hittite woman," *the wife speculated and mentioned,* "a native of the land, like these women *I speak of,* what good would life be to me? *I was better off filling my jugs with water at Laban's house than coming here to Canaan and putting up with all this stupid horse, camel,* boar, lamb and bull crap. I've never seen or heard anything quite like it!"

Chapter Twenty-eight
"Jacob's Dream at Bethel"

Isaac therefore called Jacob, greeted him with a blessing, *and congratulated his younger son for being cunning, coy, sly, dishonest and deceitful, just like him.* Isaac charged Jacob *(even though the old decrepit man was in bed and could not move an elbow):* "You shall not marry a Canaanite woman. *They all think we itinerant poachers that have migrated from Ur are merely about camel shit and bullshit. Canaanite women are often disobedient, independent and non-subservient. They think that male chauvinism is male chauvinism and many of them believe in a strange abstraction they call 'equality.'* Now go *Jacob* to Paddan-aram, to the home of your mother's father Betheul, and there choose a wife for yourself from the daughters of your Uncle Laban. *As you know our family has always believed that incest is best!*"

"*But if I marry one of Uncle Laban's daughters,*" objected Jacob, "*wouldn't I be ignorantly duplicating your stupidity all over again? Wouldn't this be more dumb incest that in the final analysis is going to fuck up our many descendents even more than our people and slaves are fucked-up mental cases right now?*"

"May God Almighty bless you and make you fertile *just like my ancestors were over in the Fertile Crescent,*" answered Isaac *from his prone position in his bed.* "Multiply so that you may become an assembly of people *big enough to fill any auditorium or open-air synagogue. You and your descendents will become an Assembly of God!*"

"*Damn it Dad, you didn't have the guts to go to Paddan-aram to get a wife!*" yelled Jacob. "*Your father sent a servant in your place. Why can't you just send a freakin' servant in my place? Why must I have to do what a flunky servant had done for you to find Mom?*"

"*Jacob,* may God extend to you and your descendents the blessing He' gave to *my Pappy* Abraham, so that you may gain possession of the land where you are staying, which He' *the Almighty had promised and* assigned to Abraham," *repeated Isaac to his quarrelsome and often petulant son.* "*We have not yet been able to steal it all from the stubborn local inhabitants. They claim squatters rights even when they bend down to take a crap!*"

Then Isaac sent Jacob on his way, *threatening to give his entire fortune to Esau if his younger son did not obey his unscrupulous commands.* Jacob went to Paddan-aram to see Laban, son of Betheul, *who was still incessantly laughing from the crazy stories Abraham's servant had described many decadent decades before.* Laban was an Aramean, the brother of Rebekah, who was the mother of Jacob and Esau. *(We know this book of Genesis is very boring, so we have to keep reminding you who is who in the sequence of numskull convoluted, repetitious plots and characters).*

Esau noted that Isaac had blessed Jacob when he sent him to Paddan-aram to get himself a wife there *at a wholesale wife and concubine discount man's store centrally situated in a bizarre bazaar.* Isaac had charged Jacob as he gave him his blessing, not to marry a Canaanite woman, and that Jacob had honored his father and mother and had gone to Paddan-aram *to search for a wife in the concubine department at the discount men's bizarre bazaar. (It is not clearly defined here whether "charged his son" means moneys or a fee extracted from Jacob or Isaac putting his' head down like an assertive bull and then snorting forward. We presume that since Isaac was lying horizontal on his deathbed, "charging his son" must have either meant some kind of nifty parental extortion or possibly giving an order).*

Esau realized how displeasing the Canaanite women were to his father Isaac, so he went to Ishmael, and in addition to the wives he had, *the first born of Isaac* married Mahalath *because Canaanite wives and women were only a shekel a dozen. This amounted to an extraordinary bargain for any enterprising local stud' meister.* Mahalath was the daughter of Abraham's son Ishmael and sister of Nahor, *which further complicated the inbred genetics of the early Hebrew family tree.*

Jacob, *having his thirst quenched at the popular local beer gardens, then* departed from Beer-sheba and proceeded toward Haran. When he came upon a certain shrine *he realized that it was always open rain or 'shrine', regardless that it never rained in that remote part of the hostile arid desert.* The sun had already set so Jacob stopped there for the night. Taking one of the stones at the shrine, he put it under his head and lay down to sleep at that spot. *Some of the stone might have shattered and penetrated Jacob's skull, since many early Biblical scholars have maintained that Jacob and most of his offspring had rocks in their head. At any rate, Jacob would wake up stoned the next morning.*

As he slept, Jacob has a dream: a stairway 'rested' on the ground *because it too was fatigued and tired.* Its top was reaching to the heavens and God's *impervious-to-danger* messengers were going up and down on it. *And as we all know, this had to be a divine vision*

138

since man will never be able to invent such an amazing device that escalates people or angels up and down from one level to another like the celestial staircase Heaven and earth had so miraculously demonstrated to Jacob.

And in the dream there was the Lord standing beside Jacob and saying: "I, the Lord, am the God of your forefathers, *even though we both know that you have only one main grandfather.* I am the God of your forefather Abraham and your father Isaac. The land on which you are lying *you ought to be telling the truth on.*"

"*Who are the individuals on that magical divine stairway?*" Jacob inquired. "*How can I get up in the world like those winged guys? Are they the sons of Hermes?*"

"Forget the small stuff!" the Lord demanded from His newfound pawn. "The *worthless* land on which you are lying *and not telling the truth on* I shall give to you and your descendents, *so just forget about the fact that neither I nor you own it.* Your descendents shall be as plentiful as the dust of the earth, *for all humans are merely dust in the wind, even in Kansas and far off Arkansas.* Through your descendents you shall spread out east, west, north and south, *so Jacob, are you ready to be stretched all over this part of Asia Minor? Notice too Jacob, I really know My' four basic directions all because of My moral compass!*"

"*That's what I need Lord, direction and a moral compass,*" said Jacob, "*but I don't think I need four different directions at the same time to be stretched all over the damned continent, north, south, east and west! Can't you just give me a magical compass instead?*"

"Jacob'," said the Lord, "*stop being such a ninny.* In you all the nations of the world shall find blessing *so don't be surprised if millions of people insist on looking inside your mouth, nose, ears, rectum, or any other orifice on your ugly body searching for this blessing that I shall place in you. Do you fathom My' words?*"

"*I don't think I want to be under such continuous public scrutiny,*" Jacob balked. "*It's worse than being a damned politician. But on the other hand, my body cavities are something that people around the world ought to look into if they desire to be Heaven blessed.*"

"Jacob, know that I am with you; I will protect you *from every schoolyard bully* wherever you may go; and I will bring you back to this land, *but remember, you still have to walk the desert and ride your camel while I bring you back to your destination.* I will never leave you until I have done what I promised you, *which means you might have to live and suffer at least ten thousand additional nasty human years."*

When Jacob awoke from his sleep, he exclaimed: *"What the fuck's going on! Truly the Lord is in this spot and I didn't take along any damned spot remover to get rid of Him. Although, I must confess, all along* I did not know it *was a sacred place, or even care to know it now."*

In solemn wonder Jacob cried out, "How awesome is this shrine! This is nothing else but an abode of God and *absolutely* that is the gateway of Heaven. *Where are all the Shriners and all of the local Moose members if this indeed is a shrine?"*

Early the next morning Jacob took the stone that he had put under his head *and when he felt a little boulder,* set it up as a memorial stone. He poured oil on top of it, *thinking of doing that since it was still oily in the morning.* Jacob called that site "Bethel," whereas the former name of the town had been Luz, *where a bunch of male Luzers and Luz women used to live.*

 Jacob then made this vow: "If God remains with me, to protect me on the journey I am making and to give me enough bread to eat and also *enough bread (money) for* clothing to wear, *I could eventually evolve out of my divine welfare state into economic independence," Jacob maintained.* "And when I come back safe to my father's house, the Lord shall be my God. *Otherwise, He' might visit some drastic calamity on my descendents and me that might be too traumatic to endure and suffer through. Who needs that kind of crazy shit just before marvelously entering slavery for four hundred years as the Lord had promised my grandfather Abraham?"*

Then Jacob reflected some more.' This stone that I have set-up' as a memorial stone shall be God's above. *I think I have been quite clever using a small stone as a memorial than having to spend days building a giant altar like my foolish father Isaac and my gutless grandfather Abraham had to do,' Jacob meditated.* "Oh Lord, of everything You' give me, I will faithfully return a tenth part to You'," *Jacob prayed out loud.* "*You shall be my authentic commission broker getting ten percent of every transaction, so send some good deals my way so that I can become even richer than I already happen to be," Jacob nobly uttered to the sky.*

Chapter Twenty-nine
"Arrival in Haran"

After Jacob resumed his journey *eastward* he came to the land of the 'Easterners', *who always turned east at crossroads and consequently after four successive right-angle turns (without the aid of a compass) always traveled in queer-looking square patterns.* Looking about Jacob saw a well in the open country, with three droves of sheep huddled near it, for droves *were driven in droves* and were watered from that well. *Jacob expeditiously thought, 'Here's a place where I can instigate some nifty trouble and insanely behave just like my crazy father and my goofy grandfather that everybody else around here calls my forefathers.'*

A large stone covered the mouth, *nose, and throat* of the well, *which gave Jacob the impression that the well might have been some sort of primitive 'wellness center'.* Only when all the shepherds were assembled there *(they came from all over the known and the unknown world, every last damned shepherd on the planet)* could they then roll the stone away from the mouth, *nose and throat* of the remote desert well. The shepherds would then water the flocks *(without giving the sheep anything to drink while giving them baths and splashing water over the pissed-off animals).* Then they would put the stone back again over the mouth of the well *after watering, splashing, bathing and rinsing the still thirsty and exhausted sheep.*

Jacob said to them, "Friends, where are you from?" *fully realizing that the sheep could not answer in words but only in bleats. Fortunately, the shepherds were capable of answering Jacob's inquiry.*

"We are from Haran," the shepherds all replied *like a babbling Babylonian barbershop quartet.*

Then Jacob asked another question, *for he was a little too inquisitive for his own damned good.* "Do you know *the bastard* Laban, son of Nahor? *Is that freak a corn' ball or what?*"

"We do know that stupid asshole," they answered *all at the same time.* "*He's by far the biggest jerk off in the whole land.*"

Jacob inquired further, "Is he well? *Has he been assassinated yet?*"

"He is," they all answered *in unison. "Unfortunately, Laban is well because he comes to this wellness center often,"* they *simultaneously agreed.* "And here comes his daughter Rachel with Laban's flock right now. *She is forced to do a man's work since Laban is too damned lazy to tend to his own flock. He's always out*

141

flockin' around as a wolf in sheep's clothing if ya' know what we mean," the shepherds all coincidentally stated and then laughed.

Then Jacob said: "There is still much daylight left; it is hardly the time to bring the animals home. Why don't you water the flocks, *and maybe this time give them something to drink in addition to bathing, splashing and washing them,"* Jacob constructively suggested. "Then you can continue *bathing, splashing, rinsing, watering and* then pasturing them *while I try to make some time and hustle Laban's exotic-looking well' endowed daughter."*

"We cannot," the shepherds replied *all together*, "until all the shepherds are here to roll away the stone from the mouth, *nose and throat* of the well. Only then can we again water the flocks. *It requires a group effort to roll back the stone."*

"Those other shepherds sound like they're licensed mouth, nose and throat specialists," Jacob admitted *with sincere admiration.* *"You probably even have a good medical plan here in your wonderful land."*

While Jacob was still talking with the shepherds, Rachel arrived with her father's sheep; she was the one who tended them (*as we have just recently told you. ibid*).

As soon as Jacob saw Rachel, the daughter of his Uncle Laban, *whom Jacob called Uncle Laban, the visitor got an immediate huge erection.* Jacob *was so motivated that he* went up, rolled the stone away from the mouth, *nose and throat* of the well *all by himself* and then *convincingly* watered his uncle's sheep *without giving them anything to drink.* Then Jacob kissed Rachel and burst into tears, *so there were millions and millions of damned tears all over the wet ground, forming a large puddle.*

Jacob told Rachel that he was her father's relative, Rebekah's son, and she ran to tell her father *because in her innocent heart Rachel actually believed that Jacob was a barbaric child molester and rapist. And besides, she had never before seen a man that could liquify himself by bursting into millions of tears to creatively form a puddle of water.*

When Laban heard the news about his sister's son Jacob, he hurried out *to the wellness center* to meet him. After embracing and kissing him, *which was the custom of incestuous gays in those lawless primitive times,* Laban brought Jacob to his house.

Jacob then recounted to Laban all that *had* happened, *for indeed Jacob knew everything that had happened to everybody since the dawn of time in the days of Adam and Eve and even about certain Neanderthal men before them. After Jacob's five-minute speech,*

Laban said to his guest, "You are indeed my flesh and blood. *You are just as full of shit and fucked-up as I am!"*

After Jacob had stayed with Laban a full month Laban said to him: "Should you serve me for nothing just because you are a relative of mine, *even though you are my nephew by marriage and not a genuine bona fide blood relative.* Tell me *my cowardly friend* what your wages should be, *and they better not be more than the cost of child labor."*

Now Laban had two daughters; the older was called Leah, the younger Rachel. Leah had lovely eyes *but was flat chested,* but Rachel was well' formed and beautiful *with nice hips, big tits, hairy pussy and a really nice firm ass.*

Since Jacob had fallen in love with Rachel, *it was love at first well' site.* Jacob answered, "I will serve you seven years for your younger daughter Rachel. *I am willing to trade hard work for good sex."*

Laban replied, "I prefer to give her to you rather than to an outsider, *even though you are a stupid outsider visiting Haran.* Stay with me *and perhaps we can have a threesome going to keep the spirit of incest alive in our demented family."*

Then Jacob said to Laban, "Give me my wife, *regardless if I don't have a wife right now that you should have to give me back.* In that way I may consummate my marriage with her *since this damned land just like mine has no lazy priests or rabbis around to perform freakin' weddings. In seven years my term of indenture will then finally be completed."*

So Laban invited all the local inhabitants and gave a feast *to show everyone just what an idiot Jacob was.* At nightfall Laban took his daughter Leah and brought her to Jacob, *who was so drunk from the feast that he couldn't distinguish Leah from her younger sister Rachel.* (Laban assigned his *exotic, erotic big-breasted* slave girl Zilpah to his daughter Leah as her *personal* maidservant).

In the morning Jacob was amazed: it was Leah *and her enticing maidservant Zilpah in bed with him* and not Rachel! So Jacob cried out to Laban: "How could you do this to me! Was it not for Rachel that I served you *seven years?* Why did you dupe me? *On second thought, look at those tits on Zilpah! Wow! What a set! This might not be such a bad fuckin' idea after all!"*

"It is the *sneaky* custom in our country," Laban said *to Jacob,* "to marry off the older daughter before marrying off the younger one. Finish the bridal week *with Leah and Zilpah in the sack, and you might not ever want to think of screwing Rachel ever again. If*

143

you then still desire *to pump the poop out of* Rachel, I will give her to you if you promise me seven additional years of service."

"Fourteen years for two wives, one of which I never wanted!" Jacob protested. *"I will go through several sets of dentures during such a long indenture." Then Jacob thoroughly scrutinized Zilpah's massive and really firm hooters. "Maybe that's not such a bad deal after all!" he exultantly exclaimed and then reiterated for Laban's satisfaction.*

Jacob *then wholeheartedly* agreed. He finished the bridal week with Leah *and Zilpah*, and then Laban gave him his daughter Rachel in marriage *since all of the hired priests and rabbis still had hangovers from the first wedding to Leah, which they had attended as guests but not as ministers. (Laban assigned his slave girl Bilhah, Zilpah's twin sister, to his daughter Rachel as her maidservant. Jacob had such a ball balling all four broads every night in the sack that he was nearly dehydrated from loss of body fluids every single morning).*

Jacob had *finally* consummated the marriage to Rachel *and either he would be worked to death by Laban or screwed to death by Rachel, Zilpah, Leah and Bilhah.* Jacob loved Rachel more than *he cared for* Leah, *but he loved having sex with Zilpah and Bilhah much more than pumping the poop out of both Rachel and Leah.* Thus Jacob remained in Laban's service another ten years *while he gladly serviced Rachel, Leah, Zilpah and Bilhah with his fleshy spear.*

When the Lord saw that Leah was unloved *unlike Rachel, Zilpah and Bilhah,* he made Leah fruitful, *so that she could be a vindictive ball buster to Jacob and be a bushwhacker to her younger buxom sister Rachel.* Rachel, however, remained barren *and had been officially 'busted' for the second time by the Lord.*

Leah conceived and bore a son, and she named him Reuben, *who later invented a famous type of deli sandwich.* Leah said, "His name means 'the Lord saw my misery'. "Now my husband will love me *as much as he loves Rachel, Zilpah and Bilhah. Damn it, I really wish I had decent-sized tits!" Leah hoped as she massaged her very diminutive breasts.*

Leah conceived again and bore a son and said, "The Lord heard *again* that I was unloved, and therefore he has given me this one also *since I haven't had sex with anyone except Bilhah is the last full year."* So Leah named him Simeon, meaning 'He heard.' *Leah named the infant Simeon because she couldn't conceive of any other mediocre name.*

144

Again Leah conceived and bore a son and she said *to her reflection in the family cesspool*: "Now at last my husband *will stop screwing around with my sister and Zilpah and Bilhah. At last the unfaithful bastard* will become attached to me, since I have now borne him three sons *but oddly enough haven't had sex with him in over two years.*" That is why Leah named the third son Levi, *which means, "He will become attached." Leah wrapped the infant in dark blue canvass material, which later bore Levi's proud name.*

Once more Leah conceived and bore a fourth son *while only having female sex with Bilhah.* She said, "This time I will give praise to the Lord"; therefore she named the fourth son Judah, which means, "I will give grateful praise." Then Leah stopped bearing children. *She visited several quack ancient gynecologists, who couldn't explain to her how she was having children without having intercourse with her husband or with any other men. When good things occur, we say that the Lord works in wondrous ways. When crazy things happen, we say that the Lord works in mysterious ways.*

145

146

Chapter Thirty
"Jacob Outwits Laban"

When *wide-hipped, big-breasted and wet-crotched* Rachel failed to bear children to Jacob, *who was putting it to her five times a night (even during her period week),* she became envious of *narrow-hipped, small-breasted frigid-crotched* Leah. Rachel said to Jacob, "Give me children or I shall die, *even if you screw me to death! You seldom screw Leah and she has children and you always pump me and I can't conceive. What the fuck's going on here?"*

Jacob retorted, "Can I take the place of God, who has denied you the fruit of the womb. *Perhaps you should wear some other kind of underwear that is more sexy."*

Rachel *cynically* replied, *"Go fuck yourself Dipshit!* Here's my maidservant Bilhah. Have intercourse with her *and pump the poop out of her hiney just like you do to me every damned night without any pregnancy resulting.* And let Bilhah give birth on my knees *so that I can massage the little bloody sucker and remove the horrible afterbirth from his slippery disgusting body.* So too then I too could have offspring through Bilhah."

Here's this ridiculous plot reappearing again! So Rachel gave Jacob her maidservant as a consort *and Jacob got all pumped up and had a sexual concert in bed with the consort.* When Bilhah conceived and bore a son, Rachel said, "God has vindicated me; indeed He has heeded my plea and given me a son. *Now pray tell how the hell do I get all of this bloody afterbirth crap off my damned knee!"*

Therefore, Rachel named him Dan *without even having the courtesy of consulting with Bilhah, the infant's biological mother.* Rachel's maidservant Bilhah *(we know her damned name, already!)* conceived again *without having sex or without even masturbating* and bore a second son, and Rachel said *(to whom?),* "I engaged in a fateful struggle with my sister, and I prevailed. *It's a good thing Bilhah's ovaries are working properly and that her crotch is juiced-up."* So Rachel named the second son Naphtali *without having the decency of consulting either Bilhah or Jacob.*

When Leah saw that she had ceased to bear children *she realized that all of Jacob's sperm were going to Rachel and again to Bilhah, whose ovaries knew what the hell to do with those horny little squiggly sperms. "He's just shooting bursts of air into me and nothing else,"* Leah complained to Zilpah. *"I'm getting all of his blank ejaculations!"*

When Leah decided that since Jacob was just shooting air and not sperm into her, she gave her maidservant to Jacob as a consort. So Jacob had *even more* intercourse with Zilpah *and he delighted in squirting sperm into her hungry crotch instead of pure air.* Zilpah conceived and bore a son, *who later turned out to be a big bore that looked like a big boar, just like a former family incestual ancestor had.*

Leah then said, "What good luck!" *So egad, she deliberately named him Gad.*

Then Leah's *horny and kinky* maidservant *Zilpah* bore a second son to Jacob, *whose magnificent sperm shooter was finally fully unclogged and working again when in the sack with her.*

Leah then said, "What good fortune," meaning, "woman call me fortunate *because I can keep Jacob riveting his tool all night long like there's no tomorrow."* So Leah named the second infant Asher, which *in addition to "purveyor of cremations" also* either means 'in my good fortune' *or 'in my hairy pink crotchola'."*

One day, during the wheat harvest, *Jacob was again feeling his oats.* But when Reuben was out in the field he came upon some 'mandrakes' (an herb thought to promote conception *and not male birds. Jacob had his own mandrake or male bird).* Reuben brought the mandrakes (*that worked like magicians*) home to his mother Leah, *who was seriously thinking about having a hysterectomy and subsequently bleeding to death from primitive surgical methods. Reuben wanted to eat the mandrakes in a sandwich.*

Rachel asked *her older sister* Leah, "Please let me have some of your son's mandrakes. *I'm too lazy to go and pick my own but I hear they're supposed to be a terrific aphrodisiac that will make me want to hump 'til I dump."*

Leah replied, "Was it not enough for you to take away my husband, that you must now take away my son's mandrakes, too! *Reuben had picked them to eat for himself' so that he could get his first boner-fide erection. Those fabulous mandrakes work like magic, you know!"*

"Very well then!" Rachel answered *her older sibling.* "In exchange for your son's mandrakes, Jacob may lie with you tonight. *I'll be horny from eating your son's mandrakes and want to be penetrated all night long so that I might achieve the ultimate ecstasy."*

That evening when Jacob came home *tired* from the fields, Leah went out to meet him. "You are now to come inside with me,"

148

Leah told Jacob, "because I have paid for you with my son's mandrakes. *I think my sister wants all the sperm from your worm."*

"What!" yelled Jacob as loudly as the fellow could bellow'. *"You traded away Reuben's first hard-on so that Rachel could get hot and horny eating the mandrakes? It's bad enough that you, Bilhah and Zilpah are stealing all of my essential juices my balls can produce! And now this stupid bullshit has to materialize!"*

So that night Jacob *exclusively* slept with Leah and God heard her prayer. Leah conceived and bore a fifth son to Jacob *and all of that crap happened in one short night (the sex and the kid) without Jacob remembering one damned thing about it, not even normally frigid Leah's multiple orgasms.*

Leah then said (*to Jacob?*), "God has given me my reward for having let my husband *screw the shit out of* and sleep with my maidservant *while I couldn't even get sloppy seconds but still somehow managed to become pregnant."* So Leah named the new son 'Issachar' *because he looked like a badly burned ember.*

Leah conceived again and bore a sixth son to Jacob, *who was extremely pissed off about his wife eating mandrakes and having sex with him without his knowledge as he slept from working exceedingly hard in shrewd Laban's fields.* Leah said, "God has brought me a precious gift. This time my husband will offer me presents now that I have borne him six *seemingly retarded* sons."

But Jacob was peeved plenty since he now had great responsibility for having additional sons *without being able to remember five minutes of pleasure making them happen.*

Leah named the sixth son Zebulun, *which means something like "thank you mandrakes."* Finally, Leah gave birth to a daughter and she named her Dinah, *which means "not enough mandrakes to make a boy with a penis and balls."*

Then God remembered Rachel *after taking some memory herbs, vitamins and minerals.* The Lord heard Rachel's prayer and made her fruitful, *so peaches, apples and strawberries appeared all over her damned sticky body.* Rachel conceived (*after secretly eating mandrakes*) and bore a son and she said, "*I bore a son!* God has removed my disgrace." So Rachel named the infant Joseph, meaning, "May the Lord add another son to this one for me *so that I will have to struggle and sacrifice more just to raise and support the pesky little bastard."*

After Rachel gave birth to Joseph, Jacob said to Laban: "Give me leave to go to my homeland. *I don't like the papyrus toilet paper you use here. It chaffs my ass and irritates my butt hole!"*

"Jacob," Laban warned his perplexed employee, "don't you do anything rash!"

"Laban," Jacob *obstinately* continued, "let me have my wives, for whom I have served you *without tennis rackets or bartenders*, and my children too, that I may depart *and work for someone much nicer and more pleasant than you.* You know very well the good service I have rendered you, *you big ugly stupid unappreciative prick!*"

Laban answered him: If you will, please...I learned through divination that it is because of you that God has blessed me. So," he continued, "state what wages you want from me, and I will pay them, *for I feel a need to courteously extend my control over you. It makes an impotent jerk like me feel more powerful having dominion over a stud such as yourself*!"

Jacob *aggressively* replied: "You know what work I did for you *and how your daughters and their maidservants nearly screwed me to death for fourteen extremely exhausting years.* You know how well your livestock *and your dead stock* fared under my care. The little you had before I came has grown into very much *ever* since the Lord's blessing came upon you in my 'company'," *Jacob reminded his chief nemesis Laban. "What am I saying? I don't own a goddamned company! Anyway,* therefore I shall now do something for my own household as well. *I intend to screw you good Laban just like you, your daughters and their maidservants have screwed me for the past damned fourteen years!*"

"What should I pay you to stay?" Laban asked. *"I can do pretty decent blowjobs you know!*"

Jacob answered, "You do not have to pay me anything outright. I will again pasture and tend your flock, *and again incessantly screw your daughters and their obliging maidservants. That gorgeous broad Bilhah and that hot whore Zilpah really make my volcano erupt until I feel I have no damned lava left!*" Jacob indicated. "Laban, I request that you do only one *special* thing for me. Go through your whole flock today and remove from it every dark animal among the sheep and every spotted or speckled one among the goats."

"That sounds easy enough to maintain your services," Laban amiably agreed. *"The spotted animals are indeed easier to spot!*"

"Only such speckled animals shall be my wages *from you*," Jacob added. "In the future, whenever you check on these wages of mine, let my *suspect and questionable* honesty testify against me.

150

Any animal in my possession that is not a speckled or spotted goat or a dark sheep got there by theft! *I swear by my goatee that I shall have no scapegoat for any spotless goat or dark sheep in my possession."*

"Very well," agreed Laban. "Let it be as you say. *You seem to be an honest and truthful liar."*

That same day Laban removed the streaked and spotted he-goats and all of the speckled and spotted she-goats *he could spot.* All those goats that were fully white or dark *were removed from his herds.* Laban left behind and he *even abandoned those goats that were wearing goatees. Laban's incompetent sons were put in charge of that remaining flockin' herd.*

Then Laban put three days journey between himself and Jacob, while Jacob continued to pasture the rest of Laban's flock *that was easy to spot from a distance because of the identifying animal markings.*

Jacob, however, got some fresh shoots of almond and poplar. *Poplar was very popular back then.* He also got some material from plane trees, *which were not plain trees at all because the 'plane trees' often flew around over the desert, which itself was a plane.* Jacob made white strips in them by peeling off the 'bark' *that he had obtained from an old growling hound dog.*

The bark was peeled down to the white core of the shoots *where the chutes would shoot out almonds.* The rods that Jacob had thus peeled he then set-up right in the watering troughs, so that the rods would be in front of the animals that drank from them, *only a rod or so away.*

When the animals were in heat *at high noon,* they habitually came out to drink. The goats mated by the rods, *the male goats having rods a full rod long.* The goats brought forth streaked, speckled and spotted kids *(in a matter of minutes),* which didn't look like Jacob's grotesque-looking kids at all.

The sheep, on the other hand, weren't on any of Jacob's hands. Jacob kept the sheep apart, *not allowing them to screw one another with their rods that were also a rod in length.* Jacob instead set these animals to face the streaked or fully dark-colored animals that formerly belonged to Laban.

Thus, Jacob produced special flocks of his own, *and who really gave a shit about this stupid fact, except Jacob, who has been dead for over a millennium now before these astounding words are being recorded.* These special flocks Jacob did not put with Laban's flock so the two herds were not allowed to mingle and to flock around with each other.

Moreover, whenever the hardier animals *(with the bigger longer rod-length hard-ons)* were in heat *at high noon on the sundial,* Jacob would set the rods in the troughs in full view of these animals. *The females saw the male's impressive rods, got excited and over-horny and then even outside the influence of estrus mated by the rods Jacob had set.*

But with the weaker animals Jacob would not waste his time and put the rods there *because the weaker animals couldn't get their rods erect, with or without Jacob's erect rod pointing in front of them.*

So the feeble animals would go to Laban, but the sturdy ones *that could easily get erections and could squirt sperm on demand* stayed with Jacob'*s rod.*

Thus, Jacob grew increasingly prosperous *and jerked off a lot in the pastures with his constantly erect rod.* Jacob came to own not only large flocks but also male and female servants, camels, asses, *and male and female asses to fondle and caress whenever the spirit moved him.*

Chapter Thirty-one
"Flight from Laban"

Jacob learned that Laban's sons were saying *and chanting all at once,* "Jacob has taken everything that belonged to our father, and he has accumulated all this wealth of his by using our father's property. *Jacob is pretty cool. We wish we had the balls to put it to our mean old man the boss way that clever Jacob has done it.*"

Jacob perceived, too, *because he had eyes, ears, hands mouth and a nose.* Jacob *sensed* that Laban's attitude toward him was not what it had previously been. *Laban now respected and feared Jacob. The son of Isaac was showing guile and cunning and Laban knew that he could no longer use Jacob and sanctimoniously give his no-longer naïve but determined son-in-law a lot of stupid bullshit every minute of every day.*

Then the Lord said to Jacob (*From the sky? In a dream? At the Bizarre Bazaar?*), "Return to the land of your fathers, where you were born, and I will be with you. *I like that place even if it is a barren desert wasteland.*"

Jacob answered, *"But Lord, You gave land to my father and forefathers that belonged to the Canaanites! Can't you just send me to Egypt, to Crete or to some other civilized place that has science, technology and culture instead? I abhor conflict but just want to live in peace."*

"Do as I say," the Lord imperatively replied. *"I'm running this show, just remember that, you little mortal twerp! You are merely a pawn on My' playing board, a meaningless trifling actor on My' immense stage. I write the entire script around here! This is My' drama you are acting in, so don't make a scene and clean up your damned amateur act!"*

So Jacob sent *a mailman (who was an actual bisexual male-man)* for Rachel and Leah to meet him where he was in the field with his flock *just walking around aimlessly in circles, knowing full well that he was not getting anywhere in life while working for a grouch like Laban.*

Jacob said to Rachel and Leah: "I have noticed that your father's attitude toward me is not what it was in the past. *I will no longer allow him to exploit me and take advantage of me. He now perceives me as his enemy and is really pissed off and seems to mean me harm!"*

"Father is angry," Leah said to Jacob, "because you have outsmarted him at his own game. You are using him to accumulate wealth, and he is not using you for the same ignoble purpose."

"The God of my father is with me," Jacob replied, "even though you two broads are with me too! It's all really sort of hard to explain."

"That's what father fears most," Rachel said. "Daddy knows what happened to Sodom and Gomorrah and he once said that he'd rather be captured and tortured by Ass-searians than to have horrific fire and brimstone shooting up his very cavernous vulnerable asshole."

"Rachel, everyone from here to Egypt knows that your father is a big unrivaled asshole," Jacob said. "You both well know what effort I put into serving your father and into servicing his two babes along with greasing the vaginas of Zilpah and Bilhah. Some days I was so thirsty from loss of body fluids that I felt like drinking the whole damned Dead Sea all because your father wouldn't go for salt. Yet your father cheated me while I cheated on both of you with sexual flings with Zilpah and Bilhah," Jacob informed his two wives. "Your father changed my wages time after time while I never changed my underwear after having all kinds of sex for twenty long years here with you two mental case daughters and your fantastic maidservants."

"You didn't change your underwear in twenty years because you never wear underwear while trying to create fruit in the womb," Leah corrected her husband.

"God however," continued Jacob, "did not let Laban do any harm to me while the ruthless bastard nearly killed me from sweating in his hot smelly pastures and screwing my testicles off pumping the poop out of you two broads as well as hitting on Zilpah and Bilhah, too! It's fuckin' amazing that I'm still alive to talk about it."

"You really know how to share your sweet-smelling juices," Rachel reluctantly admitted. "I can confirm and verify that."

"Whenever your father said, 'The speckled animals shall be your wages,' the entire flock would bear speckled young; whenever he said, 'The streaked animals shall be your wages,' the entire flock would bear streaked young, even the male animals in the flock," Jacob confided to his two sister/wives. "Thus God reclaimed your father's livestock and gave it to me. God gave me the trickery and the shrewdness to beat your old man at his own freakin' conniving game."

154

"You are even more deceitful than Daddy is," Leah marveled and remarked, *"and that is why my sister and I both love you and want to escape Daddy's inferior bullshit and listen to and obey your superior bullshit. If it wasn't for our fascination with bullshit then Rachel and I would have run away from home before you, our emotionally disturbed husband, ever arrived on the scene."*

"Once, in the breeding season," *Jacob proceeded,* "I had a white dream and really creamed myself. In the dream* I saw mating he-goats that were streaked speckled and mottled. *Immediately I knew that the he-goats were homosexual. They were he-goats that were mating. Many formerly straight heterosexual male goats modeled their behavior after the mottled ones.* In the dream God's messenger called to me, 'Jacob!' *'Here!' I mentally replied in my evasive subconscious."*

"Was the messenger in your perverted dream taking attendance in a class of one?" Leah sarcastically criticized. *"Who else would He' be addressing in your dream but you?"*

"Your stories are always so drab and unimaginative," Rachel added. *"I wish we all knew more vocabulary so that we could be more vivid in our descriptions and explanations. This lack of education really sucks!"*

"Then the messenger said," *Jacob related to his wives,* "Note well. All the he-goats in the flock, as they mate *with each other*, are streaked, speckled and mottled, for I have seen all the things that Laban has been doing to you. I am the God who appeared to you at Bethel."

"If you are indeed the Lord of my forefathers," I said, "why must You' appear to me as a subordinate messenger. Why not just appear to me as Yourself', the Lord?"

"Yeah," agreed Rachel. *"The Lord must like wearing disguises, especially messenger costumes."*

"Anyway," interrupted Jacob, *"the messenger who was the Lord said,* 'Bethel was where you anointed a memorial stone and made a vow *and a consonant* to Me. Up, then! Leave this land and return to the land of your birth!"

"Why did you stupidly smear and anoint a stone?" Leah challenged Jacob. *"Instead, you should have smeared the rich oil on the exposed parts of your body's skin to protect it from the hot desert sun! What a moron my sister and I married!"*

"It was all heavenly ritualistic symbolism and nothing else," Jacob *esoterically confessed.* "I now know that I must embark on a smear campaign to malign your father's reputation. I pledge that this retribution will happen very soon!"

Rachel and Leah *(who often spoke as one person)* answered Jacob: "Have we still an heir's portion in our father's house? Are we not regarded by our father as outsiders *because we conspire with a fool like you?"*

"Your father Laban is a real prick and a half," Jacob *attested.* *"I have labored very arduously for that dickhead for twenty years. He has now disowned his two daughters and regards me, their' valiant worthy husband as his enemy. What a conniving jerk' off!"*

"Father has a bad addictive gambling habit and pays huge sums for expensive prostitutes and hookers when actually he could get gorgeous whores and harlots around here for free," Leah *revealed.*

"Father has not only sold us," *Leah and Rachel said in unison without rehearsing a word.* "Father has even used up all the money he has gotten for us! All the wealth that God has reclaimed from our father really belongs to us and to our children. Therefore, do just as God has told you *for it is just. It's now our turn to be greedy. Let's confiscate the dirty bastard's wealth, all of it to the last shekel!"*

"Yes," Jacob *readily agreed.* *"Your father Laban needs to have his balls broken, diced and then methodically pulverized."*

Jacob proceeded to put his children and his wives on camels *(notice, his children are more important in his eyes than his wives are)* and he drove off *(without any mechanical device)* with all his livestock and all the property he had acquired in Paddan-aram. Jacob felt compelled to go to his father Isaac *(we know who his father is)* in the land of Canaan, who refused to die until his wayward son returned. *Isaac wanted to die knowing that his son had successfully connived and cheated an accomplished conniver and cheater like Laban out of his own property. Hence, Jacob's descendents would all inherit the ability of being successful and prosperous Jewish businessmen.*

Now Laban had gone away to 'shear' his sheep, *and by sheer coincidence,* Rachel *despised her old man so much that she* had meanwhile appropriated her father's household idols. Jacob had hoodwinked Laban the Aramean by not telling him of his intended flight *or that he was trying to grow angel's wings to have an intended flight out of Mesopotamia.* Thus Jacob made his escape with all that he had. Once he was across the Euphrates, he was

156

headed for the highlands of Gilead. *Then Jacob realized that he was alone and that his family riding camels was a full day behind him. Jacob waited for the camels to cross the Euphrates and then he headed for the hills (of Gilead).*

On the third day *(of the trip, not of the world)*, word came to Laban that Jacob had fled. *Nobody told Laban this vital information; words just came to Laban.* Taking his kinsmen with him, Laban pursued Jacob for seven days, *even though he never saw him that first week. The only reason Laban's kinsmen rode with him was because he owed them serious unsettled gambling debts that could only be satisfied if Laban repossessed his daughters to resell to another sucker like Jacob passing through the land looking for "a wife."*

Laban *and his kinsmen* caught up to Jacob in the hill country of Gilead, *and remarkably, they had done so by not crossing the Euphrates River as Jacob and his entourage had done.*

But that night God appeared to Laban the Aramean in a dream, *which meant that Laban might have been hallucinating or imagining paranoid things when he slept.* The dream warned, "Take care not to threaten Jacob with any harm. *Don't injure him. You can only bust his stones, and that is all and nothing else! If that can't get your daughters and property back from Jacob, then toughy-toenails! Better luck next damned time you covetous fool!"*

When Laban *and his kinsmen* overtook Jacob, Jacob's tents were pitched in the highlands; Laban also pitched his tents there, *so Jacob and Laban had a catch throwing their tents at each other. The eventful tent pitching session had taken place on Mt. Gilead.*

"What do you mean," Laban demanded of Jacob *as they pitched and threw tents back and forth,* "by hoodwinking me and by carrying off my daughters like war captives? Why did you dupe me by stealing away secretly?"

"Because you're a big first class prick and a half!" Jacob keenly replied. "Your happy horseshit ball breaking days with me are over! I hereby refuse to be used and abused!"

"You should have told me," Laban said, "and I would have sent you off with merry singing *from my gay homosexual and lesbian choir rapping* to the sound of tambourines and harps. You did not even allow me a parting kiss to my daughters and grandchildren," Laban balked, *"whom I had planned to kiss my royal ass for the next twenty years just like you' had done for me these past twenty years. What you have now done is a senseless thing that's really pissed me off!"*

"Find some other sucker to trade work for stupid poor sex!"
Jacob yelled. "I want outa' here before my dick turns into a wick
and my ass turns into grass. I'm afraid that some night I'll just be so
weak that I'll shit my ass right into the hopper!"

"I have it within my power to harm all of you," *Laban told*
Jacob and his family, who was also Laban's family. "But last night
the God of your father said to me, 'Take care not to threaten Jacob
with any harm *or I'll change your penis into a cactus and your ass*
into a chamber without a back door.' Granted that you had to leave
because you were desperately homesick," Laban acknowledged, "*but*
who really likes being sick in their home or anywhere else? I realize
Jacob that you wanted to return to your father's house, but why did
you steal my goddamned gods too?"

"I was *immensely* frightened," Jacob replied to Laban, "at the
thought that you might take your daughters away by force. *I really*
enjoy porking both of them sometimes and I especially like the
wonderful bonus of pumping Zilpah and Bilhah."

"I'm glad that my daughters and their maidservants have
brought you immense pleasure," Laban surprisingly declared. "But
what about stealing my goddamned gods?"

"But as for your gods," Jacob said, "the one you find them with
shall not remain alive! If, with my kinsmen looking on, you identify
anything here as belonging to you, take it. *Maybe the Lord took your*
gods from you. He likes collectibles and despises competition, you
know!"

Jacob, of course, had no idea that Rachel had stolen the idols.
Normally she was 'idle' in regard to idols. But Rachel saw Laban's
idols not only as a bargain but also as a real steal.

Laban then went in and searched Jacob's 'tent' *but could find*
no idols in the fabric of the tent. Then Laban searched Leah's tent
and the tents of the two maidservants; but he did not find the idols
although he derived great pleasure from gaily feeling the tents' soft-
textured fabrics.

Leaving Leah's tent, he (*Laban*) went into Rachel's tent *(after,*
of course, searching her maidservants' tents). Now Rachel had taken
the idols, put them inside a camel's cushion, and *then* seated herself
upon them. *Rachel became aroused the way the pointed objects*
stuck up her crotch and rectum, so she gyrated and wriggled around
on top of the camel cushion containing the false idols.

When Laban had rummaged through the rest of Rachel's tent
without finding the idols, Rachel said to her *beleaguered* father: "Let

158

not my lord feel offended that I cannot rise in your presence. A woman's period is upon me, *but I do not know what woman the period belongs to. To make me stand up would be a bloody curse that will certainly haunt you once a month for the rest of your doomed life."*

So despite his *intensive* search, Laban did not find his idols *that Rachel was sitting and wiggling about on like a mother duck protecting her nest of eggs.*

Jacob, now enraged *that his wife was behaving like a duck,* 'upbraided' Laban, *who was baldheaded.* "What crime or offense have I committed?" he demanded. "Why do you hound me so fiercely *without using any beagles or other sleuth-like hunting dogs?"*

"I am searching for my gods with the pointed heads that women like to sit and wiggle on," Laban replied. *"But misery and woe go to the woman who rubs my gods the wrong way with their wet sexual equipment."*

"Now that you have ransacked all my things," *Jacob vociferously hollered at Leban,* "have you found a single *or married* object taken from your belongings? If so, produce it here before your kinsmen and mine, and let them decide between us two. *Everyone will then agree that you are a bigger bull-shitter and bold-faced liar than I am!"*

"Watch your mouth while it is still part of your face," Laban *threatened without generating any actual physical harm to Jacob.*

"In *the* twenty *wretched* years that I was under you'," Jacob said, *"we' had some good sex together.* In that twenty years no ewe lamb or she-goat of yours ever miscarried *because I gave them' all abortions before they could deliver for you.* And I have never feasted on a ram from your flock *because I am allergic to ram meat, "Jacob confessed.* "I never brought you an animal torn by wild beasts. *I wanted to, but wild beasts always eat the whole torn animal and none was ever left to deliver to you.* I made good the loss myself. You held me responsible for anything stolen day or night, *even while I slept and screwed your matronly daughters and their voluptuous maidservants every single evening."*

"Get to the point," Laban disgustedly answered. *"What the hell are you trying to say? Spit it out you craven wimp!"*

"How often the scorching heat ravaged me by day while sleep fled from my eyes!" *Jacob continued and opined.* "Of the twenty years I have now spent in your household, I slaved fourteen years for your two *worthless sex-maniac* daughters and six years for your flock, all while you changed my wages time after time *for the worse. You fucked me good these last twenty years, and I now need a new asshole to prove it!"*

"That's the true meaning of life here on this repugnant earth," Laban admitted. "Screw or be screwed! Regrettably that's the way of the world!"

Jacob angrily proceeded with his bitter litany. "If my ancestral God, the God of Abraham and the Awesome One of Isaac had not been on my side, you would have now sent me away empty-handed, *you dirty bastard prick!" Jacob indicted his adversary.* "But God saw my plight and the fruits of my toil, *even though I had been a simple shepherd and not a fanciful fruit farmer.* And last night He gave me judgment to get as far away from you as possible *so that He can shoot fire and brimstone up your hairy butt hole should you dare to harm me. Heed my words Laban!"*

Laban *indignantly* replied to Jacob: "The women are mine *to screw, even my daughters.* Their children are mine, the flocks are mine *to screw, and my salt mines are mine too.* Everything you see belongs to me, *including yourself!"*

"You are the biggest fuck-off on the entire planet!" Jacob accused his father-in-law twice over, "and you don't deserve to have either a dick, a scrotum or an epididymis!"

"Jacob," Laban *harshly* interrupted, "since these women are my daughters, I will now do something for them and for the children they have borne. *I wish I knew their' children's shittin' names. Anyway,* come then, we will make an honorable pact, you and I; the Lord shall be a witness between us. *You can trust me, Jacob. My history is my honor!"*

"Your penis is your brain and your shittin' asshole is your conscience," Jacob defiantly and deftly countered.

Then Jacob took a stone and set it up as a memorial stone. *In that way on the mountain, it would be hard to reach, since Jacob didn't like anyone either breaking his stones or vandalizing his stones.* Jacob said to his kinsmen, "Gather some stones *and forget all about bronze and metal. Let's go back to the freakin' Stone Age."*

So they got some stones and made a 'mound' *for a pitcher to stand on;* and they had a meal there on the mound *of peanuts and Crackerjacks and none of them cared if they ever got back.*

Laban called the mound Jegar-sahadutha, *which means 'visiting team',* but Jacob named it Galeed, *which means 'home team'.*

"This mound, *which has no eyes or ears*," said Laban *to Jacob*, "shall be a witness from now on between you and me."

That is why the mound is called Galeed and also Mizpah, *which means 'guest team'*, for Laban said: "May the Lord keep watch between you and me when we are out of each other's sight, *which I think is really outa' sight.* If you' *Jacob* mistreat my daughters, or take other wives besides my daughters, *that is wrong. It is all right to screw all the maidservants or concubines you want but not other wives besides my two notoriously frigid daughters that you think screw like minks.* Remember that even though no one else is about, God *and this deaf, dumb and blind mound* will be witness between you and me."

Laban said further to Jacob: "Here is this mound, and here is the memorial stone that I have set up between you and me. *This area from now on will be called Galeed Memorial Park.*"

"He who is without wins, let him through out the first stone from this mound," Jacob injected.

"Jacob," Laban *haughtily* continued, "*as I told you before, and forgive me if I stutter when I repeat myself,* this mound *where we can pitch tents and stones* shall be witness, and this memorial stone *in Galeed Memorial Park* shall be witness. That, with hostile intent neither may I pass beyond this mound' into your territory nor may you' pass beyond it into mine. *So don't ever try heading me off at the pass, you despicable rebellious cock sucker!*"

"I think I'll pass on your suggestion," Jacob awkwardly joked. *"Passing is in another type of sports' game that does not involve pitching stones from a mound,"* he amusingly quipped.

Laban pretended that he had not heard Jacob's inane drivel. "May the God of Abraham and the *phony fraudulent* god of Nahor *(the men's ancestral deities which should have been gods and not simply the god of Nahor)* maintain justice between us'," *Laban finished. "Am I crazy saying shit like that, or what?"*

Jacob took the oath 'by the Awesome One of Isaac' *(whatever the hell that nomenclature means).* He then offered a sacrifice on the mountain *by bunting Rachel over to second base with Laban pitching stones from the sacred mound.* Jacob then invited his kinsmen to share the meal *of peanuts and Crackerjacks, (whatever Crackerjacks may be). Laban's kinsmen were not offered any peanuts and Crackerjacks because they were losers on Laban's losing team.*

When (*After*) Jacob's kinsmen had eaten they passed the night on the mountain *without even having the decency of wiping their asses after they passed the night along with peanuts and Crackerjacks' farts on the mountain. That is how the first inning had ended.*

Chapter Thirty-two
"Embassy to Esau"

Early the next morning Laban kissed his grandchildren and also his two daughters "goodbye" *and each yelled "Phooey! Do something about that horrible hellacious halitosis!" when those disgusting incidents happened.* Then Laban set out on his journey back home, while Jacob continued on his way *in the opposite direction heading west, for he was a west turner.*

Then God's messengers encountered Jacob. When he saw them *approaching* he said, *"Oh no! More trouble! More stupid Heavenly bullshit!* This must be God's encampment. *I wish He would quit forting around!"* So Jacob named the place Mahanaim, *which has two distinct meanings: "two camps" and "quit forting around with my life."*

Jacob sent messengers *(but not the Lord's specialized messengers)* ahead to his brother Esau in the land of Seir, the country of Edom. They went with this message: "Thus shall you say to my lord Esau: 'Your' servant Jacob speaks as follows: *If you must kill anyone, kill my messengers and leave me the hell alone. Take your wrath and hatred you have for me out on my lackey lethargic messengers."*

"But Boss," protested the main messenger, *"why must I be executed instead of you. I am innocent."*

"I am only imitating the proven foolproof methods of the Lord," Jacob emphasized. "Tell Esau that I have been detained by Laban and have been detained there until now. I own cattle, sheep and lots of asses', as well as male and female sheep, cattle and *succulent servants' male and female* asses, *too.* I am sending my lord Esau this information in the hope of gaining *your* favor. *Why should I want to gain your favor, you trashy hired help? You're just a flunky cheap-waged courier working for me!"*

When the messengers returned to Jacob *amazingly still alive,* they said *(in chorus),* "We reached your brother Esau, *also known around these parts as 'the big heel.'* He is now coming to meet you, accompanied by four hundred men *with hard-ons that want to screw your wives, your maidservants, your concubines, your male slaves and your children and animals."*

Jacob was very much frightened *and he experienced immediate diarrhea. In his anxiety he crapped himself all over the damned place. Then, without cleaning himself up, wasting no time* Jacob divided the people who were with them, *attempting to split each person in two with his staff, which wholly consisted of one traveling secretary/concubine.* He then divided his flocks, herds and camels into two camps.

'If Esau shall attack and overwhelm one camp,' Jacob reasoned, 'the remaining camp shall survive. *He will be too stupid to attack and overwhelm the second camp. All of this crazy mayhem is necessary all because my father favored me over Esau. In essence, this means that I had to slave twenty years for that enormous good-for-nothing prick Laban. Is there no psychological reward in being favored?'*

Then Jacob prayed, "O God of my father Abraham and God of my father Isaac," *for Jacob prayed out loud, much to the aggravation of all those who had to hear him. Jacob was so out of it that he actually believed that he had two fathers, his grandfather Abraham being one of them.* "You told me O Lord, 'Go back to the *native* land of your birth, and I will be good to you.' *Do you think I am a complete moron like my fathers Isaac and Abraham each was?"*

Then Jacob reconsidered his anger and frustration. "I am unworthy of all the acts of kindness that You have loyally performed for Your' *fucked-up* servant; although I crossed the Jordan here with nothing but my staff, *somehow, all these kinsmen, concubines, wives, slaves and maidservants suddenly appeared here in addition to my secretary/concubine.* I have now grown into two companies, *but I can't even remember ever being one corporation."*

Jacob gazed at the sun and reflected like a mirror some more. "Save me, O Lord. *Deposit me into a Canaanite bank if You' will!* I pray, save me from the hand of my brother Esau, *despite the fact that he has two good hands to strangle me.* Otherwise I fear that when Esau comes he will strike me down and slay the mothers and children. You' Yourself' said, 'I will be very good to you, and I will make your descendents like the sands of the sea, *all drowned underwater.'* The sands of the sea are too numerous to count *so why should I even bother to think about numbers here. I need to contemplate basic survival!"*

After passing the night there, Jacob selected from what he had with him the following presents *to bribe loyalty, mercy and trust* from his brother Esau. *There were* two hundred *neutered* she-goats and twenty *neutered* he-goats; two hundred ewes, *two hundred double-ewes* and twenty rams *from Paddan-aram;* thirty milch camels and their young; forty cows and ten bulls *and three bull elephants*; twenty she-asses and ten he-asses *all wearing tight-fitting leotards.*

Jacob put these animals in separate droves and *then* he told the servants, "Go on ahead of me, but keep a space between one drove and the next. *That way Esau will think my limited sized entourage is coming at him in droves."*

To the servant in the lead Jacob gave this instruction: "When my brother Esau meets you, he may ask you, 'Whose' man are you? Where are you going? To whom do these animals ahead of you belong?' Then you shall answer *with a major lie*, 'They belong to your *cowardly devious* brother Jacob, but they have been sent as a gift to my lord Esau; and *the craven knave* Jacob himself is right behind us. *Don't forget to fib big-time when you are accosted!"*

For Jacob reasoned, 'If I first appease Esau *and bribe him* with gifts that precede me, *my brother won't beat the shit out of me.* Then later when I face him, perhaps he will forgive me *for being favored by my father, who made me suffer for twenty long years with that no good swine Laban. Actually, it is my dying father who needs a beating from rugged Esau and not me."*

So the gifts went on ahead of Jacob *and the phlegmatic servants had to run and catch up with the gifts.* Jacob stayed that night in the camp *scared shitless of his fearsome formidable brother's wrath.*

In the course of that night, however, Jacob arose, took his two wives with the two maidservants *(as usual women's names aren't important here)* and his eleven children and crossed 'the ford' of the Jabbok, *which roughly translated into other languages means Chevrolet.*

After Jacob had taken them across the stream and had brought over all his *miscellaneous* possessions, *Jacob realized that the people were all his possessions too, so there really was no necessary distinction between people and property. They were one and the same, just like back in the time of Abraham.* Jacob was left there alone *because all of his family and people' property were seeking freedom and dignity so they very judiciously deserted him in the desert.*

Then some man *suddenly showed up on the scene and* wrestled with Jacob until the break of dawn. *The messenger of the Lord challenged Jacob to a best of two out of three falls' no-holds-barred match.* When the Lord's messenger saw that he could not prevail over Jacob, he struck Jacob's hip at the socket, *wrenching his opponent's hip socket without even using a socket wrench.* So, Jacob's hip socket was wrenched as they *wildly* wrestled *and*

thrashed about, and Jacob knew throughout the contest that he had
to ratchet-up his grappling maneuvers.

The man then said, "Let me go, for it is daybreak *and also leg'*
break time. I now have to go to ancient Greece and wrestle Proteus
followed by some grappling with Herculite, who is to be an ancestor
of a future hero named Hercules."

But Jacob said *to the apprehensive angel,* "I will not let you go
until you bless me, *but make sure your blessing is not a right cross."*

"What is your name?" the man asked. *"I always like beating the*
crap out of strangers traveling through this area without knowing
their damned names."

He answered, "Jacob *as if you already don't know you wily*
courier."

Then the man said, "You shall no longer be spoken of as Jacob,
but as Israel, *meaning 'you contended'.* You have contended with
divine and human beings and have prevailed, *so pick up your prize*
at the Lord's nearest convenience store."

Jacob then asked him, "Do tell me your name, please, *for if you*
are indeed an angel of the Lord, you are indeed a very wimpy and
lame angel."

The man answered, "Why should you want to know my name?
Just because you had been a fool and had told me yours?" With that,
the angel bade Jacob farewell *and told the patriarch-to-be he*
appeared to have a mania for the sport of wrestling that he called a
"wrestle-mania."

Jacob named the place Peniel, "meaning the face of God,"
which the angel had worn as a mask to intentionally deceive Jacob.
However, *Jacob didn't exactly know what the Lord really looked like*
so all of the crap with the mask didn't matter one iota. "Because I
have seen God face to face," he *reckoned* and said, *"yet in the final*
analysis my life has been spared by this impostor wearing a silly
God-mask!"

At sunrise, as Jacob left Peniel, he limped along because of his
recently injured hip. That is why, to this day, the Israelites do not eat
the sciatic muscle that is on the hip socket. *It is not kosher to do so*
in-as-much as Jacob's hip socket was struck at the *crucial* sciatic
muscle.

Then after thinking about his confrontation with the angel
finally Jacob realized that he had been walking alone without the
company of his wives, children, concubines, maidservants, slaves
and animals. "Where's all my damned property?" he shouted to the
clear blue sky in sheer frustration.

166

Chapter Thirty-three
"Jacob and Esau Meet"

Jacob looked up and saw Esau coming, accompanied by four hundred *nasty-looking hench*men. So Jacob divided his children among Leah, Rachel and the *two big-breasted* maidservants, putting the maids and their children first, Leah and her children next, and Rachel and Joseph last. *The family had been arranged in the order they were to be killed by Esau, should he be in a bellicose mood resulting from indigestion, from gas pains and from his extra-large hemorrhoids flaring up.*

Jacob himself went on ahead of them, bowing to the ground seven times until he *eventually* reached his brother. Esau ran to meet Jacob, embraced him, and flinging himself on his brother's neck, kissed him and wept *as was the tradition of ancient homosexual incest practitioners everywhere in the known and unknown world way back then.*

When Esau' 'looked about', *Esau looked about two hundred years old.* He saw *(Esau without a seesaw), Jacob's* women and the children. "Who are these *wandering jerk offs* with you?" he asked *the only visible male.*

Jacob answered, "They are the children whom God has graciously bestowed on your servant. *They will surely eat you out of house and home and ruin your financial condition should you claim them for your own. They are worse than vultures or locusts, and that is putting it mildly,"* the prevaricating traveler convincingly maintained.

Then the maidservants and their children came forward and bowed low; *and Esau's tongue almost fell out of his mouth when he checked out the stone-hard knockers on Zilpah and Bilhah.*

Next Leah and her children came forward and bowed low. Then Esau asked, "What did you intend with all those droves I encountered? *There are now countless mounds of sheep shit and goat shit all over my formerly pristine lands."*

Jacob answered, "It was *done* to gain my lord's favor. *Now with such excellent fertilizer all over the damned place anything you want to grow will flourish on your formerly desolate land."*

"I have enough animal crap all over my land already," Esau *lamented and retorted.* "You should keep what is yours, brother. *Animals would be okay to tolerate if they didn't have to eat and poop all the damned time."*

167

"No, I beg you!" said Jacob. "If you will do me the favor, please accept this gift from me. *I have discovered that animal crap is really an aphrodisiac that stimulates the human genitals,"* Jacob revealed the esoteric fact. *"If you smell goat crap and sheep feces together, then everyone in your camp will simultaneously feel an intense desire to get laid. The orgy could go on for 'decades', depending on how decadent you and your party become."*

"You seem to really know your shit!" Esau sincerely admitted. *"Maybe I'll reconsider your generous offer."*

"Esau, to come into your presence is for me like coming into the presence of God," *Jacob stated and fibbed.* "*I am getting all hot and bothered* now that you have received me so kindly."

"Yes, goat and sheep crap seem to mingle just fine," Esau acknowledged. *"The combined odor is more like a perfumed aroma than like a filthy stench as rudimentary logic dictates it ought to be."*

"Do you now accept the fine gifts I have brought you?" *Jacob demanded of his mercurial-tempered brother.* "God has been generous toward me, and I have *with me* an abundance of fine animals *that can produce quantities of fine fertilizer and tons of perfumed manure."*

Since Jacob so persuasively urged, Esau *heavily sniffed the air* and accepted *his brother's terms as a pint of blood surged from his abdomen and flowed directly into his stimulated genitals.*

Then Esau said, "Let us break camp and be on our way; I will travel alongside you *as long as I can smell the sweet perfumed aroma of your combined sheep and goat herds' defecation."*

But Jacob *very scrupulously* replied: "As my lord Esau can see, the children are frail *and wimpy.* Besides, I am encumbered with the herds and flocks, which now have sucklings *that really suck.* If overdriven for a single day, the whole flock will die *from getting aroused from its own aromatic manure smell."*

"That does sound like an absolute bummer," Esau amenably admitted. *"What a cruel fuckin' way to die! Just when you feel like getting laid, and then you starve to death from goddamned heat and energy exhaustion."*

"Let my lord then go ahead of me," *Jacob wisely suggested.* "Then I can proceed more slowly at the pace of the *horny* livestock, *especially the male goats and rams.* My children could also keep pace with the goats and the sheep *and perhaps enter puberty at an earlier age from immediate hormone activation.* Then later I will join my lord in Seir."

168

Esau replied, "Let me at least put at your disposal some of the men who are with me. *They appear to be quite infatuated and highly seduced by the smell of the combined goat and sheep manure, even though to me it now smells like shit!"*

But Jacob said, "For what reason *other than natural or unnatural sex?* Please indulge me in this, my lord. The arousal and the pleasure should be for my lord Esau *and not for his hirelings and his lowlife subordinates."*

So, on the same day that Esau began his journey back to Seir, Jacob journeyed to Succoth (*not far from Fuck-off*) *in quest of a good well-deserved blowjob.* There he *became quite satisfied* and built a home for himself. Jacob made booths for his livestock *and elaborate and fancy brothels for his hired harlots that voluntarily gave good head. That is why the secluded place is called Succoth.*

Having thus come from Paddan-aram *with a banjo-type instrument on his knee,* Jacob arrived safely at the city of Shechem, which is in the land of Canaan, *the Promised Land that Abraham's descendents were certain to inherit at an undetermined later date. That is to say, after one of Abraham's more gallant heirs had the balls to steal it from the Canaanites on the Lord's command.*

Jacob encamped in 'sight of the city,' *which was a remarkable insight because the magnificent city looked outa' sight.*

The plot of ground on which he pitched his tent *(after building a pitcher's mound that looked simply divine)* Jacob bought for a hundred pieces of bullion, *which was the equivalent of a hundred pieces of ass or a hundred professional blowjobs from his thriving and now-lucrative brothel back in Succoth.*

Jacob purchased the land from the descendents of Hamor, the founder of Shechem. *How so many weirdo descendents could be one weirdo founder remains a veritable mystery to this very day?* He set up a memorial stone there and invoked, "El, the God of Israel." *And so, the first word of the Spanish language had finally been created.*

Chapter Thirty-four
"The Rape of Dinah"

Dinah, the daughter who Leah had borne to Jacob, went out to visit some of the women *(who were reputed to be lesbians)* of the land *(when Dinah was old enough to walk distances on her own just after being born)*. Shechem, son of Hamor the Hivite saw her. He seized Dinah and lay with her by force *(translation: he put a hit on Dinah with intentions of getting laid, with or without her meaningless consent)*.

Since Shechem was strongly attracted to Dinah, daughter of Jacob *(is this new material or what?)*, and indeed was really in love with the girl *as his firm erection clearly indicated*, he endeavored to win her affection *by penetrating his penis deeply into her inner woman love tunnel.*

Shechem also asked his father Hamor *(we already know his damned name from a few short paragraphs ago)*, "Get me this girl for a wife *so that I can stuff her many times over with my throbbing manhood."* That comment was a really stupid and zany thing for Shechem to say to his father, who also had an enormous erection and had designs of raping the innocent girl too.

Meanwhile, Jacob heard that Shechem had defiled his *own* daughter *and now planned to also defile Dinah*. Since Jacob's sons were out in the fields with his livestock *and frenetically massaging their genitals, and because Shechem was a big strong dude that could kick Jacob's ass with one arm tied behind his back,* the patriarch held his peace. *He desired to wait* until his sons came home *before he would attempt to break Shechem's chops and bust his balls.*

Now Hamor, (the father of Shechem, *who also believed in and practiced statutory rape on female statues imported from Greece)*, went out and discussed the matter with Jacob, just as Jacob's sons were coming in from the fields. *Hamor became pissed because Jacob's sons were eavesdropping on the confidential conversation he had been conducting with Jacob.*

When the brothers heard the news *(possibly tabloid gossip)*, they were shocked and seethed with indignation. What Shechem had done was an outrage in Israel; *usually women raped the men, and also, raping tended to go against the tradition of incest as practiced since the time of Adam and Eve. Such a wicked thing as rape by a man could not be tolerated.*

Hamor 'appealed' to Jacob and his sons *and they had inclinations to rape and sodomize him because he appealed to them so much.* Hamor said, "My son Shechem has his heart set on your daughter *(while he endeavored ignoring Jacob's eavesdropping insinuating sons).* Please give her to him in marriage *so that they may legally get laid, and I assure you, after that my son will not rape your daughter and will only be raped by other women."*

"Yes," *Jacob confessed, "I was shocked when I heard that your son had raped my daughter when it should have been her that had done the raping, according to our fucked-up sacred customs."*

"Intermarry with us," *Hamor pleaded without humor.* "Give your daughters to us *so that we can enslave them to then rape all our men,* and take our daughters for yourselves *and do likewise. As you know Jacob, daughters are women, and women are mere property to be traded and exchanged for money and sex.* Thus you can live among us *and everybody could then legally rape and screw each other's wives, sisters, aunts, nieces' girlfriends and daughters at will. Then your sacred customs could evolve and gradually become more civilized!"*

"I must say, your plan is definitely worthy of consideration," *Jacob acknowledged in spite of his sons' objections.* "I'm always open-minded about new eager beavers sleeping in my tents."

"Look *Jacob,*" said Hamor, "the land is open before you, *and so too will the new open-beavers from our tribe be open to you.* You can settle and move about freely in it, and acquire landed property *and free whores for momentary wives and concubines here without any difficulty. Just let my men screw and then marry your women after first trying and approving the product."*

Then Shechem *(who suddenly appears out of nowhere)* too appealed to Dinah's father and brothers, *and they all began to get bigger erections than the ones they already had.* "Do me this favor and I will pay whatever you demand of me *for raping Dinah and for not forcing her to rape me as has been the custom in the past. For someone's in the corner with Dinah, and it's always going to be me having Dinah blow my horn.* No matter how high you set the bridal price," *Shechem the local liberal politician continued,* "I will pay you *conservative Hebrews* whatever you ask *for more of that delicious juicy pussy.* Only give me the maiden in marriage, *even though I have adroitly eliminated her maiden head with my powerful studly throbbing glory."*

Jacob's sons replied to Shechem and his father Hamor with guile, speaking as they did because their sister Dinah had *defiled*

172

both ancient and oral sex tradition by being raped and by not raping Shechem.

"We could not do such a thing," the brothers *all simultaneously* said, *which was another remarkable ability most of the ancients in that weird sector of the earth possessed.* "We cannot give our sister to an uncircumcised man *with a long skinny dick.* That would be a disgrace for us. We will agree with you only on this condition, that you become like us by having every male*'s pecker* in your tribe *of molesting jerk offs* circumcised."

"I like when my pecker throbs," Shechem stated, "*but I don't like when it throbs in pain from flesh being carved from its circumference. Do you consider yourself some kind of artistic meat sculptor Jacob? It would be then harder to find the area of my penis if you change the relationship of the diameter to the circumference through this stupid and abominable circumcision habit that you trespassers so strangely practice.*"

"*Hamor, if you and your men are willing to shed some skin,*" the brothers said *in unison,* "then we will give you our daughters and take yours in marriage, *because as you know women are commodities to be traded and are of lesser rank than men are.* We will settle with you and become one kindred people with you, *and after that, we will steal your land to fulfill the promise of the Lord that He will give us this barren desert area.* But if you do not comply with our terms regarding circumcision, we will take our daughters *and their juicy pussies* and go away, *leaving behind only our wives with their dried-up arid love tunnels for you to screw in this lousy arid wasteland.*"

The brothers' proposal seemed fair to Hamor and his son Shechem, *who wanted more young juicy pussy around and less old dried-up wives' cunts in the vicinity.* The young man wasted no time in acting in the matter since he was deeply *and madly* in love with Jacob's daughter*'s hairy juicy pink love canal.* Moreover, Shechem was more highly respected than anyone else in his clan *because he had the biggest penis in the village, and a little skin shed from his circumference would not affect his high tribal ranking one bit, as long as all the other men had to also shed some skin.*

So Hamor (*who was studying to become a priest: Hamor-rabbi*) and his son Shechem went to their town council and thus presented the matter to their fellow townsmen, *who liked the idea of getting laid more by new juicy pussy but didn't like the idea of losing skin off of their tiny dicks to do it.*

"These men *with the juicy pussy girls* are friendly toward us," *Hamor and Shechem said together to the council without any formal rehearsing.* "Let them settle in this land and move about in it freely, *as long as we can screw their juicy pussied' women while they're crazily roaming around aimlessly looking for mature sheep genitals to massage.* There is ample roaming in the country for them, *and there is ample room in their women's love holes for us, too. Ha, ha, ha!*"

"Are there any other advantages to this scenario?" asked a skeptical horny old councilman with a one-inch erection as he merely thought about getting laid on one last occasion before cardiac arrest time set-in.

"We can marry their daughters *and then trade our new wives amongst ourselves,*" Hamor said, *"and then we can give our ugly daughters and our wives with dried-up snatches to those stupid visiting itinerant cock suckers.* But the men will agree to live with us and form one kindred people with us only if we agree to *this painful business of* circumcision."

"My penis is small enough without losing any of its vital skin circumference!" protested ten elderly councilmen all at the same time.

"Would not the livestock they have acquired, all their animals, then be ours?" *argued Hamor, who also liked porking sheep, goats and pigs when he wasn't putting it to juicy pink human pussies.* "Let us therefore give in to them so that they may settle among us. *Then we can steal their livestock, screw their better juicy-crotched women and laugh our asses' off in the process while they believe they are acquiring our worthless land. All we have to do is have the rims of our dicks sliced a little bit, a small price to pay for free livestock, wet vulva and lots of great wealth. Who really gives a flying shit about ancient taboos?"*

All the able-bodied *small-dicked men* of the town council *finally* agreed with Hamor and his son Shechem', *and all of the males in the community were circumcised and instantly became soreheads, especially at the ends of their tender peckers.*

On the third day *(after the mass circumcision),* while the men were still in pain *and even had trouble pissing let alone jerking off,* Dinah's full brothers Simeon and Levi, two of Jacob's sons *(no shit),* took up their swords. They advanced against the city without any trouble and massacred all the men, *who were so busy holding their aching genitals after being circumcised that they were incapable of adequately defending themselves.*

174

After they had put Hamor and Shechem to the sword, Simeon and Levi took Dinah from Shechem's house and left. *"Those circumcisions hurt worse than if Hamor and Shechem had gotten their penises caught in crocodiles' mouths," Levi laughingly told Simeon.*

"Yes, the pain of being beheaded was a blessing to them compared to the unbearable torture they were experiencing in their private areas," Simeon replied.

Then the other sons of Jacob *(who needed a weak excuse as motivation to act)* followed up the slaughter and ransacked the city in reprisal for their sister' Dinah's rape *because they believed that the punishment should always exceed the crime. This immoral devastating massacre occurred even though the retribution far outweighed the immorality of a man raping a woman instead of a horny woman raping a man.*

The brothers seized the flocks, herds, asses, *juicy women's asses,* and anything else in the city and in the country around. They carried off all their wealth, their women and their children, and took for loot whatever was in the houses. *Thus, stealing, rape, and killing became hallmarks of archaic Hebrew morality and models for future incest-produced generations to proudly imitate and implement.*

Jacob said to Simeon and Levi: "You have brought trouble upon me by making me loathsome to the *other* inhabitants of the land, the Canaanites and the Perizzites. *They're going to want to kick our asses and un-circumcise us all by stitching skin back on our dicks!"*

"Who the hell cares?" argued Simeon. *"Just look at all the pieces of good ass, big tits and livestock we have acquired. We can scare the shit out of the Canaanites and the Perizzites by claiming that the Lord made us do it and that we were backed up by His ferocious angel/messengers."*

"I have so few men," *Jacob interrupted,* "that if these people unite against me and attack me, *I fear that* I and my family *(improper grammar)* will be wiped out."

"Should our sister have been treated like a harlot?" *Simeon balked and squawked. "Dinah's rape had to be avenged or else we might have been subjected to the Lord's wrath!"*

"Before they might attack," injected Levi, "let's make a deal with the Canaanites and with the Perizzites just like we had done with Hamor and Shechem. We'll have them rape Dinah, get circumcised, and then Simeon and I can give them the sword treatment while they're all screaming bloody murder holding their

penises in excruciating pain. Then we could take over their worthless desolate land and fulfill the Lord's promise to our mentally weak ancestor Abraham."

Chapter Thirty-five
"Bethel Revisited"

God *was passing through the territory and said* to Jacob, *who was taking a constipated dump in a rat hole,* "Go up now to Bethel. Settle there and build an altar there to the God that appeared to you while you were fleeing from your brother Esau, *in case you have forgotten his accursed name. Incidentally, if you are wondering about wandering there, I am the same God that had appeared to you then. And after you build the shrine, whatever you do, don't alter the altar!"*

So Jacob *quickly wiped his ass with nearby leaves, cactus needles and pine cones and went* and told his family and all the others that were with him: "Get rid of the foreign gods that you have among you *because the vengeful Lord is on the warpath again. I don't want fire and brimstone thrust all the way up my sensitive constipated already sore butt hole."*

"But Jacob," interrupted one of his more perceptive clansmen, *"the foreign gods do not destroy cities with fire and brimstone and they do not cause great floods, famines, plagues or other great devastation. They are not half as destructive as the Lord is when He gets His' powerful bowels in an uproar!"*

"Do exactly as I say!" Jacob insisted. "Purify yourselves. Put on 'fresh' clothes, *and make sure the nasty obnoxious clothes do not answer you back and act fresh! We are now to go up to Bethel and I will build an altar there while the rest of you watch me construct it. The Lord just instructed me to assemble the altar, which I am not allowed to alter,"* Jacob articulated. *"It is to be built* to the God that answered me in my hour of distress *when I was drinking wine and was totally delirious. This ubiquitous God has been with me wherever I have gone and keeps pestering me with exorbitant promises and intimidating threats. He just won't leave me the hell alone!"*

They (*be careful using pronouns*) therefore handed over to Jacob all the foreign gods in their possession and all the rings they had in their ears *and noses. Jacob fully knew that he could earn some serious bonus money by selling and trading the gods and the rings for slaves and prostitutes at the local bizarre bazaar.*

Then, as they set out *for Bethel,* a terror from God *(the messenger presenting Himself' as the first real terrorist on earth)* fell upon the towns round about. So, no one pursued the sons of Jacob *after he had ripped off the local merchants by trading the* poorly manufactured false gods and gold rings for slaves and prostitutes at the local bizarre bazaar.

Thus, Jacob and all his possessions in Luz *(Bethel, a town for Luzers) traveled toward* Canaan. There, Jacob built an altar *while all his people again stood around curiously watching and wildly laughing, and he named the place Bethel for the second time.* It was there *(if you remember)* that God had revealed Himself *to* Jacob when he was fleeing from his brother *(you didn't know that God had a brother, did you? And incidentally, even back then revealing oneself was not the same thing as exposing oneself.)*

Death came to Rebekah's nurse Deborah *while she was still nursing Rebekah.* Deborah's milk ducts had clogged, *triggering a massive cardiac arrest.* Deborah was buried under the oak below Bethel, *for in Bethel they had underground trees.* And so it was called Allonbacuth, *which in translation means ' inexplicable bull shit that will never be fully understood'.*

On Jacob's arrival from Paddan-aram *with his padded rams,* God appeared to him again and blessed him. God said to Jacob: "You whose name is Jacob shall no longer be called Jacob *because I like changing the names of people and places all the time at whim.* Israel shall be your name *since I think you look like a small country that will certainly be on the earth in the distant future."*

Thus, Jacob was named Israel. God also said to him: "I am God Almighty *telling you the Almighty truth.* Be fruitful *but not so fruitful you are gay,* and multiply, *because if you are gay you' cannot possibly multiply by natural means.* A nation, indeed an assembly of nations shall stem from you, *so stay away from graft and from grafters who do a lot of systematic stemming and cloning around.* Kings shall issue from your loins *and you dumb poops and nincompoops still have the testicles to produce them at will."*

"Can't You' go bother and torment some other patriarch?" Jacob pleaded to *his Spiritual Master.*

"The land I once gave to Abraham and Isaac *(which unfortunately they haven't legally or officially acquired yet)* I now *wholeheartedly* give to you. And to your descendents after you I will *wholeheartedly* give this *useless barren* land *once you legally and officially acquire it from the Canaanites by rook or by crook."*

Then God *had more important things to do and* departed from Jacob. On the sight where God had spoken 'with' him *(actually, spoken to him),* Jacob set up a memorial stone, *which he hoped would last longer than all his other memorials had lasted because he was genuinely fatigued from building and rebuilding all those temporary memorials and altering altars over and over again.*

Upon the stone he made a libation and poured out oil to *stop friction between the altar's rocks. Having amnesia and dementia* Jacob *for the second time* named the site Bethel, because God had spoken with *(to)* him there *and because Jacob had forgotten he had already named the site Bethel during his first visit to that undesirable location.*

Then they (*watch those pronouns without specific antecedents beginning new paragraphs*) departed from Bethel. *Jacob and his people enjoyed being mindless wandering nomads with no given destination, goals or objectives in mind. In this respect they were the genuine ancestors of gypsies.*

But while they still had some distance to go to Ephrath (*located next to Riffraph*), Rachel began to be in labor and to suffer great distress *as all women about to deliver happen' to do.* When her pangs were most severe, *she yelled, "I can't! I can't! I can't!" in a series of exclamatory 'contractions'.*

Rachel's midwife said to her, "*I am a midwife.* Have no fear! *Only have pain!* This time too, you *have in your belly a wild and crazy* son, *who is not only a pain in the ass but a pain in the womb too!"*

With her last breath, for she was at the point of death *and would hold that last breath for the rest of her life,* Rachel called the newborn Ben-oni *Bon-jovi,* but his father, however, renamed him Benjamin.

Thus, Rachel died, *holding her last breath for another five hours.* She was buried on the road to Ephrath *so that people, animals, and carts could travel over her on that well' traveled road.* (Ephrath today is Bethlehem).

Jacob set up a memorial stone on the side *of the road next to her grave,* and the same *famous* monument marks Rachel's grave to this *very* day.

Israel moved on and pitched his tent *as he warmed-up in the bullpen* beyond the town of Migdal-eder, *which is not on any ancient or modern map anywhere.* While Israel *(Jacob)* was encamped in that region *Reuben ate one of his energy sandwiches, achieved an erection and got laid* while he lay with Bilhah, his father's *promiscuous* concubine. When Israel heard of it, he was greatly offended *because he was left out of the action generated by a potentially wild and crazy threesome getting it on.*

The sons of Jacob were now twelve: *and the whole dozen of them somehow became the same age at the same time.* The sons' of Leah were Reuben', Jacob's first born, Simeon, Levi, Judah, Issachar, and Zebulun, *who was lead singer in a band named Led Zebulun.*

The sons of Rachel were Joseph and Benjamin. The sons by Rachel's maid Bilhah were Dan and Naphtali. The sons by Leah's maid Zilpah were Gad and Asher. These were the sons of Jacob who were born to him *(because he was a real mother in addition to being a father)* in Paddan-aram, *where old Jacob the sheepherder was a little too rambunctious and had a lot of ramifications for screwing around with all sorts of females.*

Jacob went home to his father Isaac at Mamre, in Kiriath-arba (that is, *as everybody who values impertinent trivia knows,* Hebron) where Abraham and Isaac had stayed *during their absence in a gigantic fleabag tent hotel.*

The lifetime of Isaac was one hundred and eighty years, *and the last century of his existence he wished he were dead and buried.* Then Isaac breathed his last *inhalation, finally figuring out how to die and thus effectively escaping more difficult suffering, rheumatism and arthritis.* After a full *and meaningless* life, Isaac died as an old man *(that's reasonably logical isn't it?)* and was taken to his kinsmen, *who testified that they never knew him or wanted to know him.* Then Isaac's sons Jacob and Esau buried him *in debt and they cursed their genetics and their very evident mental limitations.*

Chapter Thirty-six
"Edomite Lists"

These are the descendents of Esau (*alias a.k.a.* Edom), *who cared about as much of their ancestor Esau as we care about their stupid silly names.* Esau took his wives from among the Canaanite women, *who had the hairiest and wettest and pinkest crotches in that lackluster part of the ancient world.*

Adah, *sister of No-dah*, was the daughter of Elon the Hittite. Oholibamah, granddaughter through Anah of Zibeon the Hivite *was another wife of Esau with a fine snatcheroo notorious for pumping and thrusting.* Basemath, *the founder of arithmetic as previously mentioned,* was the daughter of Ishmael and sister of Nebaioth. Basemath bore Reuel, *who looked a little like a cross between a hypotenuse of a right triangle and a trapezoid.* Adah bore Eliphaz to Esau, *who thought his new son was a real baby griffin.* Oholibamah bore Jeush, Jalam and Korah, *the founders of the disreputable Hebrew Mafia syndicate.* These are the sons of Esau, who were born to him in the land of Canaan *(even though Esau had no vagina or ovaries). It was quite a gruesome family, indeed.*

Esau took his wives, his sons, his daughters, and all the members of his household out of Canaan, *planning to sell them to caravans of slave traders looking for bargain flesh to peddle.* Esau also took his livestock comprising of various animals *(if that's not an intelligent statement, we don't know what is!)* and all the property he had acquired in Canaan *(how do you move land?).* Esau went to the land of Seir, out of the way of his brother Jacob *and his unpredictable Lord with the formidable temper and the awesome fire and brimstone ass-singeing method that was greatly envied by the Ass-searians.* The brothers' *(Esau and Jacob)* possessions had become too great for them to dwell together, and the land in which they were staying could not support them because of their livestock *and because the sterile ground there could not even grow grass or withering weeds.*

So Esau settled in the highlands of Seir (Esau is Edom *in case you hadn't comprehended that simple fact yet, you mentally challenged readers).*

These are the descendents of Esau, ancestor of the Edomites, in the highlands of Seir *(sounds familiar, doesn't it!).* These are the names of Esau's sons, *who are at best minor supporting characters in this tedious and monotonous series of sterile stories.* Eliphaz was the son of Esau's wife Adah, and Reuel was the son of Esau's wife Basemath; *No-Dah!*

The sons of Eliphaz were Teman, Omar *the tent-dress maker,* Zepho, Gatam, *Got'em* and Kenaz. Esau's son Eliphaz had a concubine Timna, and she bore Amalek to Eliphaz, *who said his son had to be illegitimate because the infant looked normal, which in those foresaken days was completely abnormal.*

These are the descendents of Esau's wife Adah. The sons of Reuel were Nahath, Zerah, *Zero,* Shammah and Mizzah-*ry. Adah claimed to have worn five chastity belts since she had been age ten, so how these five boys were conceived or delivered remains a fantastic Biblical mystery to this very day.* These are the descendents of Esau's wife Basemath *as questionably recorded in the abridged book of Genesis.*

The descendents of Esau's wife Oholibamah, granddaughter through Anah of Zibeon, whom she bore to Esau' were Jeush, Jalam and Korah *(as just earlier mentioned because back in ancient times, most listeners were bored slow learners that really didn't give a wet fart about token appellations. They had to be continually reminded of simple-ass things like names).*

The following are the clans of Esau's descendents. The descendents of Eliphaz, Esau's first' born: the clans of Teman, Omar, Zepho, *Groucho, Harpo,* Kenaz, Korah, Gatam, *Got-em,* and Amelek.

These are the clans of Eliphaz in the land of Edom; they are the descended from Adah, *who gave birth to all of them in a hayloft, and then the infants had to descend a ladder to ground level all by themselves to become descendents.* The descendents of Esau's son Reuel: the clans of Nahath, Zerah, *Zero,* Shammah, and Mizzah-*ry.* These are the clans of Reuel in the land of Edom; they are descended from Esau's wife Basemath *who gave birth at the apex of an isosceles triangle during a wicked-ass monsoon.*

These are the descendents of Esau's wife Oholibamah: the clans of Jeush, Jalam and Korah, *who like their' ancestors and immediate blood-relatives were all products of indiscriminate inbreeding.* Such are the descendents of Esau (that is Edom *for the umpteenth time)* according to *the lists of* their *primitive, barbaric post Stone Age* clans. *With inimitable names like those that have been mentioned and documented who really needed any crappy last names?*

The following are the descendents of Seir the Horite, *who never paid for sex from any damned prehistoric prostitutes or from any ancient hookers.* Seir the Horite's family members were the original settlers in the land. They were Lotan, Shobal, *Snowball*, Zibeon, *Way-beyond*, Anah, Dishon, *Dishon-nest-tea,* Ezer, *Geezer,* Dis-han *and finally Dat-hand.* These are the Horite clans descended from Seir in the land of Edom.

Lotan's descendents were Hori *(a notorious harlot)* and Heman, *a muscular fellow without testicles having gay tendencies.* Lotan's sister was Timna, *and who really gives a rat's ass about that insignificant minute detail.*

Shobal's descendents were Alvan, *Simon, Theodore*, Mahanath, Ebal, Shepho, *Showmoorebawls* and Onam.

Zibeon's descendents were Aiah and Anah (he is the Anah who found water in the desert while he was pasturing the asses of his father Zibeon, *who was born with seven rectums that constantly ate an abundance of grass and roots). Anah's nickname was "Anus" and he always wanted to grow two more assholes so that he could then be asinine.*

The descendents of Anah *the Anus* were Dishon, *Dishon-nest-tea* and Oholibamah, daughter of Anah *the Anus (what a revelation!).* The descendents of Dishon were Hemdan, *Hemmed-in, Dishonmustturd,* Eshban, Ithran and Cheran.

The descendents of Ezer were Bilhan, Zaavan and Akan. The *closest* descendents of Dishan' were Uz, *Us',* Iran and Aran.

These are the Horite clans: the clans of Lotan, Shobal, *Snowball,* Zibeon, Anah *the Anus,* Dishon, Ezer, Dishan and *Dat-han.* They were the clans of the Horites, *who had all the right whores,* clan by clan in the *chaotic* land of Seir.

The following are the kings that reigned in the land of Edom before any king 'reigned' *or water rained* over the Israelites. Bela, son of Beor, became king in Edom *after everyone else in the place died from famine and plague;* the name of his city was Dinhabah, *Population 1.*

When Bela died, *he miraculously gave birth to Jobab and JoeBob*, sons of Zerah from Bozrat, *who somehow survived on their own for twenty years and* became kings in another part of the country known as Edom.

When Jobab *and JoeBob* died, Husham from the land of the Temanites succeeded them as king. He defeated the Midianites *in the middle-of-the-night* in the country of Moab, *where neither army rightfully belonged fighting or marching in the first damned place.* The name of Husham's city was Avith.

When Husham died, *he was dead instead of just always being dead tired.* Hadad, son of Bedad, succeeded him as king *in an empire consisting of five puny midgets.* When Hadad died Samlah from Masrekah succeeded him as king *and the empire had grown to seven distressed and depressed resident midgets having inflamed and infected anuses and colons.*

When Samlah died Shaul, from Rehoboth-on-the-River succeeded him as king *and marched all the way to Rehoboth-by-the-Sea.* When Shaul died, *he was covered with one.* Baal-hanan, son of Achbor succeeded Shaul as king *in the land of twelve distressed and depressed citizens.*

When (*Here we go with the "Whens" again!*) Baal-hanan died, Hadar succeeded him as king *and asked his kingdom, "What's the sense of living or dying? This world is a complete bullshit existence all the way from womb to tomb!"* He named his city Pau. (His wife's name was Mehetabel; she was the daughter of Matred, son of Mezahab and *Rehab the A-rab*).

The following are the names of clans of Esau individually according to their subdivisions and localities; the clans of Timna, Alvah, *Simon, Theodore*, Jetheth, Oholibamah, Elah, Pinon, *Pinned-on-the-Mat,* Kenaz, Teman, Mibzar, Magdiel and Iram.

These are the clans of the Edomites, according to their settlements in their territorial holdings, *which were all stolen or illegally acquired through fraudulent and immoral real estate and business activity.* Esau was the father of the Edomites, *and you should know that by now even if you can't read words or hear sounds.*

Chapter Thirty-seven
"Joseph Sold into Egypt"

Jacob settled in the land where his father had stayed, the land of Canaan, which still *principally* belonged to the Canaanites. This is the family history, *which is not verified in any other legitimate history books anywhere except that it appears right here in this infallible Wholly Book of Genesis.*

When Joseph was seven years old, he was tending the flocks with his brothers; Joseph was an assistant to the sons of his father's wives Bilhah and Zilpah, *who were also two helluva' good maidservants turned concubine wives. They both knew how to pump their' humps and scream "Oooh!" and "Aahhh!" and "Yes, yes!" and "Faster! Harder!" repeatedly shouting the exclamations over and over again.* Joseph brought his father bad reports about them *(his brothers or his father's wives/concubines, we know not which?)*

Israel *(Jacob's new name given to him by the Lord)* loved Joseph best of all his sons, *for he favored Joseph over his brothers (this always leads to future trouble in any family, Biblical. Greek or otherwise)* and he was the child *(missing several essential chromosomes)* of Jacob's old age. Jacob *(Israel)* had made Joseph a long tunic *without having the courtesy or the decency of giving his other sons any comparable or similar gifts. He just wanted to cause unnecessary conflict among his children as Jacob's ancestors Abraham and Isaac had deliberately done.*

When Joseph's brothers saw that their father loved him best of all his sons, *they became extremely pissed-off.* They hated Joseph so much that they didn't even greet him. *They deeply resented Israel's preferential treatment of Joseph, which in itself' was borderline immorality.*

Once Joseph had a dream, which he told to his *angered eleven* brothers: "Listen to this dream I had," *he said.* "There we were, binding sheaves in the field *that had fallen apart,* when suddenly my sheaf rose to an upright position. *It rose just like my penis does sometimes.* Your sheaves then formed a ring around my sheaf and bowed down to it *as if they were subordinate limp penises.*"

"Are you trying to tell us that you can get an erection and we can't?" one brother gruffly answered Joseph. "Stop being so fuckin' egotistical!"

"Are you really going to make yourself king over us?" his brothers asked *in unison. "We'll have you know that we can get erections also! And rock-hard firm ones too!"*

185

"Or are you trying to impose your rule on us?" *they all clamored*. So Joseph's brothers hated him all the more because of his talks about his dreams *despite the fact that he had only disclosed the essence of one dream to them.*

Then Joseph had another dream, and this one, too, he told to his brothers *since Joseph was a bit of a braggart who liked to get their goats.* "I had another dream," he *cockily* said.

"If it was a white one it probably was your first orgasm that you can't even remember because you were sleeping right through the climax," replied a jealous brother. "Too bad Dickhead!"

"This time," *Joseph proceeded,* "the sun and the moon and eleven stars were bowing down to me."

"That sounds more like a gross hallucination or a bad delusion than a prophetic dream," another brother offered. "Indeed more pathetic than prophetic! Stop with all the fuckin' hyperbole already!"

When Joseph told *(actually retold)* the dream to his father, his father reproved him. "What is the meaning of this dream of yours?" his father asked. "Can it be that I and your brothers are to come and bow to the ground before you? *I don't bow down to any man, especially my young favorite son that ain't even yet a man!"*

So Joseph's brothers were wrought up against him but his father pondered the matter, *wondering, 'What's the matter' with Joseph? Is he mentally ill or is he just basically fucked-up like the rest of us!'*

One day, when Joseph's *eleven* brothers had gone to pasture their father's flocks at Shechem, Israel *(Jacob)* said to Joseph, "Your brothers, you know, are tending our flocks at Shechem during the day *and bartending at a local saloon at night.* Get ready; I will send you to them *so that they might kill you."*

"I am ready," Joseph answered *in an exaggeration, "but instead of killing me, they will bow down to me like humble serfs."*

"Go then," Israel replied. "See if all is well with your brothers and the flocks, and bring back word. *Better yet, bring back a lot of words."*

So Jacob sent Joseph off from the valley of Hebron. When Joseph reached Shechem, a man *(possibly a pedophile)* met him as he was wandering about in the fields *without any definite destination or purpose in mind. What else is new in this rather incredible fiction?*

186

"What are you looking for?" the man (*stranger*) asked. *"I have some sweet food here in my bag if you will go away with me into the tall grass?"*

"I am looking for my brothers," Joseph *innocently* answered *the possible pedophile*. "Could you please tell me where they are tending their flocks? *They're too cheap to buy shepherding dogs to do that particular job for them."*

The man told Joseph, "They have moved on from here, *leaving sheep and lamb turds all over these formerly pristine fields*. In fact, I heard them say, 'Let us go on to Dothan *for no reason except to be just passing through wherever the hell we are with our defecating animals. The main thing is that we just make a big sloppy mess and then move on."*

So Joseph went after his brothers, *not knowing exactly where they were while he believed the perfect stranger's account of their whereabouts. He followed the animal shit trail and* caught up with them in Dothan, *which was only a one-goat-town.*

The *eleven* brothers noticed Joseph from a distance, and before he came up to them, they *by sheer coincidence* plotted to kill him, *just as Jacob had planned without ever consulting his other sons. Certainly no one in the family wanted to bow down to a young pipsqueak upstart like Joseph.*

The brothers said to one another *and listened to the same statement each was speaking,* "Here comes that master dreamer *who has yet to master the art of masturbation*. Come on," *they all said together,* "let us kill him and throw him into a 'cistern' *where he could build a chapel*. We could say that a wild beast devoured him. We shall then see what comes of his dreams. *Maybe the sun and the moon and eleven beasts will now bow down before our youngest brother and then kiss his lily-white ass."*

When Reuben heard this, he tried to save Joseph from their hands saying, "We must not take Joseph's life *but only should beat the shit out of him*. Instead of shedding his blood," Reuben continued *with a degree of compassion,* "just throw him into that cistern there in that desert *(it was a very small desert);* but don't kill him outright *while I casually hang around and watch you guys threaten to eliminate him."*

Reuben's purpose was to rescue Joseph from their hands and restore him to his father *so that Jacob might reward Reuben with a cool looking tunic, too, just like Joseph's multi-colored robe. But then Reuben considered that he didn't want to be hurled into any* desert cistern too and he immediately forgot about the idea of an expensive tunic for himself.

So when Joseph *naively* came up to his *eleven* brothers, they stripped him of the long tunic he had on *and inspected his naked body to determine if he had indeed gone through puberty.* Then the brothers took Joseph and threw him into the cistern *(Reuben only pretended to be participating).* The cistern was empty and dry, *so the fall might have killed Joseph in his rapid plummet. Obviously they certainly were not looking out for Joseph's well' being or for his 'well-fare'.*

The brothers sat down to their meal, *consisting of deli-type sandwiches prepared by Reuben.* Looking up, the brothers saw a caravan of Ishmaelites coming from Gilead, their camels laden with gum, *gumballs,* balm, resin *and resin bags* to be taken to *stadiums in* Egypt.

Judah said to his brothers, "What is to be gained by killing our brother and concealing his blood? *Let's make some 'quick-silver' and gold here! I can make a mirror with the quick-silver!"*

"What did you have in your mini-mind?" another brother asked.

"Let us sell Joseph to these Ishmaelites, instead of doing away with him ourselves," Judah suggested. "After all, he is our brother, our own flesh, *so why not put him on the damned flesh market?" Judah shrewdly suggested and advised.*

The brothers agreed. They sold Joseph to the Ishmaelites for twenty pieces of silver *and ten jars of camel polish.*

Some *of the* Medianite *day'* traders passed by, and they pulled Joseph up out of the cistern and took him to Egypt *where they could drop him into an even bigger, deeper cistern.*

When *the anxious* Reuben *felt guilty about the slave transaction he* went back to the cistern and saw that Joseph was not in it. *He finally realized that the boy the Medianites had tugged out of the hollow was indeed his younger brother Joseph. It was the queer habit of Reuben and his brothers to always toss young boys into cisterns to see how many youths it took to fill-up the vertical tank.*

Reuben tore his clothes in a rage and returned to his brothers, *who were only standing ten-feet-away.* Reuben exclaimed: "He's gone. The boy is gone! And I, where can I turn? *How the hell can I go from rags to riches?"*

"What the hell are you screaming deliriously about?" asked another brother to Reuben. "Are you having a seizure, or are you simply a demented fool just like the rest of us?"

188

The other brothers took Joseph's tunic, and after slaughtering a *scape*goat, dipped the tunic in its blood *because the brothers were basically very dippy guys.*

Then the brothers sent someone *(a perfect stranger, maybe the pedophile who had set Joseph up to meet his cruel-hearted brothers)* to bring the long tunic to Jacob, with the message: "Father, we have found this. See whether it is your son's tunic or not. *We are not tunic experts, and this one and Joseph's are the only two we've ever seen.*"

Jacob *immediately* recognized the tunic and exclaimed: "My son's tunic! A wild beast had devoured him! Joseph has been torn to pieces, *and so has my weak heart.*"

Then Jacob rented his clothes *and leased his camel.* He put sackcloth on his loins *(over his scrotum sac),* and mourned his son *for many days and many morns.*

Though Jacob's sons and daughters tried to console him, he refused all consolation, saying, "No, I will go down mourning to my son in the nether world, *although he might be in another domain of the dead exclusively reserved for naïve good souls.*" Thus did his father lament Joseph, *who was actually that moment riding in a merry caravan heading for a bigger, deeper cistern in Egypt'.*

The Medianites, meanwhile, sold Joseph in Egypt to Potiphar, a courtier of Pharaoh and his chief steward, *who also liked to screw around just like Jacob and his promiscuous family of horny sons, wives and a concubine or two thrown into the mix liked to hump and pump.*

Chapter Thirty-eight
"Judah and Tamar"

About the time Judah parted from his brothers *(they weren't at all Siamese-bounded)* he pitched his tent *at camping-grounds* near a certain Adullamite named Hirah. There he met the daughter of a Canaanite named Shua, married her *without any rabbi officiating at any ceremony and Judah thanked Heaven that she (his unimportant anonymous wife) didn't appear to be a card-carrying lesbian.* He then had relations with her *and with all of her relations.*

She *(?)* conceived and bore a son, whom she named Er. *When the unknown nameless wife of Judah was asked what her name was, she said "er," so the boy was named after his anonymous mother's pervasive indecisive nature.* Again Judah's *anonymous* wife *who everyone also called "Er"* conceived and bore a son, whom she named Onan. Then *feeling like a productive reproductive baby machine*, she bore still another son, whom she *imaginatively* named Shelah. They were in Chezib when Shelah was born, *and of course everyone knows where Chezib is located so that vital point needs no elaboration.*

The Old Testament Wholly Book of Genesis clearly proves that all women were good for in prehistoric times was producing offspring (preferably males). Judah got a wife named Tamar for Er, his first-born. *(Evidently, prior to this event Judah had dropped his own anonymous wife in some sort of separation rite).* But Er, Judah's first-born *(Is there an echo in this book?)* greatly offended the Lord *for no apparent or known reason* so the Lord took Er's life *because he had anonymously erred, unaware that he had.*

Then Judah said to Onan, *"Whatever you do, don't err or you'll wind-up dead meat just like Er did!* Unite with your brother's widow, in fulfillment of your duty as brother-in-law, and thus preserve your brother's line *of irrelevant bullshit. Er was just born, got married and now he's dead."*

Onan, however, knew that the descendents would not count as his, *which might have been a genuine blessing in disguise.* So whenever Onan had relations with his *deceased* brother's widow, he wasted his seed on the ground, *hoping that swallows would descend and swallow his seeds, not realizing that the earth might become pregnant from the left over migrant seeds.* Onan wasted his seed *in the seedy part of town* to avoid contributing offspring to his brother Er, *who was dead and wasn't able to give a shit about anything involving his brother's seeds or anybody else's seeds, including his own damned infertile seeds.*

What Onan did had greatly offended the Lord', *Who' despised jerk offs and their' abominations (long before there were bombin' nations)*, and the Lord took Onan's life too *so that his seeds were also effectively eradicated.*

Thereupon Judah said to his daughter-in-law Tamar, "Stay as a widow in your father's *seedy* house until my son Shelah grows up *and can produce seeds to plant inside you."* Judah feared that Shelah might also die like his brothers *while they tried planting their seeds anywhere they could deposit them.* So Tamar *obediently* went to live in her father's *seedy* house *in a seedy nearby tent tenement neighborhood.*

Years passed, and Judah's wife, the daughter of Shua, died. After Judah completed the period of mourning *he began feeling wild and woolly again so* he went up to Tinmah for the shearing of his sheep. Judah was in the 'company' of Hirah the 'Adullamite', *a very dull dumb fellow with a brain the size of a mite. Adullamite owned a small linoleum company that employed Judah.*

When Tamar was told that her father-in-law was on her way up to Tinmah to shear his sheep *and to trim his pubic hairs,* she took off her widow's 'garb', *calling it "unfashionable garbage."* Tinmah veiled herself by covering her shoulders with a shawl, *with the rest of her vivacious succulent body from the shoulders down remaining naked.*

Tamar sat down at the entrance to Enaim, *complaining that she had lost her admission ticket to the town.* Enaim is on the way to Tinmah. Tamar was aware that although Shelah was not grown up, she had not been given to him in marriage. *So, Shelah's seeds were meaningless even though they were not in existence yet.*

When Judah saw Tamar he mistook her for a harlot *(yeah, we've heard this story before!)* since she' had covered her face *as was the custom of all decent, despicable prehistoric harlots and pristine virgins.*

So Judah went over to Tamar at the roadside, and not realizing that she was his daughter-in-law *(the nearly blind bastard), and was too cheap to rent a roadside room for some decent sex*, he said, *"Let's forget the customary small talk.* Come', let me have intercourse with you *so that I may come too. But you must come first before I can come. Got that bitch?"*

192

She replied, "What will you pay me for letting you have intercourse with me, *you ugly cheap bastard!*"

He answered, "I will send you a kid from my flock,"*(meaning Shelah, his kid).*

"Very well," she said, "providing you leave a pledge until you send it. *I've screwed for less than a kid before. This sex better be good, that's all I got to say!"*

"What pledge am I to give you?" *asked the horny old coot.*

She answered, "Your seal and cord, and the staff you carry. *If you don't have your 'seal' with you, a walrus will do just fine as a substitute for the friggin' seal!"*

So Judah *was so hot and horny that* he gave those things to her and had intercourse with her, *and fucked her' pretty good' for the old geezer that he was.* She conceived by him, *for in those days maternity duty was not nine months but merely nine seconds.* When Tamar went away she took off her shawl and put on her widow's garb again*, thus re-entering and wearing her "unfashionable garbage."*

Judah sent the kid by his friend Adullamite to recover the pledge from the woman; but Adullamite *was (as already mentioned) a dull fellow and* could not find her. Adullamite asked the men of the place, "Where is the temple prostitute, the one by the roadside in Enaim?"

"How could the temple prostitute be in the temple and standing by the roadside in Enaim at the same time?" asked one of the more alert men. "You must be thinking of two different prostitutes."

Then other *un-erudite* men answered, "There has never been a temple prostitute here, *but that sure is a nifty idea worthy of pursuing that definitely would make sex for money a sacred thing."*

Adullamite went back to Judah and told him, "I could not find her *to get laid myself'; and besides, the men of the place said there was no temple prostitute there *but only an ugly mangy synagogue prostitute instead."*

"Let the harlot keep her things," Judah replied. "Otherwise we shall be the laughingstock of the countryside *and I, like my forefathers don't want my livestock laughing at me along with the local residents too.* After all, I did send the harlot the kid, even though you were unable to find her. *That's not my damned fault! My debt to her has been satisfied in addition to my obsessive sexual appetite."*

About three months later, Judah was told that his daughter-in-law Tamar had played the harlot and was then with child from her harlotry. "Bring her out," cried Judah. "She shall be burned *at the stake or at the hamburger. I don't need this scandal to further spoil or sully my already disreputable name!"*

But as the men were bringing Tamar out she sent word to her *deplorable ingrate* father-in-law, "It is by the man to whom these things belong that I am with child, *you blind, horny, old bastard.* Please verify," she' added, "whose' seal and cord and whose staff these are."

Judah *immediately* recognized them and said, "She is more in the right than I am, since I did not give her to my son Shelah. *He'll certainly be the kid I'll send over to her as her payment we had agreed upon. That way I can get rid of the little prick and kill two birds with one stone."* But Judah had no further relations with Tamar *or with any of her relations.*

When the time of Tamar's delivery came she was found to have twins in her womb (*another redundant twin-sibling-rivalry plot*). *"Two kids for the price of one ornery kid!" she marveled.* While Tamar was giving birth one infant put out his hand *testing the outside environment but then withdrew it back into the more comfortable and hospitable womb.*

The *experienced* midwife, taking a crimson thread, tied it on the newborn's hand, to note that this one came out first *and would inherit Judah's entire estate and gain the true resentment of his brother' as was the insane tradition back then.* But as he withdrew his hand, his brother came out; and she (*the veteran midwife*) said, "What a breach *birth* you have made for yourself'!" So he was called Perez, *and 'some day', they (the women) thought, 'he will be Prez'.* Afterward, his *reluctant* brother came out; he was called Zerah *and he eventually would also amount to one.*

194

Chapter Thirty-nine
"Joseph's Temptation"

When Joseph was taken down to Egypt, a 'certain' Egyptian *(who was sure about most everything he thought, did or said)* named Potiphar, (a courtier of Pharaoh and his chief steward) bought him from the Ismaelites that had brought him there. *So, Joseph (Jacob's eleventh of twelve sons) was bought and brought, or more specifically, brought to and again bought in Egypt.*

But since the Lord was with Joseph *and because the Lord had made Himself' invisible, the Lord was not bought and brought or brought and bought like Joseph had been brought and bought.* Joseph got along very well and was assigned to the household of his Egyptian master, *thanks to the Lord, his personal psychologist and skilled guidance counselor.*

When Joseph's master saw that the Lord was with him *(even though the Lord still remained invisible)* and that the Lord brought Joseph success in whatever he did, the master took a liking to Joseph and made him his personal attendant. *Joseph now happily had his Lord and he also happily had his master, who also seems to be the Lord's master here and now in this unbelievable Wholly Book of Genesis.*

Joseph's master put him in charge of his household and entrusted to him all his possessions, *including his wives, concubines, maidservants and personal male and female prostitutes and slaves.*

From the moment the master put Joseph in charge of his household and all his possessions, the Lord blessed the Egyptian's house for Joseph's sake *and especially because the Lord liked the way the master operated and managed his personal affairs and human properties.* In fact 'the Lord's blessing' was on everything the master owned *and the astonished master couldn't figure out what the strange brandings meant on each of his possessions.* The blessings were both inside and outside the house, *and the master was not familiar with that 'brand of blessing' that was on everything inside and outside the house, especially the brand new things that had not yet been branded.*

Having left everything he owned in Joseph's charge the *very impressed* master gave no thought, with Joseph there, to anything but the food he ate, *which coincidentally was also branded with the Lord's blessing.*

Now Joseph was strikingly handsome in countenance and body, *unlike most Egyptian men, who were ugly, baldheaded and fat-assed.* After a time, his master's wife began to look fondly *(lustily)* at Joseph and said, "Lie with me, *for if we have sex, we both certainly cannot tell the truth."*

But Joseph refused *to lie and lie.* "As long as I am here," he told his master's wife, "my master does not concern himself with anything in his house. He has entrusted to me all he owns, *which suggests that he is a fat, ugly baldheaded big-butted idiot that is too lazy to conduct his own affairs and to keep his woman satisfied.* How then could I commit so great a wrong and thus stand condemned before God? *Oh man, do I badly need to get laid!"*

Although the master's wife tried to entice Joseph 'day after day', *Joseph told her he only wanted to have sex at night when the 'master' was home in the master bedroom giving him permission.* Joseph would not agree to lie or tell the truth beside the beautiful woman, or even stay near her *because it was rumored that the master's wife had ten different kinds of lethal venereal diseases she liked to promiscuously share.*

One such day, when Joseph came into the house to do his *dirty* work, and none of the household servants were then in the house *because someone with gastritis had farted very badly, his evacuation causing a mass evacuation,* the master's wife laid hold of Joseph by his cloak saying, "Lie with me! *I need a stiff erection right now more than I need oxygen from my horrendous farting!"*

But leaving the cloak in the wife's hand, Joseph got away from her and ran outside *to escape her and the terrible fart malodor.* When the master's wife saw that Joseph had left his cloak in her hand as he fled outside she screamed for her household servants and told them, *"Look you numbskulls! Quit fartin' around!" she yelled.* "My husband has brought in a Hebrew slave to make sport of me *and of my chronic gas problem.* He came in here to lie with me, but I cried 'out' as loud as I could *because I want to be the first female umpire in the Egyptian empire.* When the *molesting* slave heard me scream for help he left his cloak beside me and ran away outside. *What a nice tight butt that cute little Hebrew rapist had!"*

The master's wife kept the cloak *(with the Lord's permission)* until Joseph's master came home. Then she told her husband the same *stupid* story *that sounded like one a five-year-old had fabricated.*

"The *handsome, muscular cute-butted* Hebrew slave that you have brought here broke in on me, to make sport of me *because I*

196

wanted to be the first female umpire in the Egyptian empire," the master's wife testified. "But when I screamed for help he left his cloak beside me and ran outside *like a true virginal coward would behave. What a royal bummer!*"

As soon as the master heard his wife's story about how the slave had treated her *and how Joseph had run away from sex*, he became enraged *without even having the Lord's help or blessing*. The master *viciously* seized *Joseph by the testicles, twirled him around over his head* and then threw him in jail where the other *sore-balled prisoners* were confined.

But even while Joseph was in prison the Lord remained with the youth; He showed him kindness *by alleviating the pain in the young man's double hernia and* by making the chief *sado-masochistic* jailer well-disposed' toward him.

The chief *S & M* jailer put Joseph in charge of all his prisoners in the jail *(a bit redundant here),* and everything that had to be done there was done under his *expert* management. The chief jailer did not concern himself with anything at all that was in Joseph's charge, *preferring to imitate the lifestyle and the indolence of his fat, ugly lazy, baldheaded big-butted master.* The Lord was with Joseph and brought success to all he *attempted and* did, *since Joseph had to learn the hard way through exploitation and through blessed sacrifice, as had everyone else that was anybody in the prehistoric and insane Hebrew Biblical tradition.*

197

Chapter Forty
"The Dreams Interpreted"

Some time afterward *(Genesis always strives to be definite)*, the royal cupbearer *(who walked around with a big two-cupped metal bra on his chest)* and the royal baker *(whose reputation was most definitely not on-the-rise because of some half-baked ideas he had implemented)* gave offense to their lord, the *eminent and tyrannical* King of Egypt.

Pharaoh was *arbitrarily* angry with his two courtiers, *but we don't know exactly why.* He placed the chief cupbearer and the chief baker in the custody of the house of the chief steward *(the same fucked-up jail where Joseph had been unjustly confined).*

The chief steward assigned Joseph to them *when he should have really assigned them to Joseph.* Joseph became their attendant *and since the two were conspiring to escape their incarceration, he could have very easily been their flight attendant.*

After they had been in 'custody' for some time *the cupbearer and the baker were eligible to become full-fledged custodians and janitors.* The cupbearer and the baker of the King of Egypt that were confined in the jail both had dreams on the same night, *as their formerly clean underwear attested with big yellow target spots splattered all over the material.* Each dream had its own meaning *that was very unclear to the cupbearer and to the baker, and in fact, just as unclear as the dried-up seminal fluid stains the two prisoners had disseminated.*

When Joseph came to them in the morning he noticed that the cupbearer *(who was no longer a cupbearer by the Pharaoh's decree)* and the baker *(who was no longer a baker)* looked disturbed. So Joseph asked Pharaoh's *former* courtiers that were with him in custody in his master's house, "Why do you look so sad today? *You should be happy you're both sentenced to die by excruciating torture! You both have a most satisfactory plan of escape from this miserable life!"*

They answered him *in unison,* "We have had dreams, but there is no one to interpret them to us. *Everyone in this insane jail is an absolute imbecile. And we believe that dreams have more truth in them than everyday reality does."*

Joseph said to them, "Surely, interpretations come from God, *but dreams come from your asinine perverted imaginations.* Please tell your dreams to me *so that I can analyze your demented subconscious minds."*

Then the chief cupbearer told Joseph his dream. "In my dream," he began, "I saw a vine in front of me, and on the vine were three branches. The vine had barely budded when its blossoms came out, *and I thought this meant that I was turning into a blooming idiot.* Its clusters then ripened into grapes."

"I hope they weren't sour grapes you were dreaming about," Joseph interrupted. "Pharaoh doesn't take well to criticism, not even of holly wood and vine."

"Well," *continued the chief cupbearer,* "Pharaoh's cup was in my hand. So, I took the *sour* grapes, pressed them onto his cup, *and without giving the grapes time to ferment into wine*, I put the cup into Pharaoh's hand."

Joseph said to the chief cupbearer: "This is what your *stupid* dream means. *Next time you ought to be sure that you stay awake all night so you don't have any more moronic dreams like this one.* The three branches are three days *because both you and the lazy baker want to establish a three-day workweek.* Within three days Pharaoh will lift up your head and restore you to your *former* post. You will be handing Pharaoh his cup as you formerly used to when you were his *appointed official* cupbearer. *Pharaoh will be fascinated by your critical sour grapes."*

"Great news!" exclaimed the cupbearer. "Pharaoh's next cup will be modeled after an athletic supporter! I already have a great designer cup idea in mind with the nifty insignia inscribed, 'My' balls runneth over'!"

"So if you' will still remember me," *Joseph calmly continued,* "when everything is again well with you, *recollect* that I was here *in this scumbag jail* with you' *telling you this marvelous pure fantasy bullshit.* Please do me the favor of mentioning me to Pharaoh so that I too can get out of this *horrific hellhole* place. The truth is that I was kidnapped *when I was a 'kid' caught 'napping' in a cistern buried in the desert.* I was taken from the land of the Hebrews, and here *in Egypt* I have not done anything for which I should have been put into a *dim* dungeon *that doesn't even have any fire-breathing dragons or malicious monsters in it. How friggin' disappointing this entire fiasco is!"*

When the chief baker saw that Joseph had given this favorable interpretation to the chief cupbearer, *the chief baker should have waited for Joseph to interpret his dream. However, he lacked patience and discipline and had a bad case of irritable bowel syndrome. Instead, the impetuous chief baker requested of Joseph,*

200

"I too had a *very odd* dream. In it I had three *wicked* wicker baskets on my head; *I also had wicker lanterns on my sandals and started dancing all over the place, too like I had a terrible fever on Saturday night,"* the baker *graphically described*. "In the top basket were all kinds of bakery products for Pharaoh *to munch on and to give to his kin so that they could become bona fide munchkins.* But the birds were *aggressively* pecking at the *bakery* products out of the basket on my head."

Joseph *knowledgably* said to the chief baker in reply, *"The baskets were probably pecks because of all the pecking done by the pecker-headed birds.* But this is what your *terrible* dream *actually* means. The three *peck'* baskets are (*represent*) three days. Within three days Pharaoh will lift up your head *after it has been decapitated.* You will then be impaled on a stake and the *pecker-headed* birds will be *ravenously* pecking the flesh from your body *and then spitting the remains into the three empty pecks."*

And in fact, on the third day, which was Pharaoh's birthday *that he celebrated once a month,* the King gave a banquet to all his staff. With his courtiers all around him, Pharaoh lifted up the heads of the chief cupbearer and the chief baker *to show everyone in attendance that two talking heads were in truth better than no quiet heads.*

Pharaoh restored the chief cupbearer to his office, so that he again handed the cup to his King. However, the chief baker was impaled, *meaning that he turned white after being penetrated by seventy sharp knives and spatulas on a sturdy board. He had lost 'all of his blood' and had no more living family or blood relatives.* This all happened just as Joseph had told the two men in his *accurate and articulate* interpretations.

Yet the *lucky* chief cupbearer *was very self-centered and* gave no thought to Joseph *after returning to Pharaoh's favor.* He had forgotten Joseph, *so this important fact makes this entire chapter rather meaningless in context.*

Chapter Forty-one
"Pharaoh's Dream"

After a lapse of two years *and a lapse of memory*, Pharaoh had a dream. He saw himself standing by the Nile, when out of the Nile came seven *submersible* cows, handsome and fat. They grazed in the reed grass, *confusing the river vegetation for a pasture.* Behind them out of the Nile came seven other cows, ugly and gaunt. The seven ugly and gaunt cows stood on the bank of the Nile *and suddenly became carnivorous.* They ate up the seven handsome cows *and had a very delicious steak-out after their stakeout. In fact, the seven gaunt cows wondered why they had ever been herbivorous.* Then Pharaoh woke up *wondering what the hell he had drunk or smoked the night before.*

Pharaoh fell asleep again and had another *alarming* dream. *In slumber-land* he saw seven ears of grain, fat and healthy, growing on a single stalk. Behind them sprouted seven ears of grain, thin and blasted by the east wind, *which as usual was going against the grain.* The seven thin ears swallowed up the seven fat healthy ears. Then Pharaoh woke up *with an eerie (ear-ie) feeling and found it was only a dream that had the potential to make his already miserable life into a veritable nightmare. 'Maybe I gotta' play 7777 in tomorrow's super jackpot pick four lottery?' he speculated.*

Next morning Pharaoh's spirit was agitated *from bouncing around in his body too much during one of his spectacular epileptic fits.* So he summoned all the magicians and sages of Egypt and recounted his *ridiculous* dreams to them, *and the wise men (guys) all had thought that the Pharaoh was psychotic before he even had the new peculiar delusions.*

Then the chief cupbearer *(who didn't know when to keep his big trap shut)* spoke up and said to *the perplexed* Pharaoh: "On this occasion, I am reminded of my negligence. *I fear that forever I shall be the biggest asshole in this asshole kingdom."*

"We all know that as a given," Pharaoh bluntly and gruffly stated. *"You don't have to remind us of your being an enormous asshole or of your notorious personal negligence. Tell me Royal Cupbearer, who the hell wants to even think about such obvious ludicrous truths?"*

"Once when Pharaoh was angry," *the chief cupbearer carefully stated,* "he put me and the chief baker in custody in the house of the chief steward. *I'm glad that my merciful Pharaoh only got angry at me once."*

"*This better be good or you too will be impaled, just like the chief baker had been sensationally eliminated,*" Pharaoh threatened the chief cupbearer. "*I'll have the chief executioner do it for me, the chief Pharaoh as my latest mischief. Ha, ha, ha!*"

"Later," *the chief cupbearer cautiously proceeded to his King,* "the chief baker and I both had dreams on the same *dreamy* night. Each of our dreams had their own meaning, *meaning the chief baker and I coincidentally happened to be both delusional and schizophrenic.*"

"*Get to the point or I'll call the chief executioner right now!*" *the chief Pharaoh candidly bellowed to the chief cupbearer.*

"There with us was a *chief* Hebrew youth, a slave of the chief steward," *said the chief cupbearer, who wanted to chiefly get himself and his chief magician friends off the responsibility and accountability hook and have Joseph impaled instead of becoming an appointed Chief-of-State.* When the *chief* baker and I told him our *perplexing* dreams, the Hebrew boy interpreted them for us and explained *in detail* their *obscure esoteric* meanings. And it turned out just as he *had* told us; I was restored to my *important* post *as chief cupbearer* but the *chief* baker was impaled *with a hundred sharp spatulas and piercing daggers.*"

Pharaoh therefore had Joseph summoned and they *(?)* hurriedly brought him from the dungeon *because no one there in their right or in their wrong mind wanted to be impaled as being Joseph's accomplice. Everyone, however, including Pharaoh, desired to see Joseph impaled because they were all into (other) body piercing.*

After Joseph shaved *his face, crotch, and armpits* and then changed his clothes *into more acceptable Egyptian garb*, he came into Pharaoh's presence.

Pharaoh then *imperially* said to Joseph: "I had certain dreams that no one can interpret *and that everyone here is afraid to interpret.* But I hear it said of you that the moment you are told a dream you can interpret it, *you callow, young, foolish, whimsical whippersnapper.*"

"It is not I," Joseph *sincerely* replied to Pharaoh, "but God who will give Pharaoh the right answer *at the wrong time for Pharaoh to comprehend.*"

Then Pharaoh said to Joseph: "In my dream, I was standing on the 'bank' of the *prodigious* Nile *looking down at my money.* Up from the 'Nile' came seven cows, *and I was almost 'annihilated'.* The cows were fat and well' formed and *avariciously* grazed in the

204

reed grass, *thinking it was uncultivated marijuana.* Behind them came seven other cows, scrawny, most ill' formed and *extremely gaunt.* Never have I seen such ugly specimens as these in all the land of Egypt. *These cows were really fuckin' ugly, I tell ya'! Fuckin' really, really ugly!* Then I woke up."

"*I get the message,*" Joseph responded. *"The cows were uglier than grotesque, even though elephants grow tusks and cows grow horns when they become horny. That's all very logical and plausible."*

"Anyway *Hebrew Asshole,*" Pharaoh continued, "the gaunt ugly cows ate up the first seven fat cows *I had mentioned.* But when they consumed them, no one could tell that they had done so, because they looked just as ugly *and skinny* as before. *There was no after to this confounding before scenario. The cows were ugly and skinny before, and then skinny and ugly after. Their physical appearances were unchanged!"*

"Sounds like each of the cows got a real bum steer out of that symbolic meal," Joseph cleverly deduced. *"Are you sure your story isn't a lot of unmitigated bull'?"*

"In another *puzzling* dream," Pharaoh sanctimoniously stated, "I saw seven 'ears' of grain *without lobes,* fat and healthy, growing on a single stalk. Behind them' *they were stalked* by seven ears of grain, which *suddenly* sprouted. The new seven ears of grain were shriveled *like my tiny dick,* thin and blasted by the east wind *that gave them a hell of a blowjob.* The seven thin ears *then* swallowed up the seven healthy ears. I have spoken to the magicians but none of them can give me an explanation *because they're all afraid of being impaled by sharp spatulas and piercing daggers if they are wrong. Perhaps the gutless prestidigitators should all start eating mandrakes."*

Joseph said to Pharaoh: "Both of the Pharaoh's dreams have the same meaning, *which means that you my King dream in double-vision stereo.* God has thus foretold to Pharaoh what He is about to do."

"What God is about to do or what Pharaoh is about to do?" Pharaoh begged for clarification. *"And please Joseph, don't be pretentious!"*

"The seven healthy cows are seven years," *Joseph claimed,* "and the seven healthy ears are seven years, the same *number prevailing* in each dream. So *Pharaoh,* also, the seven thin ugly cows that came up after them are seven years, as are the seven thin, wind-blasted ears. *It seems that seven is both your lucky and your unlucky number,"* Joseph aptly theorized and explained.

"Tell me the bad parts first," Pharaoh demanded. "I know your God is famous for vengeful devastation and catastrophe dating back before the time of Abraham."

"There will be seven years of famine. It is just as I *have* told *you* Pharaoh, *but as usual you weren't paying good attention,"* Joseph chided. "God has revealed to Pharaoh what He is about to do. Seven years of great abundance are now coming throughout the land of Egypt. But these will be followed by seven years of famine when all the abundance in the land of Egypt will be forgotten *and consummated. There won't be a 'pear-amid' you to eat,"* Joseph *declared as he pointed to the shocked assemblage of cowardly gasping magicians. The Almighty Lord's going to bust your stones good!"*

"What will happen after the seven years of famine?" Pharaoh asked in a quivering tone of voice. "My tummy's not going to like that!"

"When the famine has *totally* ravaged the land," *Joseph confidently said,* "no trace of the abundance will be found in the land because of the famine that follows it. *It's all very simple. Famine follows abundance, and then abundance follows famine if certain mandatory conditions are met.* The famine will be so utterly severe *that you will cringe to even utter a word about it,"* Joseph calmly *predicted.* "That Pharaoh had the same dream twice means that God has reaffirmed the matter and that God will soon bring it about *because He' likes to visit humans with death, suffering and destruction. Pharaoh, I feel that it is my duty to inform you that it looks like your balls are about to be broken like they've never been broken before!"*

"But my royal testicles are supposed to be sacred!" Pharaoh balked. "Your audacity is placing your life in jeopardy!"

"Therefore," *Joseph answered in an unperturbed manner,* "let Pharaoh seek out a wise and discerning man and put him in charge of the land of Egypt *so that we can have feast-or-famine-control. Even your sex lives will be affected for you all will be sex-starved just like your stomachs will be food-starved,"* Joseph boldly *predicted.* "Pharaoh should also take action to appoint overseers of land *and overseers of highways to regiment soldiers and* to regiment the land during the seven years of abundance. *All your regiments should be on a regimen,"* he counseled the Egyptian King.

206

"Seven years of famish!" shouted the very distraught chief cupbearer. "We'll all be fuckin' famished before it's ever over!"

"The overseers *of lands and the overseers of highways* should 'husband' all the food *without giving any to their parasitic wives,"* *Joseph advised.* "The overseers should collect grain under Pharaoh's authority, to be stored in the towns for food. This food will serve as a reserve for the country, *for both the army and the army reserves.* In this way Egypt will not perish in the *terrible* famine."

This *sagacious* advice pleased Pharaoh and all the officials *despite the fact that they all thought it all represented well' packaged and well' marketed horse manure.*

"Could we find another like him?" Pharaoh asked his *apprehensive* officials. "Is there another *in my land that can courageously and accurately predict doom and gloom* that is so endowed with the spirit of God?"

So Pharaoh *very directly* said to Joseph: *"You and your God are trying to fuck-up my kingdom big time!* Since God has made all of this known to you, no one can be as wise and as discerning as you are, *unless of course you are imagining this 'mammoth' catastrophe that you predict, which could in the process kill many woolly about-to-be extinct elephants," Pharaoh illogically insisted.* "You *Joseph* shall be in charge of my palace, *even though I think you're a fast-talking bull- shitter with rusty brass balls and I hardly even know you.* All of my people shall dart at your command, *stranger, so that they can stay away from your God's designated target area on His' doomed bulls-eye.* Only in respect to the throne shall I outrank you, *you rank individual!"*

"Gee your Highness, thanks for the splendid title," Joseph *gratefully replied. "This sounds much better than living in a cistern or even sleeping in a dingy dirty jail."*

"Herewith," Pharaoh told Joseph, "I place you, *a total stranger and a brash alien in this kingdom* in charge of the whole land of Egypt. *This way, if things don't favorably work out, I can have you to blame as my scapegoat."*

With that, Pharaoh took off his signet ring with its seal and put it on Joseph's finger, *in that Joseph only had one deformed finger on each of his hands.* Pharaoh had Joseph dressed in robes of fine linen *so that when he would become wet, the boy could easily be hung out to dry on a clothesline.* Then Pharaoh placed a gold chain around Joseph's neck *so that the brazen Hebrew youth could enjoy some heavy metal.*

207

Pharaoh then had Joseph ride in the chariot of his vizier *(chief 'seal' and walrus carrier of Lower Egypt),* and they *(?) boisterously* shouted "Abrek!" *("You all had better watch your fuckin' asses!")* before him' *when the newly commissioned official passed by.*

Thus, Joseph was installed over the whole land of Egypt. *Amazingly, there was enough of him to go around and to be installed all over the damned sprawling country.*

"I, Pharaoh, proclaim," he told Joseph, "that without your approval no one shall move hand or foot in all the land of Egypt. *Everyone will behave like statues until you tell them to move, sit or shit."*

Pharaoh also bestowed the name of Zaphenath-paneah on Joseph, *and its formal translation is 'chief ball' breaker'.* Pharaoh then gave Joseph in marriage Asenath, daughter of Potiphera, priest of Heliopolis, *but Joseph wished to be married to Potiphera instead of to the priest's acne-faced flat-chested daughter.* Joseph was thirty years old when he entered the service of Pharaoh, King of Egypt, *so he was really in effect drafted rather than enlisted into the service.*

After Joseph left Pharaoh's *regal* presence he traveled throughout the land of Egypt, *which he now governed as a foreigner and as a stranger.* During the seven years of plenty, when the land produced abundant crops, he 'husbanded' all the food of those years of plenty. *Joseph married the food and husbanded it all, marrying them in addition to being married to Asenath while he wished being hitched to her father Potiphera.*

Joseph placed in each town the crops *he had husbanded and had been married to.* He garnered *and gleaned* grain in quantities like the sands of the sea, *at the bottom of the ocean.* The food storage was so vast that at last he stopped measuring it, for it was beyond measure *and beyond Asenath's diminutive height of three-foot-tall, for Joseph used Asenath's length as his yardstick standard measuring device.*

Before the famine years set in, Joseph became the father of two sons, born to him by Asenath, the *hideous midget* daughter of Potiphera, priest of Heliopolis, *who was afraid of pots and had a phobia about them.* He named his first-born Manasseh, meaning, "God has made me forget entirely the suffering of my family *with or without amnesia."* The second child he named Ephraim, meaning, "God has made me 'fruitful' in the land of my affliction *even though I despise vegetarians and offensive homosexuals."*

When the seven years of abundance enjoyed by the land of Egypt came to an end, the seven years of famine set in *according to the Lord's specified famine plan and timetable.* This happened just as Joseph *had* predicted *despite the notion that nothing is ever permanent, either in the form of prosperity or famine.*

Although there was famine in all the other countries, food was available throughout the land of Egypt *and its satellite nations.* When hunger came to be felt throughout the land of Egypt the people cried to Pharaoh for bread, *for they believed that he had lots of bread in his coffers and was also very well' bred.* Pharaoh directed all the Egyptians to go to Joseph, *even the ones that didn't need bread.* The people were commanded to do whatever Joseph told them, *for they all had been systematically trained to obey arbitrary bullshit.*

When the famine had spread throughout the land Joseph opened all the cities that had grain and rationed it to the Egyptians, *who everyday ate their 'cereal' in a serial-soap opera' type scenario,* since the famine *had magically grown a hand and* had gripped the land of Egypt.

In fact, all the world came to Joseph to obtain rations of grain, *for the famine had fantastically grown other hands and had gripped the whole world and had everybody either by the balls or by their tits.*

Chapter Forty-two
"The Brothers' First Journey"

When Jacob learned that grain rations were available in Egypt *(for the Lord heavily socked it to Jacob and his family in Canaan as well as to the Pharaoh across the Nile),* he said to his *eleven remaining ornery* sons: "Why do you keep gaping at one another *like gay aliens*? I *happen to* hear," he went on, "that rations of grain are available in Egypt. Go down there and buy some for us, that we may stay alive rather than die of hunger, *which realistically seems like a better and better idea with each passing day. Why does the Lord persist in breaking my delicate fragile stones thus?"*

So ten of Joseph's brothers went down to buy an emergency supply of grain from 'Egypt', *when actually they should have been looking to buy the grain from people in Egypt.* It was only Joseph's full brother *(who always ate a lot of veggies and had a stomach and gaseous intestines loaded to capacity)* Benjamin that Jacob did not send with the rest, for he thought that some disaster would befall him *for no logical reason whatsoever.*

Thus, since there was famine in the land of Canaan also, *and whether the Lord had punished Jacob for no good reason in Canaan or had forgotten about him and his family while He was with Joseph in Egypt is uncertain and open to conjecture.* The sons of Israel *(Jacob)* were among those that came *to Egypt* to procure rations *and to look for beautiful dark-skinned hussies with eager wet pink snatcheroos.*

It was Joseph as the governor of the country, who dispensed the rations to all the people *(that came to Egypt or that were in Egypt).* When Joseph's brothers came and knelt down before him with their *frowning* faces to the ground, *the governor thought that only silly mentally disturbed sniveling retards would practice rubbing and grinding their noses, mouths and foreheads into the ground all at the same time.*

Joseph recognized his *wicked* brothers as soon as he saw them. But he concealed his own identity from them and spoke sternly to them *as if he was the Pharaoh.* "Where do you *pathetic cretins* come from?" he asked them. *"And don't dare say from your mother's vagina, either!"*

They *(the ten older brothers)* answered *all together,* "From the land of Canaan to procure food. *We need some grub in a hurry."*

When Joseph recognized his brothers *(already stated),* although they did not recognize him *(implied already!),* he was reminded of

211

the dreams he had *had* about them. Joseph said to them: "You are *dangerous* spies, *no doubt about it. I can tell by the shape of your noses after you have foolishly rubbed and grinded them into the dirt.* You have come to see the nakedness of the land *and of our beautiful dark-skinned pink-crotched women."*

"No, my lord," *the ten beggars* all *simultaneously* answered. "On the contrary, your servants have come to 'procure' food *if it has already been cured and is safe to eat.* All of us are sons of the same man, *for mothers, wives, sisters and women do not matter where we come from.* We are honest *but deceitful* men; your servants have never been spies all together, *but each of us has been a spy at least once separately."*

But Joseph *cunningly* answered them: "Not so! You have come to see the nakedness of the land *and of our beautiful dark-skinned women with eager beavers. Didn't I just say that moronic comment a moment ago?"* Joseph reiterated.

"We your servants," *they all said together the way Jacob had taught them exactly like parrots learning to repeat*, "were twelve brothers, sons of a certain man in Canaan. *His name eludes us at present, but it will come back to us.* But the youngest one is at present with our *anonymous* father, and the other one is gone *and has mysteriously disappeared somewhere in the desert."*

"It is just as I said *and not what I said was just*," Joseph persisted. "You are spies, and this is how you will be tested, *so you simpletons, get out your number two charcoal markers right now.* Unless your youngest brother comes here, I swear by the life of Pharaoh *rather than by my own precious life* that you shall not leave here *with your balls intact and your' dependent asses still attached,"* Joseph chastised his brothers. "So send one of your number, *say number five for instance* to get your brother, while the rest of you *can rest as you* stay here under arrest. Thus shall your words be tested *by this stupid lame-brained ordeal I have concocted* for their truth; if they are untrue, as Pharaoh lives, you are spies *and must be circumcised fifteen times each by the blind palace butcher."* With that, Joseph locked them up in the *military* guardhouse for three days *to protect them from nobody in particular and to protect nobody from them. In essence, the brothers had to be protected from each other and Joseph thought it would be appropriate for the confined idiots to beat and kick the crap out of one another.*

On the third day Joseph (*arrived at the area of incarceration and*) said to them: "Do this, and you shall live; for I am a God-fearing man *that likes to break balls just like Pharaoh and my father* enjoyed that specific self-satisfying enterprise," he confidentially divulged. "If you have been *honestly* honest, only one of your brothers need be confined in prison, while the rest of you *vagabonds* may go and take home provisions for your starving families *so that they might fight over the scraps of food like jackals or, in this case, like hungry rodents."*

"*You are both kind and cruel at the same time,"* one brother remarked. *"You think and behave much like the Lord and much like our anonymous father."*

"But you must come back to me with your youngest brother, *and if nature has any justice to it, you will die in the damned desert so that I won't have to be bothered with your inane insane horse shit any more,"* Joseph threatened. "Your words will thus be verified upon your return and you will not die."

To this the brothers *unanimously* agreed. To one another, however, they said: "Alas, we are being punished because of our brother. We saw the anguish of his heart *when we split open his sternum and looked inside his chest cavity.* He pleaded with us, *but none of us remember pleading with him.* We paid him no heed; *that is why this shit-eating anguish and atonement crap has come upon us."*

"Didn't I tell you," broke in Reuben, "not to do wrong to the boy, *who could do no wrong in father's eyes! How Joseph could get into father's eyes remains an enigma to this very day.* Now comes the *unpleasant* reckoning for his blood."

The brothers did not know, of course, that Joseph understood what they said, *even though they had trouble communicating with each other in their native tongue.* Joseph had earlier spoken to them 'through an interpreter' *that had the uncanny ability to 'conduct' sound right through his body.*

But turning away from his brothers, Joseph wept *because he had breathed in some pepper grains that were floating around the musty jail room.* When he was able to speak to them again, Joseph had Simeon taken from them and bound before his eyes, *and it came as no surprise since everyone had suspected that that 'binding' was bound to happen.*

Then Joseph gave orders to have their containers filled with grain, their money replaced in each one's sack, and provisions given to them for their journey home, *for what the hell, it was Pharaoh's money and provisions that Joseph was generously giving away and not his own.*

After that *distribution* had been done the *nervous* brothers loaded their donkeys with the rations and departed *thinking irrationally. They truly then understood that there was as much stupid bullshit in Egypt to contend with as there was back in Canaan.*

At the night encampment, when one of the brothers *(we can't remember which one)* opened his bag to give his donkey some fodder, he was surprised to see his money in the mouth of the bag; *whereas, he should have been surprised to see that the bag had a mouth.* "My money has been returned!" he cried out to his brothers. At that their hearts sank *into their rectums.* Trembling, they asked one another, "What is this that God has done to us?" *all together like dumb talking heads would have spoken at the Tower of Babel.*

When the brothers got back to their father Jacob *(a.k.a. Israel)* in the land of Canaan, they told him all *the happy horse shit* that had *just* happened to them. "The man who is the lord of the country," they *clamorously* said *all together,* "spoke to us sternly and put us in custody as if we were spying on the land. But we said to him: 'We are honest men *and thieves*; we have never been spies *and we wipe our asses clean every single night with cactus needles and pine cones'."*

"Tell me the rest of your fucked-up story," Jacob requested. *"My next breath might be my last one."*

"There were twelve of us brothers, sons of the same father *who is you, but we can't remember your' friggin' name,"* the brothers *said and repeated three times in a sort of mantra.* "But one is gone, and the youngest one is present with our *anonymous* father in the land of Canaan," *the brothers intoned.*

"Then the man who is lord of the country said to us: 'This is how I shall know if you *indeed* are honest men; *I will inconvenience you and break your balls good to determine the extent of your truthfulness.* Leave one of your brothers with me, while the rest of you go home with rations *for your irrational starving families that deserve to die big time'."*

"I like this no-nonsense lord guy already," Jacob admitted. "He sounds like a chip off the old block, really chipper! I wish I had a son like that such as the powerful Pharaoh has."

"When you come back to me with your youngest brother, *the lord said,* "I will know that you are honest men and not spies. Then I will restore your brother to you and *then* you may move about freely in the land," *the brothers all chanted together in a disenchanted frame of mind.*

214

"This frivolous story is so extraordinary because it is so illogical and nonsensical," Jacob marveled and loudly laughed. *"It certainly is inspired by the Lord, no fuckin' doubt about it!"*

When the *nine* brothers (*Simeon had been left behind as security*) were emptying their 'sacks' *(not their scrotums, either),* there in each man's sack was his moneybag! At the sight of their moneybags, they and their *anonymous* father were dismayed. Their father Jacob *(alias Israel)* said to them: "Must you make me childless? Joseph is gone, and Simeon is gone, and now you would take away *my youngest child* Benjamin *just because I hate the rest of you and plan to disinherit you all!* Why must such *fucked-up* things always happen to *frail and feeble little old* me?"

Then *levelheaded* Reuben told his father: "Put him in my care, and I will bring Benjamin back to you *so that you can arbitrarily favor him and arbitrarily disinherit the rest of us.* You may kill my own two sons if I do not return Benjamin to you *since I can't stand the little retarded knuckleheads as it is and sincerely wish that the disobedient annoying bratty bastards were dead anyway."*

But Jacob replied: "My son *Benjamin* shall not go down to Egypt with you *unless I know what's going down.* Now that his full brother is dead, he is the only one left *that I can use to play mind and power games with and against the rest of you idiots.* If some disaster befalls him (*Benjamin*) on the journey you must make, you would send my white head down to the nether world in grief, *but don't any of you dare touch any of my many infected blackheads! Man, do I fear the Netherlands! Everyone there goes Dutch treat all the time!"*

Chapter Forty-three
"The Second Trip to Egypt"

Now the famine in the land grew more severe *since the Lord wanted to break the Pharaoh's stones in Egypt as well as pulverizing Jacob's testicles in Canaan.* So when Jacob's family *squandered* and used up all the rations they had brought from Egypt, their father said to them, *"Show more damned basic self-discipline you unruly assholes. You have squandered all the rations you had brought from Egypt,"* Jacob admonished. "Go back and procure us a little more food *and see how much extra grain and wine you can steal on the side."*

But Judah replied: "The man *in charge over there (my brother who I never could identify or never could identify with)* strictly warned us, 'You shall not appear in my presence unless your *remaining* brother is with you.' *Oh brother, do we have a problem here! And we have to retrieve Simeon from the crazy Egyptians too!"*

"Why can't the Lord just make life easy for me?" complained Jacob. *"I'm an old fart and I don't need this heavy shit to deal with! I need asylum from insanity! That's what the fuck I need!"*

"If you are willing to let our brother *Benjamin* go with us," *Judah interrupted his father's irrational tirade,* " we will go down *to Egypt* and procure food for you. But if you are not willing, *you foolish, stupid, stubborn old man',* we will not go down. The man *(my brother who I never really knew and had once tried to kill)* told us, 'You' *flaky assholes* will not appear in my 'presence' *or appear in my gifts, either. Screw Simeon!* Your brother *Benjamin* must be with you'."

Israel demanded, "Why did you bring this trouble on me by telling the man that you had another brother? *I have to blame somebody for this shitty-assed experience, don't I! I wish I were dead! I want to die right now! Benjamin will be Big Ben before he ever gets the hell out of Egypt!"*

They *(the nine defiant brothers; remember, Simeon is still in jail in Egypt)* answered *all together*: "The *nosy* man kept asking about ourselves and our family. *He must be an Egyptian gossip columnist somewhere. He' asked us',* 'Is your father' still living? Do you have another brother? *How many times do you get laid a week? Do you still jerk off in cisterns?'* We had to answer his questions *or else he'd have had us castrated and you would then have effeminate eunuchs for sons.* How could we know *(have known)* that he would

217

say, 'Bring your *last* brother down here, *and let's party'!" the
disgusted brothers uttered together.*

Then Judah urged his father Israel: "Let the boy *(Benjamin)* go
with me, that we may be 'off and on' our way, *for I like to be off and
on as many times as I can, especially in bed with my ugly wife.* You
and we and our children will starve to death *if I am not off and on
right now,"* Judah stated *to his aged father.* "I myself will stand
surely for him. You can hold me responsible for him, *for if I am
lying, I am 'liable' to be held for libel, if only any of us knew written
language and could jot it down on papyrus scrolls."*

"*Your copious bullshit is almost convincing,*" Jacob admitted.
"*You should have been a greedy politician or a covetous priest.*"

"If I fail to bring Benjamin back and set him in your presence,"
Judah firmly continued, "you can hold it against me forever *because
I know father how you like to hold grudges just as the Lord does.*
Had we not dilly-dallied, we could have been to Egypt and back here
twice by now, *and then I wouldn't need any damned big city
Egyptian 'chiropractor' to work on my anatomy,"* Judah argued.
"*Then I wouldn't have to walk like an Egyptian!*"

Their father Israel then told them: "If it must be so, then do this.
Put some of the land's best products in your baggage and take them
down to the man as gifts to give *in his presence*: Give him some
balm and honey, gum and resin, pistachios and almonds *and some
laxatives and aphrodisiacs to clean his systems out,"* Jacob
recommended. "Also take extra money along *in case thieves and
bandits or bandits and thieves rob you along the way.* You must
return the amount that was put back in the mouths of your bags *or
the man might slit your throats after slitting the mouths of your bags.
It all may have been a mistake or a devious trick,"* Jacob theorized
and verbalized. "*The man might enjoy enacting ruses on innocent
dumb victims such as my dull-minded sons,"* Jacob cautioned his
aberrant progenies. "*We can't take that chance when dealing with
unscrupulous strangers such as this strange man in authority you
speak of. He sounds too slick to be any damned son of mine!*"

"*Is there anything else we should know or do?*" Judah
anxiously inquired. "*Can't you just die before we leave instead of
maybe during our absence?*"

"Take your brother *Benjamin* too, and be off on your way back
to the *important* man. *Be off to see the wizard.* May God Almighty
dispose the man to be merciful toward you, *and if he isn't, may God
Almighty dispose of the man. If the man is merciful,* then he may let
your *detained* brother *Simeon* go *to the bathroom* as well as

218

Benjamin," *Jacob maintained and deducted.* "As for me, if I shall suffer bereavement, I shall suffer it. *I have become used to having my stones perpetually broken by the Lord and shattered by selfish humans all my unhappy life! I'm even considering moving my entire family back to Ur in Mesopotamia."*

So the men (*brothers*) got the gifts *in their father's presence,* took double the amount of money with them, and, accompanied by Benjamin, *who was already homesick,* were off to Egypt to present themselves to Joseph, *the wizard custodian of Egyptian internal affairs.*

When Joseph saw Benjamin with them (*we really got from Canaan to Egypt in a hurry, didn't we?*), he told his head steward, "Take these men into the house and have an animal slaughtered and prepared *so that these primitive savages can eat it raw.* They are *noble barbarians that are* to dine with me at noon."

Doing as Joseph had 'ordered' *from his menu,* the steward conducted the *visiting* men to Joseph's house *located in the center of a big ghetto.* But on being led to his house, they became apprehensive *of the big slum area.* 'It must be,' they *all* thought *together,* 'on account of the money put back in our bags the first time, that we are taken inside *so that our cache of cash can be inspected by these Egyptian customs' agents that might not like our customs.* The Egyptians want to use it (*our arrival*) as a pretext to attack us, take our donkeys, steal our slaves *and egregiously piss on our faces. We Hebrews don't trust anyone' who doesn't connive, cheat or trick in the same manner as we do,'* they all simultaneously thought but dared not vocalize.

So they *(the brothers, who were also real mothers)* went up to Joseph's head steward and talked to him at the *entrancing* entrance to the house. "If you please, sir," they *all* said *in chorus,* "we came down here *to Egypt* once before to procure *cured* food. But when we arrived at a night's encampment and opened our bags, there was each man's money in the mouth of the bag, but our money in the full amount. *We want you to know that we are proud men who are thieves and not just mere beggars out looking for charity or random welfare."*

"*What are you trying to say?" the chief steward challenged. "I think you all need to take a few lessons in the fundamentals of communications somewhere. Not only are you fucked up jerk offs tongue-tied, you're all also brain tied too!"*

"We have now brought the found money back *without even reading about it in a Lost and Found column in the Memphis*

Gazette or the Nile Times. We have brought other money to procure our food with *too*," the *doltish* brothers professed. "We do not know who put the first money in our bags, *but we suspect that the whole canard was some sinister sneaky Egyptian plot or trick.*"

"Be at ease *and stop standing at attention*," the chief steward *imperatively* said. "You have no need to fear; *you only need to be a little skeptical and distrustful, that's all.* Your God and the God of your father must have put treasures in your bags. *Look in your tea bags also, for there might be some gold coins or souvenirs in them, too,*" the chief steward advised the *daft* visitors. "As for your *original* money, I received it *and am glad to report that it wasn't counterfeit. Your lives are temporarily safe with me.*"

With that, the chief steward let Simeon out *of his wild animal cage to reunite with his beastly brothers.*

The steward then brought the men inside Joseph's house *on the south side of the ghetto.* He gave them water to bathe their feet, *for he knew that according to Hebrew tradition, the toes and feet were the only parts of the body the brothers ever washed or rinsed.* The steward got fodder for their *father's* donkeys. Then the brothers set out their gifts to await Joseph's arrival at noon, for they had heard that they were to dine there. *They had been trained to always rely on hearsay.*

When Joseph came home *after visiting another slum,* they *(the new brothers in the 'hood) presented* him with the gifts they had brought inside, while they bowed down before him to the 'ground' *(the house had no floors; only dirt and gravel ground inside).* It was very hard to present the gifts while bowing down to the ground, *but the brothers were all either double-jointed or triple jointed and awkwardly performed those dual 'bow movements'.*

After inquiring how they were, he *(Joseph)* asked them, "And how is your aged father of whom you speak? Is he still in good health? *Or is the hoary senile cantankerous ball-breaker finally ready to expire on his death bed?*"

"Your servant our father is thriving and still in good health," they said in a chant *that was not too enchanting* as they bowed respectfully *and simultaneously released a large quantity of intestinal gas into the (gas) chamber.*

When Joseph's eyes fell upon *the stomach* of his full brother Benjamin, he asked, "Is this your youngest brother *that looks exactly like me? Is this the lad* of whom you told me *would grow up to be Big Ben?*"

The other brothers were lost for words, as was their habit whenever thinking or whenever serious analysis was required of them.

Then Joseph said to *'them'*, "May God be gracious to you my boy! *(Even though Joseph was solely speaking to Benjamin). May He not treat you like He has treated your ancestors and your messed-up family!"* With that, Joseph had to hurry out, *having a sudden severe diarrhea attack.* He was so overcome with affection for his *mentally deficient* brothers that he *(Joseph)* was on the verge of tears *and in the midst of accumulating some serious shit stains.* Joseph went into a private room *where he wiped his buttocks with pinecones on a hopper* and wept, *for crying out loud*!

After washing his face *but neglecting most of his grimy ass*, Joseph reappeared and, now in control of his emotions *and also his erratic bowels*, gave the order, "Serve the meal *with tennis rackets! Forget serving the meal! Serve us first!"*

The meal was served separately to Joseph *(a rank matter of Egyptian rank)*, to the brothers and *then* to the Egyptians who 'partook of his board' *and ate the wood like hungry termites since there wasn't sufficient food on the table to feed everyone.* (Egyptians may not eat with Hebrews; *that was abhorrent to them as well as to the rest of the ancient world's population).*

The *eleven* brothers' were seated by his' *(Joseph's)* directions according to their' ages, *ranks and serial numbers* from the oldest to the youngest *sibling*. They *then incredulously* looked at one another in amazement.

As portions were brought to them from Joseph's table, Benjamin's portion was five times as large as anyone else's *amount*. So they *(the brothers who were real mothers)* drank freely and made merry with him, *trying to distract Benjamin's attention so that they could behave like cannibals and successfully pilfer some of the excess raw meat heaped on his plate.*

221

Chapter Forty-four
"The Final Test"

Then Joseph gave his head steward these *foolish and ludicrous* instructions: "Fill the men's bags *and also their tea bags* with as much food as they can carry, and put each *money-hungry* man's money in the mouth of his *money*bag. In the mouth of the youngest one's *money*bag put also my silver 'goblet' *so that no one in Egypt will be able to gobble it.* The goblet should go together with the money for rations."

The steward 'carried out Joseph's instructions', *even though the instructions had no material existence, form or substance in order to be carried out of the room.* At daybreak the men and their donkeys were *taken to the local post office and* sent off *to Canaan via Donkey Express Next Year Delivery.*

They *(the not-too-bright brothers)* had not gone far out of the city when Joseph *the ball-breaker* said to his head steward: "Go at once after the *stupid* men! When you overtake them, say to them, *the bungling imbeciles,* 'Why did you repay good with evil, *you fucked-up half-ass droll simpletons?* Why did you steal the silver goblet from me? (Remember it was Joseph's silver goblet and not the head steward's silver goblet).* It is the very goblet from which my master drinks and which he uses for divination. What you have done is wrong *and heinously immoral. How the hell is my master ever going to graduate from Divination School without the cheap silver-plated goblet he uses for divination'?"*

When the *loyal* steward overtook them *(the brothers)* and repeated these words to them *(the not-too-brilliant brothers)*, they *(the brothers)* remonstrated with him: "How can my lord say such things?" *they all chanted at once as if they were trained parakeets.* "Far be it from your servants to do such a *malicious* thing! *We, the asshole sons of Jacob are but petty thieves and do not commit grand larceny.* We even brought back to you from the land of Canaan the money that we found in the mouths *and throats* of our bags," the brothers *apologetically* indicated. "Why, then, would we steal *inexpensive* silver or gold from your master's *ghetto house out in the slums?* If any of your servants is found to have the goblet, he shall die *of a swollen prostate gland that ought to violently explode inside his cancer-laden abdomen,* and as for the rest of us, we shall become my lord's slaves."

But the *adamant* chief steward *nicknamed Stu* replied, "Even though it ought to be as you propose, only the one who is found to have it *in his possession* shall become my slave *for me to mistreat, abuse, castrate, sodomize and torture.* The rest of you *ignoramuses* shall be exonerated."

Then each of them *(the brothers)* eagerly lowered his bag to the ground and opened it. *Unfortunately the brothers were too dumb and too lazy to have inspected the bags' contents on their journey out of Egypt.* When a search was made, starting with the oldest and ending with the youngest, *the steward's men took the pleasure and the novelty of feeling the healthy swollen genitals of Jacob's well' endowed circumcised sons.* The *aforementioned* goblet then 'turned up' in Benjamin's bag *as if it were a turnip that had flipped over.* At this, they *(the other brothers)* 'tore' their clothes *before continuing their pathetic suburban Egyptian tour.* Then, when each man had reloaded his donkey, they *reluctantly* returned to the city.

As Judah and his brothers reentered Joseph's house *they quickly but finally realized that he was not only their lord but also a big neighborhood slumlord.* Joseph was still there; so they *(the brothers)* flung themselves on the *filthy* ground *(for there was no floor in the slum house)* before him *(Joseph).*

"How could you do such a *naughty nefarious* thing?" Joseph asked them. "You should have known that a *deceitful tricky* man such as I could discover by divination what happened, even without my *fabulous Divination Goblet.*"

Judah *shamefully* replied: "What can we say to my lord *except words*? How can we plead or how can we try to prove our innocence? God has uncovered your 'servant's' guilt, *despite the fact that Benjamin never worked in your scummy slum-house and the dimwit is too naïve and ignorant to ever steal anything, worthwhile or otherwise!"*

"You have no remorse for your wrongdoing?" Joseph demanded to know. *"Are you attempting to exonerate your criminal younger brother?"*

"Here we are then, the slaves of our lord," *Judah explained and argued. "My lord is almost as clever as the Lord Himself' is.* The rest of us *is* no less *guilty* than the one in whose possession the goblet was found. *What the hell am I saying here? I better learn to keep my big loud mouth shut! Better yet, I better learn how to fuckin' communicate!"*

"Far be it from me to act thus!" said Joseph. "Only the one in whose possession the goblet was found shall become my slave. The rest of you *homosexual faggots* may go back safe and sound to your *decrepit* father *who art in Canaan.*"

Judah then stepped up to him *(Joseph)* and said: "I beg you my lord, let your servant speak earnestly to my lord. Please do not become angry with your servant. *Ignore the fact that I am a liar, a cheat, a thief, a conniver, a blasphemer and a proud womanizer,"* Judah confessed. *"*I believe that you are the equal of Pharaoh *without even measuring either yours or his' penis."*

"Get to the point you big blundering lummox!" Joseph angrily insisted.

"Have you a father or another brother?" *Judah requested to know.* "So we said to my lord, '*Good lord,* we have an aged father and a young brother, *the child prodigy and progeny of pop's senile old age pecker seeds.* This one full brother is *virtually* dead *from gluttony and already has the gout,* and since he is the only one by that mother that is left, his father dotes on him *with favor and mercilessly neglects the rest of us.*"

"Every family needs and has at least one spoiled brat," Joseph acknowledged. *"Without a favorite son there would be too little chaos and conflict and things would always be too normal and tranquil. Life would be too boring without family friction and I fully agree that there should be white sheep and black sheep children!"*

"Then you told your servants," *Judah proceeded,* 'Bring him down to me so that my eyes may look on him.' We replied to my lord, 'The boy cannot leave his father *because the boy is daddy's pride and joy while the old man regards the rest of the family as stagnant river scum.* The boy's father would die if the boy were to leave him. *Notice Master that I said 'the old man' instead of our father', who art in Canaan'!"*

"I thought Our Father and forefathers art in heaven!" Joseph cunningly quipped while toying with language' as was his wont.

"But you told your servants," *Judah continued,* "unless your youngest brother comes back with you, you shall not come into my presence again *with your dirty, crummy, grimy, smelly feet.* When we returned to your servant, our father *who art in Canaan,* we reported to him the words of my lord, *who is not The Lord.*"

"You know, I have only one lifetime to listen to bullshit," Joseph admonished, "so I have to be very selective distinguishing between important bullshit and trivial bullshit. Please continue, and make it as 'brief' as your stinking underwear."

"Later our father *who art in Canaan* told us to come back and buy some food for the family," *Judah uttered.* "So we reminded him, 'We' cannot go down there *to that uncivilized land of uncircumcised lunatics for such a picayune purpose.* Only if our youngest brother is with us can we go, for we may not be able to see the man in charge if our youngest brother *Benjamin* is not with us *in Egypt.*"

"What does all this have to do with the price of incense in the underground black marketplace?" Joseph vociferously challenged. "Quit clowning around and say something having substance instead of words just having simple-minded form."

"Then your servant *our father who art in Canaan* said to us," *Judah cautiously emphasized and framed,* 'As you know, my wife bore my two sons, *which is all that women are really good for.* One of them, however, 'disappeared' *without ever having attended any magicians' kindergarten or prep' school.* I had to conclude that he *(Joseph)* must have been torn to pieces by wild 'beasts' *and rabid wildebeests*; I have not seen him since," *Judah attested.* "If you now take this one *(Benjamin)* away from me, I'll not only be hurt. *I'll be really pissed.* If some disaster befalls him *(Benjamin),* you *(brothers)* will send my *(Jacob's)* white head down to the nether world in grief *along with all of my numerous scabby blackheads."*

"Has your father ever consulted a competent skin doctor?" Joseph indulgently laughed. "He sounds like he needs to change his diet and to stop eating so many sweets and honey in the land of milk and honey."

Judah continued his solemn oration to Joseph. "If then the boy is not with us when I go back to your servant my father *who art in Canaan,* whose very life is bound up with his (Benjamin's), he *(Jacob)* will die as soon as he sees that the boy is not with him," Judah declared. *"That is why you (Joseph) must keep our youngest brother (Benny) here in Egypt with you. Then the rest of us (brothers) can inherit Jacob's fabulous fortune."*

"I'm still concerned about your father's horrendous skin problems," Joseph claimed with a grim expression on his singular countenance. "That whitehead' and those myriad blackheads sound debilitating and possibly life-threatening. Have you tried rubbing his wretched skin with ultra-wet vagina juice?"

Judah cleared his throat. "And your servants will thus send the white head of our father *who art in Canaan* down to the nether world in grief, *and hopefully, all of Jacob's numerous blackheads will die when his body ceases to function."*

226

"*Your family is really very badly fucked up!*" Joseph accused the brothers. "*All you Biblical guys do is bust each other's balls all day long! Is this some kind of self-destructive family tradition or something? Don't you ever learn anything from history or from past experience?*"

Judah was acting a little aggravated at the doubt and cynicism expressed in Joseph's caustic tone of voice. "Besides," *Judah said,* "I, Your servant, got the boy from our father *who art in Canaan* by going surely for him saying, 'If I fail to bring him *(Benjamin)* back to you father *(Jacob)*, you *(Joseph)* can hold it against me *(Judah)* forever. *But to tell you the truth I don't really give a regal shit anymore!*"

"*You should have more respect for your old man even though he persists and delights in breaking your super-sensitive testes by favoring your brother Benjamin!*" Joseph chastised.

Judah grunted and mumbled some indiscernible jargon. "Let me, your servant," *he said,* "therefore remain in place of the boy *(Benjamin)* as the slave of my lord, *or we might have to get 'The Almighty Lord on the case to bust 'my lord's' chops once and for all.* Please let the boy go back *home* with his *stubborn obnoxious vulgar* brothers. How could I go back to my father *who art in Canaan* if the boy were not with me *to be slandered, ridiculed and 'outfoxed'*?" Judah pleaded. "I could not bear *to chicken-out or even duck down* to see the anguish that would overcome my father *who art in Canaan.*"

Chapter Forty-five
"The Truth Revealed"

Joseph could no longer control himself. *His bowels were irritated and swollen and his kidneys and bladder were working too well for his own good.* In the presence *and gifts* of all his *estranged* attendants, he cried out, "Have everyone withdraw from me *as I wipe my rear-end and clean up this horrible mess I have made by barfing!"*

Thus no one else was about when he *(Joseph)* made himself *(actually his mother and father had made Joseph)* known to his brothers, *who had been too stupid to recognize him or his unique expressions and mannerisms.* But his sobs were so loud that the Egyptians heard him *(all over the country), wondering what his (Joseph's) sob story might be.* So the news reached Pharaoh's palace *before Joseph finally revealed his identity to his unobservant brothers. It didn't matter that the news reached Pharaoh's palace since the palace had no ears to hear the news and had no brain to understand the idiotic gossip.*

"I am Joseph," he *methodically* said to his brothers. "Is my father still in good health?" *(Joseph hadn't realized he had asked that same question before about the brothers' father, who also happened to be his father).* But his brothers could give him no answer, so dumbfounded were they at him *just like they had been when Joseph had asked them no questions at all.*

"Come closer to me," he told his brothers. *"I need a hug!"*

When they *(the brothers)* had done so, he *again* said: "I am your brother Joseph," *since the ancient Hebrews took pride in repeating themselves over and over until their dumb dense listeners finally understood what the hell they were saying.* "You *blood rabble* once sold me into Egypt *when you had gone to the well once too often."*

The not-too-swift brothers finally began comprehending the significance of Joseph's words. They were indeed slow learners and fast talkers, even as most people are today.

"But now do not be distressed," *Joseph elaborated and consoled,* "and do not reproach *or approach* yourselves for having sold me here. It was really for the sake of saving lives that God sent me ahead *of you so that our family could survive the famine that the Lord has inexplicably and irrationally rendered all over the region."*

"Wow!" the brothers exclaimed all together. "That was nice of Him! We have to ration and rationalize because He's irrational!"

"For two years now the famine has been in the land," *Joseph explained,* "and for five more years tillage will yield no harvest. *I wish we Hebrews were smart enough to have science and invent irrigation, but as you know, we are all stupid unimaginative assholes dependent on a Lord that continuously punishes the hell out of both us and our enemies."*

"Then we are better off not wasting our time planting crops that won't grow," the brothers all said simultaneously. "What the hell are we saying?" they all shouted in a weird refrain. "We're stupid shepherds and not dumb farmers!"

"God therefore sent me ahead of you *to prepare you for the impending disaster He has been generating,"* Joseph disclosed. "I am here to ensure you a remnant on earth and to save your lives in an extraordinary deliverance *that should have never happened in the first damned place if the Lord didn't enjoy watching us suffer and toil needlessly."*

"You're right on target," the brothers agreed. "Why must we suffer and be persecuted thus? It's almost as if Abraham, Isaac, Jacob and the Lord were all one and the same crazy person!" the visiting siblings all remarkably stated in unison.

"So, it was not really you *but God who had put me in that cistern through what you have assumed was your evil effort,* and He made me come here *to solve the famine crisis that He had visited upon us and upon Egypt,"* Joseph clarified. "And He has made of me a father to Pharaoh, *but don't any of you bother asking me how that is possible because it's a holy mystery to the entire world!* I am lord of all' his household and ruler over the whole land of Egypt *all because of this idiotic famine and because of Pharaoh's fragmented deranged dreams. I am Lord of this land just like Abraham, Isaac and Pop always wished they were. But those three incompetent fools couldn't even gain control of a desolate place like Canaan!"*

"Wow!" the brothers again exclaimed. "You're the most successful Hebrew ever just because we deposited you into a cistern and were accomplices to the Lord's crazy scheme!" they all whooped together.

"Hurry back then to my father *(who is also your father, so why didn't I say our father, who art in Canaan)* and tell him *this sensational revelation*: 'Thus says your son Joseph: God has made me lord of all Egypt. *Actually, I guess the Lord has made me lord.* Come to me without delay *even though you are an old codger and might cardiac-out while journeying across the hot arid desert,"*

Joseph commanded his brothers. "*If you do not die,* you will settle in the region of Goshen, *a long way from the nearest ocean.* You will be near me, *despite the fact that my brothers hate your guts and resent me because of the discriminatory practice of your bad habit of favoritism.*"

"*Should we tell big Daddy anything else?*" the brothers *curiously asked.*

"*Tell him to* bring you and your children and grandchildren, your flocks and your herds, and everything that you own *along. Tell Pop you all must come to Egypt so that some day our people can be slaves here. It is the Lord's inexplicable mysterious will that must be fulfilled!*"

"*Wouldn't it be a lot easier for all of us to be executed by your imperial guards or simply commit suicide?*" *the frustrated brothers all requested together.*

"Since five years of famine still lie ahead," *Joseph interrupted,* "I will provide for you there *at Goshen far from the ocean* so that you and your family and all that are yours may not suffer want. Surely, you can see for yourselves, *and you do not need to wear eyeglasses although you are often blind to the truth,*" Joseph *admonished his frequently aberrant siblings.* "Benjamin can see for himself, *so he doesn't need any emergency eye operations, either.* He knows that it is I, Joseph, who am *(is)* speaking to you. *I repeat, as is our bad habit of constantly reiterating,* tell my father *(our father, who art in Canaan)* all about my high position in Egypt and all that you have seen *to allow Pop to brag to all his gullible Canaanite neighbors,*" Joseph *boasted and pontificated.* "But hurry and bring my father down here *where the beaches are so hot that your asses and his fat butt will fry like sizzling bacon.*"

Thereupon he *(Joseph) shrank down to the size of a tiny dwarf* and flung himself on the neck of his brother Benjamin and wept. Benjamin *shrank down to the size of an infant* and wept in Joseph's arms. Joseph then *had a homosexual inspiration* and kissed all his brothers *at the same time,* crying over each of them' *as they were lying prone upon the ground.* Only then were his brothers allowed to talk with him *(Joseph) because he finally gave them permission to do so.*

When the news reached Pharaoh's palace that Joseph's brothers had come, *it didn't matter since the palace had no ears as has already been explained. However,* Pharaoh and his courtiers were pleased *with that irrelevant knowledge.*

231

So Pharaoh told Joseph *without even visiting him*, "Say to your brothers: 'This' is what you shall do: Load up your animals and go without delay to the land of Canaan. There get your father and your families, and then come back here to me *because in the future Egypt will need more slaves and lackeys.* I will assign you the best land in Egypt, *regardless that all the land is horrible because of this miserable famine and drought your insane Lord has created and perpetuated.* You will live off the fat *of the skinny* land! *This I guarantee and promise!*"

"Is there anything else I should tell my brothers that are right here at your feet right now listening to our ridiculous numbskull conversation?" Joseph asked the mighty King.

"Instruct them further," *Pharaoh said, ignoring Joseph's brothers lying on the ground (floor) near his filthy feet.* "Do this. 'Take wagons from the land of Egypt *(why not just say Egypt?)* for your children and your wives *(children were more important than women in Egypt as well as they were in Canaan)* and transport your' *decrepit, ailing invalid* father on the way back here, *as Joseph had ordered.* Do not be concerned about your belongings, *for I will send my soldiers to steal them.* The best *of the worst* in the whole land of Egypt shall be yours'."

The *now-illuminated* sons of Israel *saw merit in the Pharaoh's words and in the Lord's new strange enigmatic plan and* acted accordingly. Joseph gave them the wagons, as Pharaoh had ordered, and he supplied them with provisions *and a bevy of horny kinky prostitutes* for the *long* journey *home.*

He *(Joseph)* also gave to each of them 'fresh clothing' *that nastily spoke back to its owners.* To Benjamin Joseph gave three hundred shekels of silver and five sets of garments *to use when sleeping with and to pay for the bevy of horny kinky prostitutes.* Moreover, what he *(Joseph)* sent to his father were ten jack-asses, *one for each of his jack-assed-brothers (except Benjamin).* Each jackass was loaded with the finest products of Egypt and *there were also* ten jennies' *(?)* loaded with bread and grain and other provisions for the *arduous eastern* journey. *However, no silver-plated goblets were secretly hidden in the ten jennies.*

As he *(Joseph)* sent his brothers on their way he told them, "Let there be no recriminations, *incriminations or discriminations* along the way."

So they *(the brothers)* left Egypt and made their way to their father Jacob in Canaan *(is this a new character or a new setting, or what?)* When they *(the brothers)* told him *(Jacob, alias Israel),*

"Joseph is still alive *and well in Egypt*; in fact, it is he who is the ruler *and the yardstick* of all the *doomed* land of Egypt," he was dumbfounded, *just like the old fool was before he heard the good news.* He *(Jacob, a.k.a. Israel)* could not believe them *(his sons) and their testaments (Old and New).*

But when they *(the brothers)* recounted to him *(Jacob) that this story has severe pronoun-antecedent and other grammatical problems* and all that Joseph had told them, his *(Israel's)* spirit was revived. Then Jacob saw the wagons that Joseph had sent for his transport, *and he fainted while thinking and worrying about how wonderful it was that he was eventually going to die while suffering the difficult hot trip to Egypt.*

When Jacob finally returned to consciousness, he said, "My son Joseph is still alive! *I feel strong enough to get laid one last time! Bring on the contingent of horny kinky prostitutes! Then* I must go and see him *in Egypt* before I *dramatically* die *from too much sexual excitement!"*

Chapter Forty-six
"Migration to Egypt"

Israel *(Jacob, who looked a lot like a small nation)* set out with all that was his *including his concubines, slaves, whores and newly acquired luscious prostitutes.* When he arrived at Beer-sheba *(he had lost everybody else along the way), he stopped at the local beer garden to down some tasty and refreshing suds.* Jacob *next* offered sacrifices to the God of his father' Isaac, *who was the God of his forefather Abraham, who was also Israel's (Jacob's) God.* At that place God, speaking to Israel in a vision by night, called, "Jacob! Jacob! *Listen to Me' you uncouth sleepy bones! Get your lazy old butt in gear!"*

"Here I am," he *(Israel/Jacob)* answered. *"How did You' know I was here? I was trying to hide from You' to have some decent peace of mind and fewer near-death experiences before I die! But unfortunately You' are ubiquitous!"*

Then He *(God)* said: "I am God, the God of your father. *I think I was Abraham's God, too, if I recall!* Do not be afraid' *Jacob* to go down to Egypt. *I've been hanging out there lately guarding over Joseph and it's a pretty safe place even for a visiting God to reside.* In Egypt I will make you a great nation *although everyone now knows you as Israel, a humble Hebrew," the Lord revealed.* "I will also bring you back here, after Joseph has closed your eyes *and opened your mind. Hopefully, we can steal some advanced civilization and new-fangled inventions from the Egyptians so that the Hebrews can develop a half-decent more modern civilization! Then you could become conquerors instead of lowly pastoral victims and potential slaves. It all depends on My' whim at that particular moment!"*

So Jacob departed from Beer-sheba *and left the bustling beer garden half-tanked.* The sons of Israel put their' *intoxicated half-dead* father and their wives and children on the wagons that Pharaoh had sent for his *(their)* transport. They took with them their livestock *but left their myriad dead stock behind to be eaten by hungry famine-stricken beer garden patrons.* They also took *and transported* the possessions they had *illegally* acquired *and stolen* in the land of Canaan *(Just say Canaan, will ya'!).*

Thus Jacob and all his descendents *(not to mention slaves, concubines and blood relatives)* migrated to Egypt *to become immigrants and legal aliens.* His *(Jacob's) deviate* sons and his grandsons, *a few who were actually grand* and his daughters and

235

granddaughters *(none of whom were grand)* he took with him *to travel to travail in Egypt.*

These are the names *(as if you're really remotely interested)* of the Israelites, Jacob and his descendents, who migrated to Egypt *in quest of a better life than that which existed in Canaan, the land of the Canaanites that the Lord had promised Abraham, Isaac and Jacob.*

Reuben, Jacob's first born, and the sons of Reuben: Hanoch, *Hanukkah*, Pallu, Hezron, *Enron* and Carmi.

The sons of Simeon: Nemuel, Jamin, *Jasmine, Jazzman,* Ohad, Jachin, Zohar, and 'Shaul', son of a Canaanite woman *that always had cold shoulders and gave one to everyone she encountered or slept with.*

The sons of Levi: Gershon, *Gershwin,* Kohath, *Strauss,* and Merari.

The sons of Judah: Er, *Error, Erroneous,* Onan, Shelah, *Juan,* Perez, *Zero* and Zerah. However, Er and Onan had died in the land of the Canaanites *and were killed for making up false deeds to properties that didn't belong to them.* The sons of Perez were Hezron and Hamul, *but who really cares about this elementary family tree crap?*

The *irascible* sons of Issachar, *who as you might recall, looked like a burned-out ember:* Tola, *Toledo, Ohio,* Puah, Jashub and Shimron.

The *bellicose* sons of Zebulan: *Led,* Sered, *Sir Ed,* Elon, *Elite* and Jahleel.

These were the sons whom Leah bore to Jacob in Padaan-aram, along with his daughter Dinah, *who 'bore' some of them too when she wasn't in the corner blowing somebody's erect horn. That's why in prehistoric times women were considered 'bores' to be bored and stroked by their boorish husbands. Around* thirty-three *or so* persons were in all, *classified* male, female *and neuter.*

The sons of Gad: *Egad, Jihad, Sinbad, Sindbad, Singood, Singgood,* Zephon, *Siphon,* Haggi, *Old Haggi,* Shuni, Ezbon, Eri, A-rod, *A-dick* and Areli.

The sons of Asher: Inmah, *Inmahcar, Sidney, Australia,* Ishvah, Ishvi, *Ish-vi-here* and Beriah, with their sister Serah; and the sons of Beriah: Heber and Malchiel. These were the *listless* descendents of Zulpah *on the list.* Zulpah was the man who Laban had given to his daughter Leah *as a present;* these she bore to Jacob, sixteen persons in all.

The sons of Jacob's wife Rachel: Joseph and Benjamin, *the favored two.* In the land of Egypt Joseph *remained pure and never had sex* but somehow became the father of Manasseh and Ephraim, whom Asenath, daughter of *pot-bellied boorish* Potiphera, priest of Heliopolis 'bore' to him. *As you might have guessed, Asenath was a bore to Joseph, who never did bore and stroke her according to his claim.*

The sons of Benjamin: Bela, *Bella-Bella*, Becher, *Benji*, Ashbel, Gera, *Geratol,* Naaman, Ahiram, Shupham, Hupham, Ard *and Ardvaark.*

The *always barking* sons of Dan: Hushim and *Hushpuppy.*

The sons of Naphtali: *Denale, Denali*, Jahzeel, Guni, *Goonie*, Jezer, *Old Jezer*, Shillem and *Shell-em-good.*

These were the *perverted* sons of Bilhah, whom Laban had given *as gifts* to his daughter Rachel; these she bore to Jacob, seven persons in all.

Jacob's people who migrated to Egypt, his direct descendents, not counting the wives of Jacob's *horny and kinky* sons, numbered *approximately* sixty-six *to eighty-one unlucky ill-starred* persons in all.

Together with Joseph's sons who were born to him *(without any women involved)* in Egypt, two persons, the people *mentioned* comprising Jacob's *psychotic* and *dysfunctional* family. In all they totaled *either* seventy *or eighty-one* persons *even though Basemath was already dead to figure it all out.*

Israel *(Jacob)* had sent Judah *as a courier* ahead to Joseph so that he *(Jacob)* might meet him *(Joseph)* in Goshen, *far from the ocean.* On his arrival in the region of Goshen, Joseph hitched the horses to his chariot, *for the Egyptians were technologically superior to the post-Stone Age Hebrews that were desperately searching for pride, dignity, toilet paper and identity through the practice of their primitive pastoral religion.*

As soon as he *(Joseph)* saw him *(Jacob)*, he flung himself on his neck *(as was the bad custom of the era)* and wept a long time in his arms, *all along wishing he were the town crier instead of the Pharaoh's main man.*

And Israel *(Jacob)* said to Joseph, "At last I can die, now that I have seen for myself that Joseph is still alive. *I can fully attest that living after the age of one hundred and thirty is a lot of fucked-up bullshit!"*

Joseph then said to his *envious* brothers and *to* his father's household: "I will go and inform Pharaoh *that his country's future slaves have arrived*. I shall also tell him: 'My' brothers and my father's *fucked-up* household, whose home is *a tent* in the land of Canaan, have come to me. The men are *primitive prehistoric* shepherds, having long been keepers of livestock *and 'wood stock'*. They have brought with them their flocks and herds, and everything else they own *including some nice-looking harlots and attractive whores'*."

"*Brother Joe,*" said Judah, "*what else are you planning to tell Pharaoh?*"

"When Pharaoh summons you and asks what your occupation is," *Joseph sagely advised*, "you must answer *honestly and forget your innate propensity for lying. This is no time for being facetious or frivolous, or you all might die by being killed.*"

"*What should we say?*" Judah persisted.

"*Say* we are servants *just like our pre-Bronze-Age* ancestors have been *primitive* keepers of livestock from the beginning until now. *I caution you, my clumsy pastoral brothers,*" Joseph *emphasized and empathized*. "In order that you may stay in the region of Goshen *far from the ocean, you must be very careful*. All shepherds are abhorrent to the *intolerant* Egyptians. *Their advanced culture detests all those from inferior civilization that feign barbaric pride and that show and demonstrate rude and crude Hebrew arrogance.*"

238

Chapter Forty-seven
"Settlement in Goshen"

Joseph went and told *his listless buddy* Pharaoh, "My father and my brothers have come from the land of Canaan, *which they do not own and which they have never owned.* They have come with their flocks, their herds, *their slaves, prostitutes, pimps, whores, concubines, harlots* and everything else *legal and illegal* that they own. *And I must relate that* they are now in the region of Goshen, *far from the ocean.*"

He *(Joseph)* then presented to Pharaoh five of his *mentally challenged* brothers whom he had selected from their full number. When Pharaoh asked them what their occupation was, they answered *all together,* "We, your servants, like our *ill-fated* ancestors are shepherds with animal crap *all over the bottom of our smelly sandals.* We have come," they continued, "in order to stay in this country *to see if we can somehow pilfer its wealth away from you as we had tried to do in Canaan but subsequently failed.*"

"We Egyptians don't want to get sheep and goat shit all over our goddamned feet!" objected Pharaoh rather strenuously. *"Then we'll stink just as bad as you Hebrews do and have to wash our damned smelly feet all day long!"*

"Pharaoh," the unimpressive brothers said all at once, "there is no pasture for your servants in the land of Canaan, so severe has the famine *that the Lord has visited upon us* been back there. Please, therefore, let your servants settle in the region of Goshen, far from the ocean. We'll give you all of the lamb chops you need or want! And we'll even occasionally bust your chops if that's okay with you!"*

Pharaoh said to Joseph, *"I fuckin' hate lamb chops even more than I hate having my chops busted, I swear by Cheops! But because I like you Joey Boy* your brothers may settle in the region of Goshen *far from the ocean,* and if you know any of them to be qualified, you may put them in charge of my own livestock. *I just had my chief shepherd executed for walking into my palace with cruddy sheep shit on the bottom of his sandals. That is what happens when one gets too careless and develops a Khafre (carefree) attitude."*

Thus, when Jacob and his sons came to Joseph in Egypt, and Pharaoh, king of Egypt heard about it, Pharaoh said to Joseph, *"Joey baby, everything's gonna' be cool.* Now that your father and your *fucked-up* brothers' have come to you, *we have set them up to eventually become our slaves.* The land of Egypt is at your disposal;

even at your garbage disposal; settle your *incompetent and incontinent* father and your *mentally challenged* brothers in the pick of the land, *which is best suited for future institutionalized slavery."*

Then Joseph brought his father and 'presented' him *as a gift* to Pharaoh.

Pharaoh asked him *(Jacob),* "How many years have you lived? *You look like you should have died seven decades if not centuries ago!"*

Jacob *humbly* replied: *"Believe it or not kind Pharaoh, I still get an occasional erection, and that's what really keeps me going on a daily basis. As for your pertinent question,* I have lived as a wayfarer to the age of one hundred and thirty years," *Jacob disclosed.* "Few and hard have been these years of my *wasted* life; *however,* they do not compare to the years that my *worthless degenerate* ancestors *also* lived as *asshole aimless* wayfarers." Then *the regretful* Jacob bid Pharaoh farewell and withdrew from his presence *before he himself involuntarily became a gift of human property.*

As Pharaoh had ordered, Joseph settled his father and brothers in Egypt, *which was a very unsettling experience for Joseph to pursue.* He gave them holdings on the pick of the land, in the region of 'Rameses', *far from Paddan-aram.* And Joseph sustained his father and brothers and his father's whole household, *which almost bankrupted (in the process) Pharaoh's royal treasury.* Even the youngest got food *and extra spending money for hookers and gambling. Joseph personally saw to that.*

Since there was no food in any country because of the extreme severity of the famine *the Lord had maliciously produced,* the lands of Egypt and Canaan were languishing from hunger *(not to mention the people in those lands languishing from starvation).* Joseph *confiscated* and gathered in all the money in Canaan and in Egypt. He put the money in Pharaoh's palace *and stacked it all in a big pyramid.*

When all the money in Canaan and Egypt was spent, *the pyramid of coins and shekels had suddenly and coincidentally disappeared. Joseph's risky 'pyramid scheme' had failed.* All the Egyptians *(that had not yet died in the severe famine)* came to Joseph and pleaded *all at once,* "Give us food or we shall perish under your eyes, *and the stench from our rotting bodies will give you a very serious eye infection. All our money is gone, lost in the livestock market and in your incomprehensible complex 'Khufu' pyramid scheme'!"*

240

"Since your money is *permanently* gone," Joseph replied, "give me your livestock, and I will sell you bread in return for your livestock."

"Don't you mean you will trade us bread for our livestock?" yelled back a disgruntled Egyptian merchant. "Selling is the wrong terminology to use! Let's employ the correct language here! You specifically meant trading or bartering and not selling!"

"I stand corrected because I don't like being admonished when I'm sitting down!" Joseph sincerely apologized.

"So they *(the Egyptians, how many of them we don't know or even care to know)* brought their livestock to Joseph, and he 'sold' *(traded or bartered)* to them food for their' horses *because Joseph liked to horse around with fancy chariots a lot.* He also traded for their flocks of sheep and herds of cattle, and their donkeys, *becoming a very proficient animal flesh trader and animal slaughter activist.*

Thus he (Joseph) got them through the year with bread for all of their livestock, *swindling them (the native Egyptians) out of a small fortune in livestock.*

When that *very profitable* year ended *for Joseph,* they *(the impoverished indigent Egyptians)* came to him *(Joseph)* and said: *"You fuckin' ripped us off you lousy chiseler!* We cannot hide from my lord that, with our money spent and our livestock missing has been *wickedly* turned over into my *lord's new money pyramid," they all said and protested together (for the Egyptians were now being corrupted by the Hebrews' business practices that were detrimentally infesting the formerly pristine town).* Nothing *of value* is left to put at my lord's disposal. *Apparently* the only things left are our *fatigued* bodies and our *mortgaged-to-the-hilt* farm land."

"Have you losers ever done any striptease dancing in beer gardens?" Joseph wondered and asked. "You can make minimum wages there if you know how to take off your garments in a way that pleases the tough audience. You'll get paid in grain and you'll get laid in straw," Joseph added. "I hear some patrons are generous tippers and even put olives and papyrus leaves down the tight underwear of dancers that are recognized as good strippers."

"My lord," said the *infuriated* Egyptians *all together,* "this is a time when we must get serious about the prospect of dying. Why should the native residents and our useless land perish before your very eyes *in favor of these repulsive resilient Hebrews that cause trouble wherever they roam*? Take we Egyptians and our land in exchange for food. *We will gladly trade our bodies and some good sex for some basic nourishment."*

"Do you mean you actually want to live and suffer some more?" Joseph *incredulously stated and then laughed.* "What a bunch of wifty knuckleheads you pretenders are! Don't you understand that you all would be better off dead? You ought to regard it as a pleasure to have an opportunity to finally escape more harsh suffering on this despicable planet."

"We will become Pharaoh's slaves and our *personal* land his property," *the Egyptians pleaded and bitched.* "Only give us seed that we may survive and not perish, and that our land may not turn into a *total* waste. *We want to be crazy in the head just like those goddamned lucky favored troublemaking Hebrew trespassers are!"*

Thus Joseph *shrewdly* acquired all the *formerly productive* farmland of Egypt for Pharaoh, *who would rather screw hordes of whores and other loose women than worry a wet fart about silly things like his dedicated native people dying all over the damned country while the uneducated coarse Hebrews were being treated like the King's privileged guests.*

The famine was too much for *the average* Egyptian to bear. Every Egyptian sold his field, so the land passed over to Pharaoh, *who was screwing all the women while Joseph was screwing all the landowners out of their houses, life savings and homesteads.* The *native* people were reduced to slavery, from one end of Egypt's territory to the other, *stretching all the way to Goshen not far from the ocean.*

Only the priests' lands Joseph did not take over. Since the priests had a fixed allowance from Pharaoh and lived off the allowance that Pharaoh had given them, *Joseph figured it would be too difficult to swindle them out of their favored property.* So the priests did not have to sell their *indigenous* land, *although they used most of their' allowance to court horny kinky prostitutes at the local beer garden and at the greedy Pharaoh's widely acclaimed decadent orgies.*

Joseph told the *Egyptian* people: "How does it feel to be skillfully fucked by a real pro? Now that I have acquired you and your land for Pharaoh, here is your seed for sowing the land. But when the harvest is in, you must give a fifth of it to Pharaoh *so that I can bankrupt you even more than you are being bankrupt right now with fabulous high-interest loan shark rates!"*

"Why don't you just give us the royal salami some more!" *jeered the incensed crowd in unison.* "We're all mighty pissed off

242

because we've all been pissed on by you and our fuckin' arrogant jerk off Pharaoh!"

"While you keep your four-fifths as seed for your fields," *Joseph shouted from a safe balcony while standing over the protesting voices,* "keep that share as food for yourselves and your families."

"You're about as generous as an unkempt swine with not enough to eat in his crap laden trough!" the angry crowd shouted in unison at Joseph.

"If you don't start cheering me soon instead of complaining," Joseph threatened, "I predict that you all will be executed in the bizarre bazaar marketplace at dawn!"

"You have saved our lives!" *the Egyptians yelled in chorus. "We are tired of being free men!* We are grateful to my lord, *who art in Egypt* that we can be *benevolent* Pharaoh's *loyal* slaves."

Thus Joseph made it a law for the land of Egypt, which is still in force, that a fifth of its produce should go to Pharaoh *to spend on loose women and on horny kinky prostitutes.* Only the land of the priests did not pass over to Pharaoh *because the priests were Pharaoh's cronies and his drinking pals that joined the King in celebrating his legendary wild and crazy orgies.*

Thus Israel *(Jacob, not the country)* settled in the Land of Egypt, in the region of Goshen-*by-the-Sea, far from the ocean.* There they *(his crude and rude people) illicitly* acquired property, were fertile, *more so than the land,* and increased greatly *by virtue of proper dieting and good sex.*

Jacob lived in the land of Egypt for seventeen years. The span of his life came to a hundred and forty-seven years *of toil, grief, misery, suffering, sacrifice and all the other cruel joys of human existence on this screwed-up globe.*

When the time approached for Israel to die, he called his son Joseph and said to him: *"Quit fuckin' the poor Egyptian people!* If you really wish to please me," *the father said,* "put you hand under my thigh *so that I may enjoy one final erection and possibly be rewarded with one small final orgasm. What a way to go!"*

"But father, if you don't orgasm you will continue to live," Joseph stated. "I will see that you don't shoot your messy seeds all over my hand or for that matter all over the damned place!"

"Your hand under my thigh will be a sign of your constant loyalty to me," *Jacob explained to his sometimes' recalcitrant son.* "Do not let me be buried in Egypt *where the dirt is too fertile to contain my decaying remains. I want you to bury me in Canaan where the land the Lord promised my forefathers has not yet been delivered to us because the Lord is now hanging out in Egypt with you!"*

"Father, you're making no sense at all," Joseph critically indicated, *"and I think you're being too irrational and delirious on your deathbed!"*

"When I lie down with my ancestors," *Jacob said,* "we won't be able to have any more sex because all of us will be dead. *So what's the sense of lying down with my ancestors? That's what the fuck I want to know!"*

"Father, you definitely are now being a definite dimwitted psycho!" Joseph exclaimed. *"Who needs to listen to this stupid shit?"*

"Have me taken out of Egypt and buried in their burial place *back home,"* gasped Jacob. *"I want to be with my grandfather Abraham and with my father Isaac."*

"I will do as you say," *Joseph sobbed, "only because I'm afraid you'll put a wicked curse on me if I don't enact your wishes. Even on your deathbed you still could be a prick and a half!"*

But his father *further* demanded, "Swear it to me *or I will curse you for the rest of your days, you disobedient little bastard!"*

So Joseph swore to him. Then Israel bowed at the head of the bed *and joined his ancestors in nowhere' land, but then he came back to life and did not die as he had planned.*

244

Chapter Forty-eight
"Jacob and Joseph's Family"

Some time afterward, Joseph was informed *(by an unknown source)*: "Your father is failing *biology but the old stubborn fart still breathes and his spirit refuses to expire.*" So he *(Joseph, not the unknown source)* took along with him his two "*I don't give a shit*" sons, Manasseh and Ephraim *for immoral support to visit Jacob.* When Jacob was told *(by a second unknown source),* "Your rich *favored* son *that has gotten rich on his own without the aid of your squandered inheritance* has come to *see* you," he *(the old clutching tenacious coot)* rallied his strength. Jacob sat up in bed. *His old decrepit body was a hundred times more erect than his withered shriveled penis was.*

Jacob then said to Joseph: "*You have come to watch me die like the faithful son you are.* God Almighty appeared to me, *a regular loser* at Luz in the land of Canaan, *which He had promised Abraham, Isaac and me. I am tired of all His hollow, hallowed broken promises! My life has been plagued with disappointment and failure just as surely as the Lord's harrowing famine has weakened Canaan and Egypt.*"

"*What did the Lord have to say?*" Joseph curiously asked. "*He's been pretty cool with me. I can't complain, and I'm not even on my damned deathbed.*"

"First He blessed me, *but I don't think the blessing has worked too well. Somewhere along the line it has badly backfired.* He said, 'I will make you fertile and numerous,' *but Joseph, I have been fertile but have remained but one person all these fuckin' miserable years. I haven't been able to interpret the second part of His nebulous prediction. Damn it, son, I'm still Jacob, but now, thank Heaven, I'm finally dying whether my accursed name is Jacob or Israel.*"

"*Maybe the Lord meant that by being fertile your warped and cursed genes will produce many unfortunate offspring in the future,*" Joseph, *an expert on symbolism clarified.* "*Your honored sons shall constitute the forthcoming twelve tribes of Israel.*"

"*Then the Lord added,*" Jacob remembered and said to Joseph and his two disinterested sons, "I will raise you into an assembly *of twelve post Stone Age* tribes, and I will give this land to your descendents *as I have also vaguely promised Abraham and Isaac.* After you *become deceased,* they will have this land *from the Canaanites* as a *treasured* permanent possession."

"How will this miracle happen?" I (Jacob) asked the Lord.

"Your two *grand*sons, therefore, who were born to 'you' *(a male)* in the land of Egypt before I joined you here, shall be Mine'," *the Lord said, "because I have no wife yet to have children of My' own. Devoted goddesses are hard to find these days. They avoid this famine part of the world as if it was a plague."*

"What do you actually mean Lord?" I (the senile Jacob on his deathbed) asked and repeated to Joseph.

"Ephraim and Manasseh shall be Mine' just as much as Reuben and Simeon are Mine'. *Mine', Mine', Mine, I say! Not hearsay! I say! Do you get it now Jacob? How thick and dense your cranium must be!"*

"Okay," I granted, "You're super lonely and You' want to take my kids and grandsons that I've never before seen away from me because You' favor me and will likewise favor them. No big loss," Jacob declared.

"What did the Lord say next?" Joseph inquired.

"Progeny born to you after them *(Ephraim and Manasseh)* shall remain yours *and remain to Israel,"* Jacob related to Joseph. "But their inheritance shall be recorded in the names of their two brothers."

"More complicated incomprehensible soap opera bullshit!" Joseph protested. "Father, you would have had better luck if you were tossed down a cistern by your other' sons like I had been hurled into one by my envious brothers!"

"Joseph," Jacob interrupted from his deathbed, "I do this because when I was returning from Paddan-*aram with my sheep,* your mother Rachel *got fed up with life and with me* and died. *This was* to my sorrow during the journey into Canaan while we were still a short distance from Ephrath, *which, as you know is not on any damned map anywhere.* And I buried her *(Rachel)* there on the way to Ephrath (that is, Bethlehem. *In the old days, a place was often two places just like Joseph's father was really two people', Jacob and Israel).*

When Israel *(Jacob)* saw Joseph's *punk pugnacious* sons, he asked, "Who are these *young hooligans? They look like they're active juvenile delinquents!"*

"They are my *disobedient troublemaking* sons," Joseph answered his father. "And God has given me them here *so that I can enjoy the pleasure of suffering just as you have endured over the years."*

246

"Bring them to me," said his father, "that I may bless them *despite the fact that I am bankrupt, near death and a financial failure on my deathbed. On second thought my blessing might indeed truly be a vile curse.*"

(Now Israel's *gray* eyes were dim from old age, *just like his brain was dim from old age.* He could not see well. *His vision was very poor as it also had been for his family's welfare during his whole life span). Although he wished he still lived in 'Asia Minor', Jacob was now totally 'incontinent'.*

When Joseph brought his sons close to him *(Jacob),* he *(Jacob)* kissed and embraced them *(Ephraim and Manasseh), and the two boys both simultaneously yelped: "Phooey! More nasty genetic halitosis!"*

Then Israel *(Jacob)* said to Joseph, "I never expected to see your face again, *but now that I have, I am thoroughly disappointed in how fate ingeniously operates.* Now God has allowed me to see *on my deathbed* your *juvenile delinquent decadent* descendents as well, *and now I am doubly disappointed and my fatigued spirit is absolutely ready to die.*"

Joseph removed them *(Ephraim and Manasseh)* from his father's *bony* knees *(Jacob was lying in bed, and the two corpulent but petulant boys weighed three hundred pounds each).* Joseph *then respectfully* bowed down before him *(Jacob)* with his face to the ground *(there was no floor in the house (tent), only dirt, sand and gravel as usual) and the visitor got plenty of dirt up his nostrils.*

Then Joseph took the two *insolent ungrateful children,* Ephraim with his right hand, to Israel's *(Jacob's)* left *side,* and Manasseh with his left hand *clenched in a fist, in a cumbersome fashion* to Jacob's *immediate* right. He *(Joseph)* led them *(Ephraim and Manasseh)* to him *(Jacob).*

But Israel *(Jacob),* crossing his *arthritic* hands, put his right hand and laid it on the head of *the grimacing* Ephraim, although he was *a tad younger than Manasseh was.* Then Jacob placed his left hand on the head of *the snarling* Manasseh, although he was the first-born. *All of this was done (according to family tradition and the Lord's arcane will) to show that Ephraim was mistakenly blessed (cursed) while Manasseh (the first-born) would be disfavored (blessed) Does this plot pattern seem all-too-familiar? Biblical history predictably repeats itself!*

Then he *(Jacob)* blessed them *(Ephraim and Manasseh)* with these *uninspiring* words:

"May the God in Whose' unpredictable and mysterious ways my 'fathers' Abraham *(Jacob's forefather or grandfather)* and Isaac *(Jacob's father)* walked,

The God Who' has been my shepherd *in our inferior pastoral existence, shunning science and technology and the Bronze Age* from my birth to this day,

The Angel that has delivered me from all harm *and that has kept me away from the reward of death,* bless these boys

That in them *(Ephraim and Manasseh)* my name *(Jacob or Israel)* be recalled,

And the names of my *two* 'fathers', Abraham and Isaac,

So forget my two wives that were both mothers, my sons' wives, whoever those second-class females were.'

"I pray that they *(Ephraim and Manasseh)* may become teeming multitudes *and not ornery crowds or riotous mobs* upon this *reprehensible* earth, *for the Lord needs more worshipers to expand His' insane policies in regard to human life on this atrocious planet!"*

Joseph saw that his father had laid his right hand on Ephraim's head *(the second born. It didn't matter whether the first-born was mentally retarded or not. The first-born was always supposed to be favored through inheritance but it always seemed to turn out the reverse).*

Joseph took hold of his father's *trembling* hand to remove it from Ephraim's head and *rightfully* place it on Manasseh's head *(who Joseph favored).*

Joseph *with fervent conviction* said, "That is not right, father. The other son is the first-born *and should be favored, causing hatred and resentment among brothers' as has been our hallmark family tradition.* Lay your hand on the head of Manasseh. *Do something right for a change before you die you vile mentally inferior dirtball!"*

But his father *(Jacob), who was in the advanced stages of senility,* resisted *Joseph's rational request.* "I know it son," he said, "I know it, *but I must be an avid ball-breaker right to the very end.* That one too *(Manasseh)* shall be a tribe *where the bullshit shall run rampant. I predict it here on my deathbed. He too shall be great and deceiving, just like Abraham, Isaac and me!* Nevertheless, his younger brother *(Ephraim)* shall surpass him *(Manasseh).* His *(Ephraim's)* descendents shall become a multitude of more *fucked-up* nations!"

248

So when he *(Jacob)* blessed them *(Ephraim and Manasseh)* that day *and said in a low raspy tone of voice*, "By you shall the people of Israel *(me)* pronounce blessings *(curses and cursing)*. May they say, 'God make you like Ephraim and Manasseh, *and may the best man win'!*" He (Jacob) placed Ephraim before Manasseh *just to break Manasseh's balls and the balls of all of first-born in Manasseh's future generations.*

Then Israel *(Jacob)* said to Joseph *in a hoarse hardly audible voice*: "I am about to die, *thank Heaven!* But God will be with you and will restore you to the land of your fathers, *although we both know that you are much better off in Egypt as an authority figure than in the Promised Land of your fathers that still belongs to the damned Canaanites," Jacob weakly uttered.* "As for me, I give to you *(Joseph)*, as to the one above his brothers, Shechem, the *worthless deserted* city that I had captured from the Amorites with my *rusty* sword and *my flimsy* bow. *Shechem too was hit big-time by the oppressive famine, and it is completely abandoned. You deserve to own it, son!"*

Chapter Forty-nine
"Jacob's Testament"

Jacob called his sons and said: "Gather around, so that my *demented senile* mind may tell you what is to happen to you in the *inglorious* days to come, *for I have been hallucinating many delusional* things. You will be the ancestors *in a long line of assholes that are genetically sure* to follow." *Then the dying Jacob proceeded.*

"Assemble and listen *to my exaggerated bullshit,* sons of Jacob, listen to Israel, your *feeble, irrational lunatic prevaricating* father," *Jacob uttered as he began stating his last will and testament.*

"You, Reuben, *king of deli sandwiches,* are my first-born, my strength and the first fruit of my manhood, *for I remember that particular orgasm very well despite my failing mind. You are* excelling in rank and excelling in power, *whatever the hell that fucked up jargon means!" Jacob disclosed. "We really need more damned words in our lackluster language; you inbred hedonistic idiots all know that!" the patriarch emphasized.*

"Unruly as water, you *(Reuben)* shall no longer excel, for you climbed into your father's bed, *had homosexual relations with queer men while you were supposed to only be screwing horny whores and kinky prostitutes, and therefore* defiled by my couch *and by my crotch, much* to my great sorrow." *Jacob then took a deep gasp.*

"Simeon and Levi, brothers indeed, *blue canvass material* and weapons of violence are those *knaves'* knives. *May you both contract life-threatening' venereal' diseases' and suffer the fuckin' consequences." There was a momentary pause as Jacob struggled to inhale his next breath.*

"Let not my soul enter their *(Simeon and Levi's)* council *chambers,* or my spirit be joined with their company, *which makes absolutely no freakin' sense at all, deathbed or no damned deathbed. Life's a bitch and then you die and disintegrate. It's blatantly that simple," the father lamented.*

"For in their *(Simeon and Levi's)* fury they 'slew' *a slue* of men, and in their willfulness they maimed oxen, *and let me tell you, not by 'oxidant', either. That's why your accursed descendents will be more 'Oxidental' (Occidental) than Oriental," the old fool stated.*

"Cursed be their *(Simeon and Levi's)* fury so fierce and their rage so 'cruel' *as tainted poisoned crullers are deadly!" Jacob blurted out.*

251

"I will scatter them *(Simeon and Levi)* 'in Jacob *(me)*', and disperse them throughout Israel, *so now all I have to do is figure out how the two of you will enter my body and then I can die, hopefully with you two imbeciles situated inside me. In addition, we all still have to learn how to use pronouns correctly when we speak,"* Israel advised.

"You Judah, like a lion's whelp, you have grown up on prey *and venison, you frisky denizen.* My son, he crouches like a lion recumbent, *feeling incumbent to attack.* The king of beasts-who would dare rouse him, *except maybe his horny wife!" the old idiot babbled.*

"The scepter shall never depart from Judah, *for as we all know scepters have no legs and cannot walk, run, sprint or depart anywhere,"* the expiring fellow ranted.

"Or the mace shall not depart from between his *(Judah's)* legs *or else he would be severely 'penal-ized'. After my imminent death, all of you please bring some order and logic to this thoroughly fucked-up world,"* Israel begged.

"While tribute is brought to him *(Judah)*, he receives the people's homage *and the faggot men's gay homosexuality,"* the father declared.

"He (Judah) tethers his donkey to the vine, and his purebred ass to the choicest stem, *the stupid ass! Learn to ride a damned horse and forget about that asinine donkey of yours!" Jacob* pleaded.

"In wine he *(Judah)* washes his garments *because he can't distinguish between water and wine when it comes to rinsing things off.* His robes are washed in the blood of *sour* grapes *before he disrobes, the dizzy fool,"* the crazed old gent uttered.

"His (Judah's) eyes are darker than wine, *so he shouldn't fight with his fists so often against skilled boxers or against back alley pugilists.* His teeth are whiter than milk *because he paints them, the conceited bastard,"* the demented codger opined.

"Zebulun, *who 'led' his people, since they obviously refused to have 'led Zebulun'.* Zebulun shall dwell by the seashore *but not near Goshen far from the ocean (this means a shore for ships that might unexpectedly 'barge in' from time to time).* And his flank shall be based on Sidon, *unless, of course, Zebulun is out-flanked by ambitious flankers,"* the confused clansman prattled.

"*I'm thoroughly amazed that all you assholes are still standing around listening to my idiotic litany.* Issachar is a rawboned asshole," *Jacob continued, "whose hot embers are crouching low*

252

between the saddlebags. Get off your ass once in a while and ride a chariot like your more ambitious brother Joseph does."

The old man's parched tongue licked his lips. "When he *(Issachar)* saw how good a settled life was, and how pleasant the country *but how hostile the people he said, 'Holy shit!' and* he bent his shoulder to the burden and became a toiling 'serf' *without any surf nearby to comfort his lost ailing soul."*

"Dan shall achieve justice for his kindred, like any other *wild and uncivilized* tribe of Israel *(me)," Jacob maintained.*

"Let Dan be a serpent by the roadside, *which is one level above being a yellow-bellied snake in the grass. Dan shall create a new generation of vipers. This bullshit is what I predict as part of my legacy," the failing coot insisted.*

"That bites the horse's heel, so that *the heel makes* the rider tumble backward. What the fuck am I thinking and saying?" *he blabbered.*

"I long for your deliverance, O Lord, *O Lord do I long for deliverance," Jacob driveled.*

"Gad shall be raided by 'raiders' *(egad, how about using the more sophisticated words marauders or plunderers, here),* but he shall raid' *(attack?)* at their' heels *but not at their more vulnerable Achilles' heels," Jacob jabbered.*

"Asher's produce is rich, and he shall furnish *dainty* dainties to kings, *you big sweetie with your satin underwear, you!"*

After groaning and grunting, Jacob persisted, "Naphtali is a hind let loose, *which then indiscriminately craps on the ground* and then brings forth lovely 'fawns' *to faun each other and then watch them 'faunacate'."*

"Effervescent Joseph is a wild 'colt' *that joined the Egyptian cult.* He is a wild colt by spring, a wild ass on the hillside, *looking for wild-ass parties and outrageous orgies with the Pharaoh and his chief priests," Israel yapped.*

"Harrying and attacking, the archer opposed him *(Joseph), but that was an 'arrowneous' (erroneous) thing on his part to do.* But each one's bow remained *as* stiff *and firm as a good erection,* as their arms were unsteady *as real jerk offs' hands and arms are upon achieving a well-earned climax," the dying man illogically articulated.*

"By the power of the Mighty One of Jacob, because of the Shepherd, the 'Rock' of Israel *and other types of acceptable music,* the God of your father, Who' helps you blunder *as I and my forefathers have blundered incessantly,"*

"God Almighty, Who' blesses you *with false land promises, floods, famines and other wicked devastations,"*

"With the blessings *(curses)* of Heaven above, the blessings of the abyss that crouches below *(whatever that obscure terminology means),"*

"The blessings of *big succulent* breasts and *wet and hairy pink* wombs, the blessings of fresh grain and *poisoned* blossoms,"

"The blessings of everlasting mountains, *or the blessings of robust female chests that look like everlasting mountains,* and the delights of the eternal hills, *where all of us got laid in the prime of our youths,"* Jacob triumphantly proclaimed.

"May they *(the bountiful blessings)* rest on the head of Joseph, on the brow of the prince *that lives* near his *inferior and totally inadequate* big *bullying* brothers," *Israel demanded.*

"Benjamin is a ravenous wolf *that looks like a raven having a wolf's appetite*; mornings he devours the prey *without even praying; and during the* evenings he distributes the spoils *and then wipes his hairy ass with the spoils he does not distribute,"* the baffled patriarch recklessly gabbed.

All these *offspring were the founders* of what were the ten *primitive, archaic* tribes of Israel *(Jacob).* This is what their father said about them, as he bade them farewell and gave to each of them an appropriate *meaningless and obscure* message.

Then he *(Jacob)* gave this charge: "Since I am about to be taken to my 'kindred' *to be a kindred spirit with them,* bury me *and my debts* with my fathers in the cave that lies in the field of Ephron the Hittite. The *secret* cave is *clandestinely camouflaged* in the field of Machpelah, facing on Mamre, *somewhere* in *a remote section of* the land of Canaan," *the dying Israel solemnly declared.* "This is the field that Abraham *(my grandfather)* bought for a burial ground from Ephron the *hypocritical* Hittite, *who really mercilessly ripped old Dishonest Abe off!"* Jacob reviewed.

"That sounds like a rather grave situation indeed, Father," Joseph said and evaluated. "Tell us more about this well' concealed cave that you have alluded to."

"Abraham and his wife Sarah are buried there, and so are Isaac and his wife Rebekah. *It's really a pretty neat secluded off-the-beaten path cemetery.* I buried Leah there, also. Abraham had purchased the field and the cave from Ephron the Hittite, *but there is no deed or document confirming the transaction,"* Jacob informed Joseph and his apathetic brothers. *"So like everything else in my*

254

empty and sorrowful life, even my burial site is in dispute. Thus shall be the legacy of the Hebrews. "

When Jacob had finished giving these *invaluable opaque* instructions to his *attention-deficit* sons, he 'drew' his feet into the bed *symbolically using black crayons to draw his feet*, breathed his last, and was *immediately* taken to his kindred' *spirits by unknown supernatural forces or possibly by unknown, invisible, unidentified flying objects.*

Chapter Fifty
"Jacob's Funeral"

Joseph threw himself on his father's face', *breaking Jacob's nose in two places and thus hastening the patriarch's death by means of suffocation.* Joseph wept over him *(Israel)* as he kissed him, *licking away the blood from Jacob's broken nose.* Then he ordered the physicians in his service to embalm his father, *even though Jacob was still barely alive but comatose.*

When they *(the physicians/funeral directors)* embalmed Israel they spent forty days at it, *learning their craft by on-the-job-training,* for that is the full period of embalming *that it took slow learners to master.*

The *more maudlin* Egyptians 'mourned' Jacob for seventy *mornings.* When that period of mourning was over Joseph spoke to Pharaoh's courtiers: "Please do me this favor," he said, "and convey to Pharaoh this request of mine, *a fast song I would like to hear the King's royal rappers perform.* My father, at the point of death, made me promise on oath to bury him in the *remote, obscure, opaque* tomb that he had prepared for himself 'in the *inhospitable* land of Canaan'!" *Joseph sobbed. (Just please say Canaan, will you!)* "May I go up there to bury my father and then come back? *I promise to be a good boy while away from Egypt!"*

Pharaoh, *who never received the message from the not-too-swift royal courtiers* replied *from the other side of the city*: "Go and bury your father *along with his foolish debts, as he made you promise on 'oath', the big old dead oaf!"*

So Joseph left Egypt to bury his father, *smartly remembering to take Jacob's body along with him.* With him went all of Pharaoh's officials that were senior members of the *royal supreme* court and all the other dignitaries of Egypt, *whom Pharaoh hoped would die on the dangerous journey to Canaan.*

Joseph's whole household, his brothers and his father's household *also* went *on the several-hundred-mile-long funeral procession into the barren desert wasteland.* Only their' children and their flocks and herds were left in the region of Goshen, *far from the nearest ocean.* Chariots, too, and charioteers pushing their chariots *(for they had no horses)* went up with him; it was a very large retinue.

When they *(the traveling funeral procession)* arrived at Goren-ha-atad, *the capital of Goran-ha-atad-small-place,* which is beyond the Jordan River, *and beyond our comprehension,* they held there a very great and solemn memorial service *for a baby pet kitten that had died from neglect along the way.*

Then Joseph observed seven days of mourning for his *stone-cold* father. When the *pastoral* Canaanites that inhabited the land saw the mourning at Goran-ha-atad, they said *all together,* "What *the fuck's going on down there?* This looks like a solemn funeral the Egyptians are having, *but it might be a sinister Hebrew trick in disguise to steal our valueless land and to circumcise the circumference off our sensitive peckers!"*

That is why the place is named Abel-mizraim. It is *shaped like a circumcised penis and* is located *just* beyond the Jordan River.

Thus Jacob's sons did for him as he had instructed. They carried him to the land of Canaan, which still belonged to the Canaanites outside of the little field and cave *that had been bought from Ephron the Hittite.* They *(the sons)* buried him *(Jacob)* in the *remote* cave in the *rural* field of Machpelah, facing on Mamre, the field that Abraham had bought for a burial ground from Ephron the Hittite, *who was no relation to or friend of Ahab the Arab.*

After Joseph *and his brothers* had *finally* buried Jacob, he returned to Egypt with his brothers and with *the hookers and whores and* all *the other creeps and weirdos in his gaudy-looking entourage* that had gone up with him for the burial of his father.

Now that their' father *(Jacob)* was dead *and buried,* Joseph's brothers became fearful. The brothers thought, *(not only did they speak the same words simultaneously but also they thought the same thoughts coincidentally),* 'Suppose Joseph has been nursing a *terrible* grudge against us and now plans to pay us back in full for all the wrong we did him!' *they all communicated using primitive mental telepathy.*

So they *(the brothers)* approached Joseph and said, "Before your father died *(who is also our father, who art in the cave),* he gave us these *specific* instructions: You shall say to Joseph, 'Jacob begs you to forgive the criminal wrongdoing of your *criminal* brothers, who treated you so cruelly *before, during and after the felonious cistern incident.* Please, therefore forgive the crimes that we, the servants of your father's God, had *grievously* committed. *If you do, we'll kiss your lily-white ass every single day for hours at a time."*

When they *(the brothers)* spoke these words to him, Joseph broke into tears *because a spider had entered his robe and had chewed up half his scrotum.*

258

Then his (*Joseph's*) *zany* brothers proceeded to fling themselves down before him *pretending to be arachnids*, and they said, "Let us be your *personal tarantula* slaves*! We'll make for you web sites all over the world and our fucked-up followers will eagerly dance the tarantella!*"

But Joseph replied to them: "Have no fear, *you 'Euphrates' cats'*. Can I take the place of God? Even though you *cruelly* meant harm to me, God meant it for good, to achieve His' present *obscure* end *and purpose*, the survival of many people *as we stay out of harm's way of the Lord,"* Joey explained to his former kangaroo court. "Therefore *brothers* have no fear. I will provide for you and *for your no-good lazy parasitic* children, *too*." By thus speaking kindly to them *(his criminal brothers)*, he *(Joseph)* reassured them *that they would not be deservedly slaughtered.*

Joseph remained in Egypt *while Jacob's remains remained in the cave up near Canaan*. He stayed *in mourning* with his *fellow family members.* Joseph lived a hundred and ten years *of grief, anguish, agony and pure aggravation.* He saw Ephraim's children to the third generation, and the children of Manasseh's son Machir were also born on Joseph's knee, *as Joseph held his knee up to Machir's wife's vagina when she prolifically delivered.*

Joseph said to his *criminal* brothers (*Where were they? When? We need a damned setting here*!): "I am about to die. God will surely take care of you and lead you out of this land to the land that He' had *fraudulently and facetiously* promised on oath to Abraham, Isaac and to *our father who is in Canaan* Jacob."

"Who gives a rat's shit!" the criminal brothers all inharmoniously yelled together. "Who gives a rat's ass's shit!" they repeated in true bona fide Hebrew fashion.

He *(Joseph) diplomatically ignored their justified protests and calmly* continued: "When God thus takes care of you, *I hope He' does you in good and gives you the royal Heavenly shaft.* You must bring my bones up with you from this place. *Hey Bros', where the frig' are we' anyway? What the hell's the goddamned setting? I'm now just as confused as parsimonious Abraham, Isaac and Jacob were on their deathbeds!*"

Joseph *sadly* died at the age of a hundred and ten. *(Must we' tell you again that insignificant fact!).* He was embalmed and *gently* laid to rest in a coffin in Egypt. *All of his brothers had developed severe allergies to embalming fluids and were coughin' around the coffin every morning for the full forty days of official mourning.*

259

About the Author

Jay Dubya is author John Wiessner's initials (J.W.) and also his pen name. John is a retired New Jersey public school English teacher, having taught the subject for thirty-four years. John lives in Hammonton, New Jersey with wife Joanne, and the couple has three grown sons. The book *So Ya' Wanna' Be A Teacher* chronicles Jay Dubya's public school teaching career.

Jay Dubya has written other adult fiction besides *The Wholly Book of Genesis* and its companion book *The Wholly Book of Exodus*. *Black Leather and Blue Denim, A '50s Novel* and its sequel, *The Great Teen Fruit War, A 1960' Novel* are humorous "coming of age" adventure books. *Frat' Brats, A '60s Novel* completes Jay Dubya's action/adventure trilogy. *Pieces of Eight, Pieces of Eight, Part II, Pieces of Eight, Part III* and *Pieces of Eight, Part IV* are short story/novella collections featuring science fiction, paranormal and humorous plots and themes. *Nine New Novellas, Nine New Novellas, Part II, Nine New Novellas, Part III* and *Nine New Novellas, Part IV* are also sci-fi/paranormal story collections.

Ron Coyote, Man of La Mangia is adult humor and a satire/parody on Miguel Cervantes' *Don Quixote*, published in 1605. *Mauled Maimed Mangled Mutilated Mythology* is adult satirical literature that retells twenty-one classic myths in parody form. *Fractured Frazzled Folk Fables and Fairy Farces* is adult humor that reorganizes famous children's tales as does its sister book *Fractured Frazzled Folk Fables and Fairy Farces, Part II*. Other satirical humor books authored by Jay Dubya are *Thirteen Sick Tasteless Classics, Thirteen Sick Tasteless Classics, Part II, Thirteen Sick Tasteless Classics, Part III* and finally *Thirteen Sick Tasteless Classics*, Part *IV*.

John has also authored a trilogy of young adult fantasy novels, *Enchanta, Pot of Gold* and *Space Bugs, Earth Invasion*. *The Eighteen Story Gingerbread House* is another children's work written by Jay Dubya.

Jay Dubya likes '50s rock and roll music and he also enjoys pop' songs by the Beach Boys, Beatles, Fleetwood Mac, the Eagles, the Rolling Stones, ELO, John Mellencamp and by John Fogerty. When not writing or listening to music Jay Dubya likes watching *76ers* basketball and *Phillies* and *Yankees* television' baseball games.